Translation as Mission

THE MODERN MISSION ERA, 1792–1992
AN APPRAISAL

a series edited by Wilbert R. Shenk

THE MODERN MISSION ERA, 1792–1992
AN APPRAISAL

A SERIES EDITED BY WILBERT R. SHENK

Translation as Mission
Bible Translation
in the Modern Missionary Movement

by

William A. Smalley

MERCER

ISBN 0-86554-389-5

Library of Congress Cataloging-in-Publication Data

Smalley, William Allen.
    Translation as mission : Bible translation in the mod-
ern missionary movement / by William A. Smalley.
    xv + 287pp. 6″ × 9″ (15 × 23 cm.) — The modern mis-
sion era, 1792–1992: an appraisal.
    Includes bibliographical references and indexes.
    ISBN 0-86554-389-5
    1. Bible—Translating—History. 2. Missions—His-
tory. 3. Bible—Versions—History. 4. Carey, William,
1761–1834. I. Title. II. Series.
BS450.S52   1991
220.5′09—dc20   90-26724
                                                                        CIP

CONTENTS

LIST OF TABLES

General Introduction

The modern mission movement emerged during the last years of the eighteenth century. Publication of William Carey's manifesto *An Enquiry Into the Obligations of Christians to Use Means for the Conversion of the Heathen* in 1792 has often been cited as the symbolic starting point. That same year the English Baptists, prodded by enthusiastic upstarts like Carey himself, formed the Baptist Missionary Society and the Carey family sailed for India the following year. During the next twenty-five years, groups of Christians in Great Britain, Europe, and North America, newly awakened to their missionary "obligations," founded an impressive array of mission societies.

Roman Catholic missions had suffered a major setback when Pope Clement XIV ordered dissolution of the Jesuits in 1773. After 1825 Roman Catholic missions began to recover as old missionary orders were revived and new ones were created.

The modern mission movement takes its name from the so-called modern period of world history, which began with the Enlightenment and the social, political, religious, and economic revolutions during the last third of the eighteenth century. The modern mission initiative would lead to far-reaching changes in the location and composition of the Christian church. During the final years of the twentieth century, more than half of all Christians were to be found outside the region that had been the historical heartland of Christianity for nearly fifteen hundred years. New centers of Christian strength and vitality were now to be found where missionary initiatives had been focused in widely scattered places in the Americas, Africa, and Asia. One must speak of missionary initiatives to indicate that from the beginning missionaries were joined in this endeavor by colaborers indigenous to a particular culture. Without such remarkable collaboration the enterprise would have had a quite different issue. As it was, modern missions fundamentally changed Christian identity.

The most important development in the eighteenth century was the Enlightenment—a powerful constellation of fresh ideas that released forces affecting all areas of human existence and inexorably extended to all parts of the globe. Through the core ideas it birthed, the Enlightenment redirected the course of human development. It was a European phenomenon and the Enlightenment fostered in Europeans a new spirit and outlook. In the words of Peter Gay, "In the century of the Enlightenment, educated Europeans awoke to a new sense of life. They experienced an expansive sense of power over nature and themselves."[1] This "new sense of life" was to have many ramifications. The Enlightenment Project was carried along by a dynamic Western messianism.

Before the end of the eighteenth century Enlightenment ideas had been translated into a political program--first in the formation of the United States of America, especially as enshrined in its constitution, but more radically in the French Revolution of 1789—based on liberal, democratic, and nationalist ideals. These revolutionary ideas have continued to reverberate throughout the world ever since, toppling one *ancien regime* after another.

The Enlightenment challenged religion with special intensity by its aggressive doctrine of the powers and possibilities of human reason joined with an attitude of radical skepticism. Religion increasingly was on the defensive. Some theologians sought to accommodate themselves to these new demands, fashioning a theology that conformed to the canons of the new science. Others reacted by intensifying their faith experience through movements such as Pietism and the Evangelical Revival. Where people managed to hold in tension inward piety and outward concern for the world, these renewal movements became engines of wide-ranging innovation, the modern mission movement being one of the most evident fruits.

As the end of the twentieth century approached it was increasingly agreed that the modern era had passed and the postmodern period had begun. Although it was too early to delineate fully the characteristics of the new epoch, some features were becoming evident. Intellectually, the long-dominant Enlightenment view of scientific knowledge had been superseded. Science was no longer understood to be sole arbiter of knowledge by virtue of holding the keys to inviolable "scientific" laws to which all branches of human knowledge had to answer. Science itself was now understood to be a product of culture and subject to historical conditioning.

---

[1] Peter Gay, *The Enlightenment— An Interpretation, vol. 2, The Science of Freedom* (New York: Alfred A. Knopf, 1969).

Politically, the postmodern era signaled the end of some five centuries of Western hegemony in the world. From the sixteenth century onward Western powers gradually came to dominate the world through economic, military, political, and intellectual means. The Spanish and Portuguese crowns, with the blessing of the church, were the first to take territories and create colonies in other parts of the world. Dutch, British, French, Danes, Germans, Italians, Russians, Americans, and Japanese all followed with their own colonial ventures. The American defeat in Vietnam in 1975 and rout of the Russians in Afghanistan together with the collapse of the socialist system in the 1980s signaled that a far-reaching geopolitical realignment was under way. In the postmodern world a restructuring of the international economic and political order had begun.

The advent of the postmodern period coincided with an epochal shift for the Christian church. Viewing the entire sweep of Christian history, some scholars have discerned just three periods, each defined by the geographical ''center'' and the sociopolitical tradition that predominated.

According to this view, the first stage of Christian expansion and development extended from the time of Jesus Christ to 70 C.E. This was the Jewish phase. The destruction of the temple in Jerusalem in 70 C.E. effectively ended Jewish influence on the Christian movement.

The Christian story then entered its second phase, the Hellenic-European, which lasted until well into the twentieth century. Europe soon became the geographical heartland. Christian expansion which endured was almost exclusively in European Christendom. World War II was a watershed in world affairs as well as for Christendom. Among conciliar Protestants, formation of the World Council of Churches in 1948 marked a new beginning. For Roman Catholics Vatican Council II, convened in 1962, represented a definitive transition. Conservative Protestants felt the impact of the approaching end of the old era as a result of major international events such as the Berlin Consultation on Evangelism in 1966 and the Lausanne Consultation on World Evangelization in 1974. For each ecclesiastical tradition the story was the same. The time of European dominance was coming to an end and church leaders from other parts of the world increasingly filled leadership roles.

This transition from the Hellenic-European phase to the postmodern was a direct result of the modern mission movement. In this respect the modern mission movement contributed in no small measure to bringing about an end to historical Christendom. The line of development from Jerusalem in

33 C.E. was from a pronounced particularity toward a global communion of diverse peoples held together by their loyalty to Jesus Christ.

Viewed in this light the nineteenth century represents one of the truly seminal periods of Christian history. The great motivating center of the modern mission movement was the vision that "the earth will be full of the knowledge of the Lord as the waters cover the sea" (Isaiah 11:9b). The basis for fulfilling that vision, as William Carey and others argued, was the final instruction given by Jesus to his motley band of followers to "go and make disciples of all nations" (Matthew 28:18-20). Carey's generation managed to impress on the Christian church that it had a present duty to continue fulfilling the apostolic mandate. The modern mission movement was led in each generation by a small coterie of people gripped by the hope of seeing all peoples of the world give their allegiance to Jesus Christ. By the nineteenth century the geographical and political implications of such an undertaking were largely known. Steady progress in technology made it appear feasible.

The task before us in this book—and its companion volumes—is to essay this movement through closer analysis of certain key themes, paying special attention to the long-term direction of its development. Critics have charged that the modern mission movement was little more than a sustained attempt to impose Euro-American culture on the peoples who came under its sway. They assert that this effort was simply the religious dimension of the wider quest for Western hegemony in the world. Closer study confirms that this unfolding story was indeed marked by ambiguity and complexity. To be sure, the missionary drama was played out on the same stage as the powerful political and economic developments of the period; missions have been stained by their association with Western imperialism. By virtue of its global reach the movement became a primary carrier of modernity and the artifacts and institutions associated with modernity early became hallmarks of missions. But there is more to be said. Missions released influences that contributed to the subversion and eventual overthrow of colonialism in its many forms.

No aspect of the modern mission movement illustrates better the way in which it produced unintended effects than does Bible translation. In *Translation as Mission*, William A. Smalley gives us a comprehensive account in of the "Bible movement" which viewed itself as strictly an accessory to missions. From the beginning the Bible societies eschewed controversy and forged guidelines designed to minimize conflict with various Christian traditions and to maximize cooperation in the translation, production, and distribution of the Christian Scriptures. From this modest beginning came a movement that commanded the widest possible cooperation among Christians worldwide. Especially in the twentieth century Bible translation became a sophisticated participant in linguistic science. By the end of the twentieth century Bible translation was increasingly recognized to have been an important contributor to the renewal of indigenous cultures by assisting them in reducing their languages to writing, thereby infusing them with a sense of pride and dignity. In short, the mission of translation made a remarkable impact that went far beyond anything the founders in the early years of the nineteenth century could have imagined.

The authors of the volumes comprising this series geographically and culturally represent the North Atlantic. They acknowledge the limitations this imposes. There are indeed other perspectives from which the modern mission era must be studied in order to complete the picture, and the past generation has seen an impressive growth of studies by scholars from Asia, Africa, and Latin America. This series, The Modern Mission Era, 1792–1992: An Appraisal, is offered as a contribution to an enlarged and enriched understanding of what will increasingly be seen as a shared experience.

—Wilbert R. Shenk, general editor

ACKNOWLEDGMENTS

In writing this book I profited by residence at the Overseas Ministries Study Center, New Haven, Connecticut, and by a Research Fellowship at Yale Divinity School, with access to the Yale library system. I also received help from the United Bible Societies Translation Information Clearing House, the United Bible Societies Translation Service Center, and the American Bible Society Library, all in New York. Staff members of these various institutions have been unfailingly helpful.

The following individuals commented on an earlier draft of much or all of the book: Marjorie Bromley, H. Myron Bromley, Charles W. Forman, Donald N. Larson, Mildred L. Larson, Norman A. Mundhenk, Eugene A. Nida, and Philip C. Stine. Daniel C. Arichea, Jr., Barbara F. Grimes, Joseph E. Grimes, Jacob A. Loewen, Carol V. McKinney, Lois Malcolm, William Mitchell, David Rising, A. Christopher Smith and Ross Smith also offered comments on selected parts. From such people I frequently got criticism, correction, fresh insights, new leads, bibliographic tips, encouragement, caution and other essential help.

As editor of the series of which this book is a part, Wilbert R. Shenk proposed that I write it, and has offered numerous valuable suggestions.

I am very grateful for all of this help.

CHAPTER 1

Translation and the Bible

Nothing has ever been translated as frequently, into as many languages, and over as long a span of time as the Bible, and so close is the identification of Bible with translation that for many people in the world their translated Bible is the Bible. It is God's word in KiKongo or Quechua or Cantonese. The modern missionary movement of the past two hundred years did not begin the identification of Bible with translation, not by two thousand years, but it cemented the relationship by sheer numbers of languages and the geographical extent over which it was involved.

Full-scale translation of part of the Bible began, so far as we know, in the third century before Christ, when books of the Old Testament were translated into Greek, the translation which became the Bible of the Greek-speaking Christians in the first century A.D. Translation into other languages then followed at irregular intervals over the next centuries, increasing radically in the last two, until all over the world there are now at least 1,200 ongoing projects where people are translating the Bible, or parts of it, or retranslating or revising existing translations.[1]

All of this translation activity has taken place in spite of the fact that the Bible is difficult to translate well. Any translation is a highly complex activity, but translating a technical article about some aspect of nuclear physics from Russian to English, or the reverse, is normally easier than

---

[1]The United Bible Societies reported being associated with 527 ongoing projects in 1988 (United Bible Societies, "World Translations," v), and the Summer Institute of Linguistics reported 848. (Information Services Department, "General Statistics"). There are, of course, some translation projects not associated with either institution, but there is also some overlap between the two figures, and the Summer Institute of Linguistics figure includes projects in which translation has not yet begun but "preparatory linguistic studies are currently in progress."

translating the Book of Job from the ancient Hebrew in which it was written into English, or translating the Gospel of Matthew from the original Koine Greek into Navajo. Nuclear physicists working in English and Russian share carefully defined scientific concepts which enable them to translate much more directly than can translators of the Bible, who have to cope with vast time and cultural distance, incompatibility of literary styles, and greater differences in linguistic structure.

Before we consider the role of Bible translation in the modern missionary movement more specifically in later chapters, we need therefore to look broadly at what translation does for and to the Bible, providing a perspective without which much of the later discussion would be relatively meaningless.

Accessibility and Distortion

Since the Bible was written primarily in Hebrew and Koine Greek, ancient languages used today by only a tiny minority of the world's population, other people obviously must either learn those languages or use a translation, if they are to read the Bible. The first type of alternative is the one followed in Islam,[2] where converts who speak other languages than Arabic learn to read and recite the Qur'an in Arabic if they are to use it at all, many doing so without understanding much of what they read. But right from the beginning of Christianity, the second alternative was largely followed. Converts outside of Palestine did not use Hebrew for the Old Testament (which was their full Bible at first), but Greek, and early on the New Testament, together with the Old, was translated into several other languages. And as the faith has spread ever more widely, the Christians' Bible has continued to be a translated Bible in almost all churches except Greek-speaking ones, and even there the Bible has been translated into Modern Greek, the New Testament several different times.

So in spite of the difficulties inherent in it, translation of the Bible is critical for Christians, and when it is done well the Bible becomes potentially accessible to all people who read any of the languages of the many translations. The degree to which a translation makes the original message accessible is also the measure of that translation, and that potential accessibility is what motivates most Bible translators to devote years of their lives to the task.

---

[2]Sanneh, *Translating,* 211-34.

Accessibility through translation, on the other hand, does not come without cost, for a translation is always something less and something more than the original, much as the translator works to minimize flaws. Perfect translation is impossible because no two languages are the same, no two cultures are the same, the world views of no two peoples are the same. A translation is always an approximation of the original. Some degree of accessibility and distortion are therefore the anticipated product and inevitable byproduct of all translation. The skillful translator seeks to maximize accessibility and minimize distortion of all kinds, but skewing can never be absolutely eliminated.

Accessibility has been counted more significant than the distortion which goes with it by those thousands of people who have translated the Bible through the centuries, and by the churches which have used their translations. Translation of the Bible, or parts of it, has almost always resulted in net gain for people who wanted access to it. They have not usually even been aware of most translational imperfections, or assumed that translational problems they sensed were just in the nature of the Bible.

Something of this drive for accessibility which keeps translators of the Bible at their difficult task could be seen, for example, when Benjamin Rittiwongsakul was retranslating the New Testament into his native Sgaw Karen language in northern Thailand in the 1960s. He had a Karen Bible, translated in neighboring Burma and first published in 1853, but had long been troubled by the fact that he could understand his English Bible better, even his ancient King James version. On the other hand, his attempts to retranslate the New Testament into Karen were being resisted by Karen church leaders in Thailand, people who sincerely felt that the Karen Bible was perfectly clear, and that he was tampering with God's word.

One day one of these church leaders passed by the place where Rittiwongsakul was working and was invited to sit in. He began to look at a copy of the draft manuscript, comparing it with a copy of the traditional Karen Bible with which he was familiar. Then after several long minutes of study and comparison he looked up and said quietly, ''Now I see what you are doing.'' And pointing to the manuscript, he said, ''You can understand this one!''

For the first time this Christian pastor realized that ''understanding'' the Karen Bible was possible to a degree he had never dreamed of, just by reading the biblical text itself. He had previously often ''understood'' the older Karen translation in the sense that it reminded him of what he had learned in training for the ministry, or in church, like "baptism of repentance unto the remission of sins"[3] may remind readers of the King James version of what they have been told it means without being intelligible in itself. He had thought that the archaic language or the obscurity of the translation style was what the Bible was like.

The older Karen translation, however, in spite of its weaknesses, had nevertheless made the Bible accessible in a significant way to several generations of Sgaw Karen, and the translation had become the foundation of a large and vigorous church in Burma, plus a smaller one in Thailand. Undoubtedly the translation had been less obscure a hundred years earlier, before the Karen language had changed a great deal. But even now it was still easier to learn the meaning of the Bible and be reminded of that meaning through this murky translation than through an unknown foreign language. So it was better than nothing. On the other hand, although Rittiwongsakul's new translation was making the Bible clearer it would also inevitably subtract something from the Bible as well.

The contemporary controversy over sexist language in much past translation of the Bible into English highlights the subtle pervasiveness of distortion in translation, and how the perspective of the observer often governs whether or not it will be noticed. Certainly the original Hebrew and Greek Scriptures have a prevailing male focus due to the culture of the times in which they were written, but until recently translators have sometimes added to the maleness of the language already in the Bible by using male expressions to translate gender-neutral or essentially female wording of the original: "So God created *man* in his own image . . . male and *female* created he them."[4]

In the King James version *teknon* "children" is translated as "sons" in John 1:12, "to them gave he power to become the sons of God," and in some other places where it does not refer to males alone. The indefinite pronoun *tis* "anyone" is often translated "man" or "any man" in the King James, and sporadically in other translations like Luke 9:23 in the Revised Standard Version: "If any man would come after me . . . ," and John 6:50 in the New English Bible: "which a man may eat, and never die."

---

[3] Mark 1:4.

[4] Genesis 1:27 (emphasis added), Revised Standard Version. Please note that the citation of an unfortunate wording in this or any other translation of the Bible does not mean that it is a poor translation overall. Many factors comprise the quality of a translation, and all translations have their weaknesses.

Male-based figures of speech such as "man" for "human beings," the part representing the whole, were natural English idiom at the time the translation was made, when people did not question male dominance as much as many do now, nor sense the male terminology as exclusive, either. The degree of distortion has increased, therefore, as readers have changed.

Translators, furthermore, have sometimes actually downgraded women in the Bible. The apostle Paul frequently referred to people in various churches as *diakonos* in Greek, which meant "person who serves, who ministers to the needs of others," and which at some point in the early development of the church became the term for a position in the church hierarchy: deacon. In the King James version when Paul refers to a man by this term it is translated "minister" or "deacon," but in reference to the woman Phoebe, although her role was clearly that of a leader, the term was translated "servant."[5] *The Living Bible* even translated it as "a dear Christian woman"[6] which is not even close in meaning, as well as downgrading Phoebe's standing in the church.

A different perspective on all of this may be gained from Thai and many other languages where, unlike English with *he* and *she,* there is no gender distinction in third-person pronouns, so that pronouns referring to God who is spirit, who is neither male nor female, have no gender implications at all. Instead, in Thai the system of first-and second-person pronouns presents an elaborate and finely graded series of distinctions which depends on the social relationship between speaker and hearer. To the translator, because Jesus is God he must be addressed with pronouns and other terms which imply sacredness and royalty, as well as deference on the part of the one speaking to him. That is also what the modern Thai Christian and even the Buddhist reader expects in the Bible, and that is what the older translations had.

However, for such people as the Pharisees to address Jesus in such high terms in the translation is entirely out of keeping with the relationship actually pictured between them and Jesus in the gospels. To them he was a Rabbi, a religious teacher, and as such to be respected except when they were angry with him, but nothing more than that. If they had been speaking Thai their pronouns would certainly not have reflected deity unless they spoke in mockery. No solution to this translation dilemma avoids distort-

---

[5]Romans 16:1.

[6]Mickelsen and Mickelsen, "Male Dominance," 26; Arichea, "Phoebe."

ing the Thai Bible in one way or another. The translator must decide either to distort the picture of what took place in Jesus time or seem to downgrade Jesus' divinity for the modern reader.[7]

Some scholars emphasize the distortion which occurs in translation to the point where they despair of the worth of translation:

> And how can a translator hope to capture in English what is obvious in Hebrew—that *'Adam* was so named because he was taken from *'adamah,* which is *'adom* like *dam*? It simply does not "mean" the same thing to say he was called *Man* (*'adam*) because he was taken from the *earth* (*'adamah*) which is *red* (*'adom*) like *blood* (*dam*).[8]

The example is taken from the passage "And the LORD God formed man from the dust of the ground. . . ."[9] Clearly the magnificent Hebrew play on words, which admittedly has intriguing theological implications, is lost in translation. Even when translations explain the play on words in a footnote, which may help a few readers, the net loss is still heavy. The issue from the standpoint of the present book, however, and from the missiological standpoint, as well as from the standpoint of the church which uses the Bible for its edification, is whether loss of the play on words is reason not to make accessible to the reader the story of creation in which it is embedded.

But in spite of many critics who bemoan the "impossibility" of translation, a large part of the modern missionary movement has found translation to be essential as a foundation of the church's life and ministry. And in spite of many critics who emphasize the loss that occurs in translation,[10] a large number of the churches which the missionary movement has helped to spawn have unequivocally accepted the Bible as accessible in the language of the people. Bible translation has played a major part in the establishment and spread of the church, particularly of its Protestant branches.

Translation as Communication

Fundamental to understanding accessibility of the Bible in any missiological sense is the concept of communication, of how that which is in

---

[7]Hatton, "Pronouns" and "Maha-Katoey."

[8]Minkoff, "Problems," 37.

[9]Genesis 2:7, New International Version.

[10]Mounin, *Les Belles Infidèles,* summarizes and discusses some of the arguments.

the mind of one person is partially recreated in the mind of another. Translation is one of many types of human communication, one way of using language.[11] Language, in turn, is the most complex form of communication available to human beings, made up of several simultaneous interrelated layers of structure including sound and/or writing system, grammar, meaning, and others. Translation multiplies the complexity by the degree to which two or more languages differ in grammar, meaning structures, styles and conventions of use. Serious translation of complex material like the Bible is therefore one of the most difficult communication processes in human experience.

Communication itself, whether through language or some other medium, is also complex. It is often thought of as "transmitting meaning" or "sending messages" from one person to another, from a "source" to a "receptor," but is actually much more than that, as we can illustrate with this sequence of interchanges:

> Now the elder son was out in the fields and on his way back, as he drew near the house, he could hear music and dancing. Calling one of the servants he asked what it was all about. "Your brother has come" replied the servant "and your father has killed the calf we had fattened because he has got him back safe and sound." He was angry then and refused to go in, and his father came out to plead with him; but he answered his father, "Look, all these years I have slaved for you and never once disobeyed your orders, yet you never offered me so much as a kid for me to celebrate with my friends. But, for this son of yours, when he comes back after swallowing up your property—he and his women—you kill the calf we had been fattening."
> The father said, "My son, you are with me always and all I have is yours. But it was only right we should celebrate and rejoice, because your brother here was dead and has come to life; he was lost and is found."[12]

The servant's understanding of what was happening, whatever it may have been, was not simply transmitted into the son's head unaltered as a result of their conversation. Instead the son processed what he heard, fitted it into his memories and experience, and interpreted it in light of his frustration and resentment over his brother's earlier behavior. He created a

---

[11]The term *language* is used here in its primary sense: spoken and written language, sometimes called natural language, as opposed to forms of communication like "body language," "computer language," and other metaphorical extensions.

[12]Luke 15:25-32, *The Jerusalem Bible*.

meaning which was only partly the same as the meaning intended by the servant. He was not just a passive listener; rather his role as receptor in the communication event was just as active as that of the servant as source.

So it was with the father when he heard the son's outburst of resentment. He interpreted it within his joy, and in his reply he sought to refocus the son's memories and values, tried to influence him to interpret differently this information to which he was reacting. That is, he tried to get the son to create a different meaning for himself. The father did not tell the son anything the latter did not already know, but worked to stimulate him to think differently about it.

And Jesus, as he told the story, was not ultimately giving his hearers information about a father and two sons. In Luke's context he was stimulating them to change the perspective with which they viewed his behavior when he befriended and ate with people who were religiously contaminated, ritually impure.[13] He wanted his hearers, the Pharisees, to understand his actions in a way more congruent with his own motives in performing them than what they were doing.

Communication is an interaction between people, in which they take reciprocal roles as source and receptor, sometimes alternating the roles rapidly, as in conversation. The source (whether one who keeps the role for hours as in a book, several minutes as in a speech, or for only an utterance or so) expresses meaning through some medium like language, gesture or other activity. The receptor sees or feels or hears the expression and interprets it within her or his thought processes, memories, beliefs, values, knowledge, perception of reality, prejudices, emotions, and other mental equipment. The receptor creates a meaning stimulated by the expression coming from the source. In the case of written communication the source and receptor are usually separated in time and space, altering the dynamics in important ways, but not eliminating the factors. In the case of the Bible read by a modern receptor, that time and space distance is enormous.

The people involved in any communication event think and have feelings. They think and feel partly independently and partly in concert. Communication is efficient, is working well, when they are able to keep close together in their thinking and feeling, or at least perceive the other's thoughts and feelings accurately. Each is stimulating the other to think and

---

[13]Luke 15:2.

feel in harmony, negotiating a state of shared thinking and feeling. Often the results are not that, of course, as when communication breaks down because one or both do not understand, misunderstand or reject. But even such failures do not necessarily mean that the communication event was useless. Even though the participants do not "understand" each other, or disagree, one or the other may have been stimulated to think something new, fresh, or valuable, although remote from what the other intended at the time.

We are not conscious of most of the complexity of communication, language and translation as we use them. We talk or write or translate without being aware of most of the choices we are making on many levels, or knowing why we make them. As we write we repeatedly change the wording, vaguely perceiving the changes to be improvements, but are often unable to analyze why. As the draft becomes "smoother" and "more coherent," we are causing different elements of structure to be in greater harmony with each other in the discourse as a whole, but cannot explain much of the process.

In St. Mark's gospel, for example, there is an account of Jesus travelling in foreign territory and meeting a woman of the country who begged him to heal her daughter of demon possession. Jesus told her in reply, "It isn't right to take the children's food and throw it to the dogs."

Then in the *Good News Bible* and similarly in some other translations, " 'Sir,' she answered, 'even the dogs under the table eat the children's leftovers!' "[14]

This story is a powerful one, but the use of "Sir" in this translation seems discordant, sounding cold, as though the woman were lecturing Jesus. I would find "Oh, yes Sir!" to be more in harmony with my impression of the woman—warmer, more earnest. But I cannot explain why, and other readers might not agree. *The Jerusalem Bible* has "Ah, yes, sir!" which does not sound natural to me at all, but literary or archaic. Phillips's *New Testament in Modern English* has "Yes, Lord, I know," which carries a deeper tone of humility, and may be the most suitable of all these translations. But again my judgment is based on a vague sense of appropriateness, or usage which I cannot define. The translator works constantly with such uncertainties created by the complexities of communication, language and translation.

---

[14]Mark 7:27-28.

Here is the problem of distortion again, and again there is no question but that the value of having the story accessible in English far outweighs the loss felt in the way the interpersonal exchange between Jesus and the woman is translated. The issue for translators, however, is how to reduce the loss as much as possible, perhaps in this particular instance to eliminate it altogether for all practical purposes.

Eavesdropper or Direct Receptor

One of the issues on which translators often disagree the most is about what features of the original text should be made most accessible in translation, and where the greatest loss should be tolerated. If the poetic structure of a Psalm is to be made accessible to the modern reader, for example, that will probably obscure the message of the Psalm. If the message is to be made as clear as possible, that will certainly obscure the original poetic structure.

One of the most crucial decisions of that kind concerns the role into which the reader is cast. Is the translated communication to take place now, directly involving the modern reader as a primary receptor, or is the reader a secondary receptor, an eavesdropper listening in on a communication in which an ancient people were the primary receptors?[15] Is God (or are God's agents) talking to us today through the translation of the Bible or are we listening to a message delivered to someone else a long time ago?

Translation aside for the moment, these two kinds of receptors can be illustrated, although rarely in pure form, in the biblical exegete and the preacher. The exegete studies the meaning of the biblical passage in its original historical and cultural setting, whereas the preacher hears and passes on a message for today. If they are responsible receptors in the biblical communication, neither discounts the significance of the other role or point of view. Many preachers, in fact, draw heavily on exegesis as a foundation for seeking the current implications of the text.

Many biblical scholars who are also translators tend to place the modern reader in an eavesdropper role, overhearing an ancient communication. One example of this is the way many of them carry over into the translation indications of different sources within a Bible passage. The *Jerusalem Bible,* for example, uses "God," reflecting Hebrew *elohim* "gods, god," in Genesis 1. Then it has "Yahweh God" beginning with Genesis

---

[15]Bird, "Sexist Language."

2:5, reflecting a sequence of two Hebrew words. The first is *yahweh,* the name for the particular God of the Jewish people, revealed at Sinai. The second is *elohim* again. Then "Yahweh" is used beginning in chapter 4, reverting to "God" again in 4:25. The Revised Standard Version, similarly but more traditionally for English, has "God," "LORD God," "LORD," and "God," respectively, to reflect the same differences in Hebrew.

In such cases as these shifts in the terms for God, translators are sometimes trying to show that Genesis is a compilation of different communication events by different sources who used the different terms. They show the shifts of sources in these somewhat artificial ways to help the modern reader overhear the multiple voices of the original. A characteristic weakness of eavesdropper translation of this kind, however, is that any significance in these differences in the names for God is lost on most modern readers, who interpret them as synonyms, alternative ways of referring to the same deity in the larger context, which of course they are in the original also. Such modern receptors thus create a meaning more in keeping with their experience with written documents in spite of the translator's efforts to the contrary.

More extreme and problematical, however, is a translation like the American Standard Version, of which the following is a sample:

> And you *did he make alive,* when ye were dead through your trespasses and sins, wherein ye once walked according to the course of this world, according to the prince of the powers of the air, of the spirit that now worketh in the sons of disobedience; among whom we also all once lived in the lusts of our flesh, doing the desires of the flesh and of the mind, and were by nature children of wrath, even as the rest:—but God, being rich in mercy, for his great love wherewith he loved us, even when we were dead through our trespasses, made us alive together with Christ (by grace have ye been saved), and raised us up with him, and made us to sit with him in the heavenly *places,* in Christ Jesus: that in the ages to come he might show the exceeding riches of his grace in kindness toward us in Christ Jesus: for by grace have ye been saved through faith; and that not of yourselves, *it is* the gift of God; not of works, that no man should glory.[16]

In a translation like this the concern of the translators to overhear the original communication greatly reduces the accessibility of the text for the modern reader. They have tried to match the form, especially the order of

---

[16]Ephesians 2:1-9.

words in the Greek original, as much as they can. The passage is one, long, tortured English sentence, following the Greek syntax, but more difficult than the Greek because Greek has a grammatical structure more suited to keeping it clear.

In addition to that, "you" and "ye" are both used in the translation, taken from an archaic form of English in which *ye* is the subject form of the second person plural pronoun and *you* is the object form, like modern English *I* and *we* as against *me* and *us*. The distinction is made in the translation in part[17] because Greek has such a grammatical distinction between second person subject and object, although it is completely unnecessary in English in this and most passages, and most readers do not know what the archaic difference between the two words used is supposed to signify anyhow.

The passage is also liberally sprinkled with incomprehensible phrases or ones only dimly understandable without some special training: "course of this world," "prince of the powers of the air," "sons of disobedience," "children of wrath," all literal translations of Greek phrases.

On the other hand, words in italics in this translation are a small concession to the modern reader. They are not used for emphasis, as in normal English practice (another distortion), but are supplied to help make minimal sense of the text. However, the fact that the words are visually set apart in italics like this manifests an eavesdropper concern again. The use of italics is supposed to tell the eavesdropper that there are no corresponding Greek words as such.

Certainly such a translation as this American Standard Version makes the Bible more accessible to the reader of English who does not know Greek or Hebrew than do the Greek or Hebrew texts themselves. On the other hand, its low level of consideration for the modern receptor makes the translation usable only up to a point, only with grave loss and severe distortion to the message. The reader has to strain to overhear, and gets only muffled parts of what is going on.

On the other hand, those translators who perceive themselves primarily as facilitating communication between God (or the writers of the Bible who speak for God) and the modern reader want the translation of the Bible to address the modern situation directly in modern terms. One extreme example is *The Cotton Patch Version* of parts of the New Testament, done

---

[17]The other reason is that a pseudo-Elizabethan English is used throughout the translation.

by Clarence Jordan to reflect his understanding of the Gospel as applied to the American South of the 1960s:

> Fourteen years later, because of an insight I had, I went again to Atlanta with Barney, taking Titus along with us. There I laid before them the message which I preach among Negroes. (I did this privately before the executive committee, so that what I was doing—or had done—might not be wasted.) But not even Titus, the Negro professor who was with me, was compelled to abide by Southern traditions. . . .[18]

More recently there are translators who want to enable the modern female reader or hearer of the Scriptures not to feel excluded from the message, trying to compensate for the male bias in the world view which prevailed when the passages were written. In this they go beyond correcting translations which introduced male imagery where the original text has no gender implications, or actually has feminine ones. They make the original male-oriented imagery inclusive in the translation:

> And the Word became flesh and dwelt among us, full of grace and truth; we have beheld the Word's glory, glory as of the only Child from [God] the Father [and Mother]. (John bore witness to the Child, and cried, "This was the one of whom I said, 'The one who comes after me ranks before me, for that one was before me.' ") And from the fulness of the Child have we all received, grace upon grace. For the law was given through Moses; grace and truth came through Jesus Christ. No one has ever seen God; the only Child, who is in the bosom of [God] the [Mother and] Father, that one has made God known.[19]

In this text, adapted from the Revised Standard Version, the most conspicuous change, of course, is the addition of the words "God" and "Mother." Others include the use of "Child" where the Revised Standard Version has "Son," and repetitions of "the Word" where the Revised Standard Version has masculine pronouns.

It is clear, however, that the people who did the adapting were not only seeking to help modern readers who are sensitive to issues of female exclusion feel that the Bible is addressed to women directly, as well as to men, but were also trying to maintain an eavesdropper role, marking many of the inclusive language changes with brackets and italics. Thus they tried

---

[18]Galatians 2:1-3, Jordan, *Paul's Epistles,* 95-96.

[19]John 1:14-18, *Inclusive Language Lectionary.*

to let the receptor have it both ways, to know both what the original communication was, and also what it is, as they understand it. Changes from male pronouns to nouns, as from "his glory" to "Word's glory," were not so marked, however.

In contrast to that policy of typographically showing the larger changes in this way, compare the same passage in another version:

> And the Word became flesh and lived among us, full of grace and truth. We saw the glory of the Word, glory as of a unique Child of God. John witnessed to the Word, and cried, "This is the one of whom I said, 'The one who comes after me ranks before me and was before me.' "
>
> From this fullness we have all received grace upon grace. For the Law was given through Moses, but grace and truth came through Jesus Christ. No one has ever seen God. But the beloved of God, who lives in God's bosom, makes God known.[20]

It is not possible to overhear the male imagery of the original communication in this translation at all, as the perspective of the modern receptor in direct communication has been adopted more singlemindedly. This translation is also stylistically more accessible than the previous one, smoother and more readable without the intrusive brackets, italics and notes. But a characteristic loss from doing translation in the mode of the modern receptor hearing directly, of masking the intermediary communication, is that the historic basis for the faith may be blurred; the events when people of old heard God speak may be superseded. In making the Bible fit the modern context the biblical context may be distorted.

These two receptor types are not mutually exclusive, of course, but poles along a continuum. The translators of the American Standard Version would not have translated at all if they had no interest in accessibility by the modern reader, and they gave that reader a little extra help now and then when the eavesdropping got hard. And Clarence Jordan, who translated the *Cotton Patch Version,* was much concerned with maintaining the implications he heard in the original communication. But the positions of these two particular translators are nevertheless very far apart, and other translators, most of whom lie between, nevertheless disagree sharply sometimes about which position a translation should take.

But whichever receptor the translator envisions, the exclusion of the other means some degree of distortion. So it is with all translational choices,

---

[20]Haugerud, *Word for Us,* 1.

on all levels of the work. The distortion should be kept to a minimum, but it cannot be eliminated.

The Bible Translator in the Communication Process

In many of the examples presented so far translators probably made conscious choices. However, because the complex interrelationship between human beings which we call communication is manifested in highly complex language, and then multiplied in translation, the translator is normally working with hundreds of variables or potential variables on many levels at a time, completely unaware of most of them. Just as we are usually unconscious of the grammar of our language as we talk, translators produce what seems to work best, sound best, ''feel'' best as an equivalent for the original, often without knowing why. They struggle with the problems of which they are aware, but for other problems their judgment works subliminally.

This means that training, experience and personal skills are of great importance for any translator, who must have a good understanding of the original meaning plus an ability to express that meaning as accurately and effectively as possible for the type of person who will use the translation. It usually means that more than one person should work on a translation so that their skills may complement each other.

When a missionary is translator, native speakers of the language must also be involved to produce idiomatic wording, no matter how well the missionary knows the language. In many translations of earlier days in the modern missionary movement, native speakers helping with the translation have sometimes not had the education or background to do much more than answer the missionary's questions about language usage. Although that still applies in a few cultural situations, today native speakers are increasingly taking the primary role in translation, with missionaries supplying background information on the language and culture of the original when the native speakers lack that. In some situations, of course, there are native speakers in non-European languages who are more qualified in all respects than any missionary who might be inclined to translate into their language.

The primary types of training and experience that are needed on a translation team are biblical exegesis and interpretation, translation theory and method, insight into the language and culture of the translation, skill in writing and editing, and a critical ear for the nuances of language as appropriate to the audience for which the translation is being made. Each of these requirements is complex and difficult, but skillful, balanced and co-ordinated exercise of all of them helps to increase accessibility and diminish distortion.

Translators come from many different backgrounds, however. Of those who translate into their own language many have ministerial training, and some of them are seminary professors. But other backgrounds are also common, so that at one translators' training program in Asia all the following occupations were represented among native-speaker translators: minister, priest, seminary student, professional translator, journalist, nurse, military officer, homemaker and school teacher. Such people are selected to be part of a translation team when they seem to be the most capable available people, or select themselves to be translators because they want to respond to a need they perceive.

Similarly, except for those members of the Summer Institute of Linguistics who will be involved directly in translation, and a few others, people do not normally become missionaries in order to be Bible translators. They enlist as pastors, teachers, even agriculturists, doctors or nurses; but in time some are selected to be translators because they seem to be the most capable available people, or select themselves because translation is needed, and there is nobody else to do it. Typically they have some skill required for the translation team, and have worked in the language of the translation for several years, usually knowing it better than many of their missionary colleagues.

So Bible translators are something of a motley crew when matched against ideal criteria. Biblical scholars sometimes consider themselves to be the most qualified to translate, but a lifetime of writing for an audience of fellow scholars may be no preparation for writing a translation intended for ordinary people in the churches. Scholars may also have an unsuitable understanding of the translation task. A journalist, on the other hand, may write well, but lack the needed biblical background as well as the necessary understanding of the principles of translation.

Correspondingly, sometimes the work translators do is not adequate. Some translations have been unusable, or below satisfactory standard, because of inaccuracy or too high a level of distortion. But often, by the grace of God, people who do not seem to be qualified rise to the task, do good work with the help of others who complement their skills, and produce a translation which once more makes the Bible accessible, and sometimes highly attractive to a people.

Some translators grow immeasurably in the process. In one case a translation consultant met with two missionary translators in an early stage of their work, discussing it with them, and checking the reaction of native speakers to samples from drafts which had been prepared. These men knew their English Bibles very well, but had little training in formal biblical studies. They spoke the language of the translation fluently, but lacked necessary translation principles. They wanted to translate literally, and the results were correspondingly largely incomprehensible to native speakers, even the ones who had been their "translation helpers."

The consultant made suggestions for different ways of approaching the translation problems they were finding, pointing out possible solutions when the translation seemed difficult or misleading for the native speakers. Although he did not know the language, he was able through this process to help the translators begin to see a more adequate approach, indirectly beginning to teach some translation principles. Soon both translators noticed that the native speakers were much happier about the changes than they had been with the earlier work. But then one of the translators remarked, "If you translated like this it would take a long time, wouldn't it?" They occasionally commented wistfully on the need to translate quickly. They had little concept of the complexity of the task they had undertaken.

But in spite of this naive and inauspicious beginning, over the years that followed one of these men did learn to translate "like this," and grew into a very competent translator. As he learned translation theory and technique, and gained experience in them, his translation made the New Testament highly accessible.

As the world has changed since the beginning of the modern missionary movement, and as knowledge of many kinds has grown, part of the process of translating the Scriptures has likewise become different for many translators. Such changes will be discussed more fully at different points in this book but perhaps the most fundamental development is that today training and knowledge are available to the translator on a massive scale, mediated by agencies who specialize in giving such help. As illustrated in the preceding incident, translation staff from the Bible Societies and the Summer Institute of Linguistics in particular are available to train translators and help them avoid some pitfalls that plagued their translational predecessors.

A few Bible translators like Jerome, John Wycliffe, Martin Luther, William Carey and Adoniram Judson became famous, usually for reasons which go beyond their work as translators. But for the most part translators are not remembered long, or are remembered only in a tiny corner of the world. People accept their Bibles or Testaments or portions (full books of the Bible), and take these for granted without being conscious of the tremendous debt they have to the people who did the translation.

The translators made no money. They often worked in debilitating heat or cold. Those who were missionaries may have suffered diseases unknown in their homelands. And some died. For many their translation work was done on the side, late into the night after a day of ministering to people in other ways. It was a task often undertaken with great love, but at great sacrifice. Although some translators had the reward of seeing thousands of copies of Scripture portions, Testaments or Bibles sold and used, others never lived that long.

They worked by the grace of God and believed they were doing the will of God, driven by the hope that the Bible would become accessible to people among whom they lived and worked. Many of the missionary translators among them were also buoyed in their painstaking work by their fascination with the language and culture into which they were translating, which they were constantly exploring in the desire to express God's word better. Many contributed to the wider understanding of those languages and cultures.[21]

As we look back at some of their work now, we wish it had been better. Sometimes the distortion was pretty bad, but even many of those ''inadequate'' translations were used in a major way by the Spirit of God in spreading the Church of Jesus Christ and enriching the lives of Christians. And we know from the English King James version that a translation of the Bible with serious flaws can sometimes nevertheless be an enormous blessing to many people.

Each translator has helped to make the Bible or part of the Bible accessible to varying degrees in one of more than 1,910 languages.[22] Together many of their translations are studied in hundreds of seminaries and Bible schools, read in thousands of churches, memorized by millions of

---

[21]Wonderly and Nida, ''Linguistics.''

[22]See chap. 2, table 1.

people. And through it all, as we shall see in later chapters of this book, this motley crew of translators with their different skills and abilities undergirded by the Spirit of God, has made an enormous impact on the world.

CHAPTER 2

Translation and the Spread of the Church

The complicated task of translating the Bible has sometimes followed the church in its expansion into new languages and sometimes preceded it, has sometimes been an outgrowth of mission activity, sometimes the entering wedge. Before the modern missionary movement of the past two hundred years the church almost always came first, with translation sometimes following long after. St. Patrick, for an extreme example, took the gospel to Ireland in the fifth century but the first Irish translation was not published until 1602.

The Gospel of Matthew was first published in Malay in 1629, the first portion of the Bible ever printed for evangelistic purposes in a non-European language, and the Bible has been translated and retranslated several times since, but there is still no Malay church to speak of. The church has never followed among ethnic Malay of Malaysia. More typically, in the early years of the modern missionary movement and the preceding century, the church followed soon after translation, or developed simultaneously with it. Later the order was sometimes one way, sometimes the other, but either way the spread of Bible translation and of the church are normally roughly coextensive.

Occasionally when translation came first the conversion of significant numbers of people to Christian faith followed considerably later. In the early nineteenth century, for example, the Chinese government outlawed even the teaching of Chinese to foreigners. The penalty was death, and the Chinese instructor who helped Robert Morrison learn classical literary Chinese and translate the Scriptures carried poison to commit suicide if he were ever discovered. Morrison's first Scripture publication in 1810 was printed with a false cover page to help conceal its nature. But by mid-century the dam had broken and a post-translation church was being established. After that numerous translations into other Chinese languages were produced, and translation then followed the church once again.[1]

A church whose members believe it was founded by St. Thomas, the apostle, had existed among Malayalam-speaking people in South India for centuries, with Syriac as its church language, when the first translation of the gospels was published in Malayalam in 1811.[2] This first translation was made from Syriac by two priests of the church stimulated by Church of England missionaries. Unfortunately the work was not usable, as it was neither accurate nor readable because the translators did not understand their task. A better translation was therefore undertaken from Greek into Malayalam by Benjamin Bailey, an Anglican missionary working with Malayali colleagues, and the New Testament was published in 1829. Although this translation had many flaws "perhaps no single event contributed more to the renewal of life among the Thomas Christians."[3] Here translation followed long after the ancient church but preceded the revitalized one.

Epochs in the Development of Bible Translation

The history of Bible translation is punctuated by a few great shifts when major new factors started new directions, each new era from then on running concurrently with those which began earlier. None of them has ended yet.

The era of spreading the faith (300 B.C.–*).* When people began to translate books of the Old Testament into Greek about 300 B.C., the Jewish community was expanding into the Gentile world. Greek was the great universal language of the eastern Mediterranean area, the language of culture and politics, the one people used for communication beyond their national or ethnic community. Alexandria, Egypt, was a major center of the Greek-speaking civilization, and that was where the translation was done.[4]

So the Septuagint, the first major translation of the Old Testament (actually the Bible as it then existed), followed the faith as it expanded into another culture and into other countries, even before there was any Chris-

---

[1]Nida, ed., *Thousand Tongues,* 70-71.

[2]Ibid., 271.

[3]Neill, *Christianity in India,* 243.

[4]Other translations were made by Jews into Aramaic (first-century A.D.) and Samaritan (second-century A.D.).

tianity. And then during the first century after Christ, when this translation became the Bible of Greek-speaking Christians, the Septuagint was the translation which Paul and others used as the church grew to the north and northwest of Palestine, where the faith followed the translation.

The Christian church spread rapidly in the first centuries. By A.D. 400 it was strongly established in the eastern Mediterranean countries, especially those of Asia, adjacent areas of Europe and the coast of North Africa. It extended to a lesser degree also into other parts of Europe, to Ethiopia, and to Asian countries like Persia, the Arabian peninsula and India.[5]

Scripture translation of the time reflected both this expansion of the church and the fact that Greek and Latin were the primary languages of that civilization. The Old Testament was the only authoritative Scripture at first, and the Greek Septuagint continued to be the most important translation of it for a long time. The New Testament canon began to jell in the third century, and it was eventually included in translations of the Christian Bible.

In those early years several translations were made into Latin also, the first one in the first century. Others were made into Syriac, a major language of the eastern Mediterranean, extending over to the Mesopotamian valley (the first of these translations in the second century). Then translations were made into several forms of the Coptic language in Egypt (the first one in the third century), and into Ethiopic south of that (the first one in the fourth century).

Also in the fourth century Ulfilas produced his great missionary translation of most of the Bible into the Gothic of the Danube area to the north, a language of the "barbarian" tribes. Like many modern translators, Ulfilas had to develop a writing system for Gothic before he could translate.[6] In some other ways the Gothic translation was not typical of modern missionary circumstances, however, as Ulfilas was the grandson of Christians captured and carried away as slaves by the Goths, and was therefore translating into one of his own languages for a people among whom he had grown up.

East of the Mediterranean countries Nestorian Christians, whose church language was Syriac, were the most far-ranging missionaries in the world in those early centuries. By A.D. 635 they had reached China, and a church existed there until the fourteenth century. In A.D. 640 missionaries made a

---

[5]Barrett, ed., *Encyclopedia*, 23-24; Aland, *Christianity*, 52-54.

[6]Walker et al., *Christian Church*, 148.

translation of the gospels in Chinese for the emperor of China, but it and other translations of parts of the Bible from this period of Christian presence in China were apparently never printed, perhaps not even copied much, even though methods of printing existed in China before the Nestorians died out there.[7]

Arabic in the eighth or ninth century and Persian in the fourteenth were other important additional translations into new languages as they also followed the expansion of the church.

The Era of European Vernaculars (405–). The completion of the Latin Vulgate by Jerome in A.D. 405 is the symbolic beginning of another era in Bible translation. The Vulgate was one of the great translations of all time in several respects, and became the standard Bible of Roman Catholic Christianity for over a thousand years, its supremacy confirmed in 1546 at the Council of Trent in reaction to the threat of the Reformation. At times the Vulgate seemed even to supersede in authority texts in the original languages, and for a long period translations were generally made from it in preference to making them from those original languages.

Ironically, however, part of the innovative greatness of the Vulgate itself was the fact that it was the first translation since the Septuagint to be fully based on the original Hebrew text for the Old Testament. Until that time that Greek Septuagint translation was the primary text from which Old Testament translations were made instead. The Vulgate was also the first translation done by someone who discussed and argued for principles of translation, or at least whose arguments are still preserved, as Jerome defended his work vigorously against Augustine and others.

The centuries following the completion of the Vulgate were centuries of consolidation for Christianity in Europe and the establishment of the church of Rome as the dominant political power in the western part. With the exception of a very few cases like Chinese, Arabic and Persian mentioned above, translation of the Bible into new languages was a European activity. It extended northward from both the Eastern and the Western churches into Georgian and Armenian (fifth century), Slavonic (ninth century), German (eleventh century), Dutch (twelfth century), Spanish (thirteenth century), Norwegian (fourteenth century) and Hungarian (fifteenth century), to cite only some examples.

---

[7]Nida, ed., *Thousand Tongues,* 70.

Most of the translations were done by native speakers translating into their own vernaculars, in their own countries, with translation still following the church, often far behind. One important early case was Armenian, spoken in what is now the southern USSR, where the church was founded about the beginning of the fourth century and where a translation of the New Testament was completed one hundred years later in 410. The writing system was devised by Mesrop, who was also involved in the translation, and who has traditionally been considered to have devised the writing system and translated the New Testament into neighboring Georgian as well.[8]

The most important instance where translation and the beginning of the church did coincide closely was in Slavonic under the brothers Cyril and Methodius, with the Bible completed by A.D. 880 This was a missionary translation but unusual again (from a modern point of view) because it was not a translation into the dialect spoken where the missionaries were working. The brothers were Greeks who had been brought up in Macedonia, the bilingual border area between the Greeks and the Slavs, so they spoke the Macedonian dialect of Slavic as well as Greek from childhood. However, at the time when they devised a writing system and translated the Scriptures and liturgy into Slavic, they were missionaries in Moravia (farther north in the area of present-day Czechoslovakia), where a different Slavic dialect was spoken. They nevertheless translated primarily into Macedonian Slavic, which the Moravians understood.

As a result, this newly written Macedonian Slavic through which the Slavic peoples became literate in their own language rose to the level of a literary language (now called Old Church Slavonic) throughout a great deal of the Slavic-speaking region. In subsequent centuries the spoken Slavic dialects became more extensively differentiated, some of them into different languages like Russian and Czech. The literary language started by Cyril and Methodius, in turn, became the forerunner of church and liturgical languages of the Orthodox churches in the Slavic-speaking areas, languages still so used at the present time although they are no longer intelligible except to those people who especially study them.[9]

Translation into European vernaculars later gained much greater impetus under the Reformation and has not ended yet. The most recent ad-

---

[8]Ibid., 20, 152; Neill, *Christian Missions*, 47-48.

[9]Dvornik, *Slavs*, 80-84; Matejka, "Slavonic."

ditions to the European languages in which at least one book of the Bible has been translated were in 1984 when portions were published in the Zürich form of German and into Mallorquin, two vernaculars spoken in Switzerland. Much more important than these, the process of revising and of preparing new translations for new generations of speakers of ever-developing European languages continues to grow.

The Era of Printing (1450–). Nothing has been more important to the growth of Bible translation than the European reinvention of printing with movable type in 1450.[10] Gutenberg's first Bible, an edition of the Latin Vulgate, was printed in 1456. His first German Bible, the first printed Bible in any contemporary vernacular, followed in 1466. Some other existing translations were published in the next decades at an increasing pace, as were translations into new languages before long.

Before printing, every copy of any translation in any language had to be made by hand, letter by letter, a phenomenal task from twentieth-century perspective. Every copy of the Septuagint used by early Christians, every copy of the Syriac, the Coptic, the early Latin translations and the Vulgate, the Slavonic, and the other translations down through the centuries had been produced by people (usually monks) creating another single manuscript from the manuscript in front of them or dictated to them. It is astounding how many copies were made in this way, and how they spread all over Europe and the Middle East.

Printed editions, on the other hand, could be run off quickly in the thousands of copies, which made them more easily available and cheaper. Printing therefore made possible a much wider distribution and use of translations, and stimulated the spread of literacy.

The invention of printing in the West was followed shortly by increased Bible translation stimulated first by the Renaissance, with its new humanism, its new interest in scholarship, and its new concern for local languages and cultures, and by the Reformation. Martin Luther was born in 1483, just thirty-three years after the invention of printing. The Reformation emphasis on the vernacular and Luther's own translation of the Bible gave impetus to a chain of new translations. With Luther, also, Protestant translators now usually returned to translating from the original Hebrew

---

[10]Printing by movable type was invented in China in the eleventh century, but was not reinvented in Europe before 1450.

and Greek, rather than from the Latin Vulgate which had become the usual practice.

The change did not come without cost. The early part of this era was a time of persecution and even martyrdom for some Bible translators. Luther stayed carefully out of the Pope's reach while he did his translation, but Tyndale, whose English translation was a great forerunner of the King James version, was strangled and his body burned in 1536.

Persecution did not stop the effort, however, and later the new interest in translation jumped the boundaries of Europe, foreshadowing developments in the modern missionary movement. The evangelistic work of John Eliot among the Massachuset Indians just north of Boston, for example, prodded him to become one of the first really missionary Bible translators in the West in a thousand years. He devised a writing system for the language and began translating as part of his attempt to establish the church among the people. When the Bible was produced in 1663 it was the first complete Bible in any language published in North America.[11]

The Bible Society Era (1804–). With the beginning of the Bible society movement Bible translation began to accelerate. The Bible societies would not have been possible without printing, nor would the acceleration have been as great without the modern missionary movement which began at the same time. This period around the turn of the century experienced an explosion of organizing activities on all aspects of Christian ministry as then conceived, both at home and abroad, and concern that people have and read the Bible was a major part of this new vision. The Bible society movement and the missionary movement were both products of this new vision, and became tightly intertwined in carrying it out. Without the missionary movement the Bible societies might have expended their energies primarily on providing Scriptures for people who spoke English and the other European languages.

The Bible society which first set the tone and pace for the era was the British and Foreign Bible Society, its name reflecting the missionary mood that spawned it in 1804.[12] The impetus for the founding was the need for Welsh Bibles, which existing Christian literature organizations could not meet; but the proposal to organize so as to fill this need produced a spark of vision from one of the people present: ''and if for Wales, why not for

---

[11]Nida, ed., *Thousand Tongues,* 286.

[12]The first Bible society was the Canstein Bible Society in Germany.

the Kingdom; why not for the whole world?"[13] The first publication by this new society that very same year was the Gospel of John in Mohawk, an American Indian language. Other Bible societies were soon established in other countries on the model set by the British and Foreign Bible Society, although few had an international scope, and none matched the international character of the British society for more than a century.

Bible societies became the most important links between translators who were increasingly at work all over the world, on the one hand, and the printing press on the other. They were also sources of financial assistance. Translators could send their manuscripts to a Bible society, which would print the books and send them where they were needed, subsidizing the cost to make the price low enough for individual readers to afford. The subsidy and Bible society expenses were borne by Christians in the home country of the Bible society, people who wanted to contribute to the spread of the faith through the Bible. The Bible societies were also crucial players in the development of the eras yet to begin.

The Era of Professionalized Translation (1943–). The promotion of professional expertise, the development of translation theory and of translation procedures based on such theory, began when Eugene A. Nida joined the American Bible Society staff in 1943.[14] Up to that time the Bible societies had given what advice they could to translators, and had sought to ensure the value and quality of each translation as well as they knew how, but had no developed and articulated theoretical base for doing so. Nida, as a linguist and anthropologist as well as a student of ancient Greek literature, quickly proceeded to amass the necessary data and develop ways of conceptualizing and teaching the process of translation.[15] In time he also recruited a professional team of linguists and biblical scholars to serve with him as consultants to translators all over the world. Later they would be internationalized, working under the auspices of the United Bible Societies.

Nida came to the American Bible Society from the fledgling Summer Institute of Linguistics, which together with the Wycliffe Bible Translators, was founded by William Cameron Townsend to promote profession-

---

[13]Fenn, "Bible and Missionary," 388-89.

[14]North, "Nida."

[15]Nida's 1947 book *Bible Translating,* his first on the subject, shows the range of information about different languages being amassed, and the beginning of the development of procedures and of the rationale for them.

alized translation in yet another way. It recruited and trained people to specialize directly in translating the Bible instead of filling typical missionary roles as evangelists, medical workers and educators while doing Bible translation on the side.[16]

In addition to the development of translation theory and procedures, and to providing consultant help for translators, professionalized translation has been communicated to translators through extensive published materials and through innumerable training programs conducted all over the world by both the UBS and SIL. SIL in fact gets its name from the linguistic training programs for missionary translators with which it started its work.

In this era, also, translation has preceded the church into a number of societies to an unprecedented degree, largely through SIL, but also as others followed the SIL example. Especially in Latin America there are churches which grew up in response to the life and ministry of Bible translators living in an area and working in the language, and in response to their translation itself.[17] Frequently the earliest converts were people who helped the missionaries to learn the language and to translate Scriptures into it.

The Interconfessional Era (1965–). Beginning with the Luther translation into German, completed in 1532, for nearly four hundred and fifty years translation of the Bible into new languages was primarily a Protestant activity. Under the threat of the Protestant advance the Roman church often drew its boundaries more tightly around the Vulgate, opposing much vernacular translation of the Bible, although not stopping it altogether. The Bible society movement, furthermore, did not normally include Catholics, although it served a wide range of other churches.

When Roman Catholic missionaries went to the New World in the sixteenth century a number of the priests plunged into learning vernacular languages, and into writing grammars and catechisms, because they could not use Latin to communicate with native Americans.[18] This activity did

---

[16]The Netherlands Bible Society followed this pattern on a small scale for a period. To give one example of the large share of the missionary translations into new languages produced by SIL, twenty-four of the thirty-two new languages added to table 1 in 1987 were work done by its members. This included four of the six new Testaments (United Bible Societies, "Language Report").

[17]See, e.g., Slocum and Watkins, *Seed*; Larson and Dodds, *Treasure*; Rossi, *City*.

[18]Wonderly and Nida, "Linguistics," 64-69.

not extend to the translation of the Bible, however, as shown by the fact that the first published Scripture translation in an American Indian language of Latin America did not appear until 1829, and then was not done in the Catholic church. It was the Gospel of Luke in Aymara, a language of Bolivia, translated by Vincente Pazos-Kanki in London at the request of the British and Foreign Bible Society. Pazos-Kanki was spotted as probably coming from Latin America while riding a London bus.[19]

Catholic delays in making Scriptures available in vernaculars were rooted in theology and church behavior established before the advent of printing, with attitudes also colored by the still-current low literacy level of many European populations. Lack of vernacular Scriptures did not mean that the Roman church was not communicating the Bible in any form, however. Down through the centuries in Europe stories from the Bible had been transmitted orally, enacted in plays, and pictured in church windows. Characters from the Bible stood as statues in the churches. Catechisms in vernacular languages were memorized. These patterns were carried over also into the new places where Catholic missionaries worked.

In sharp contrast to parts of this Catholic tradition, the Reformation grew up around the written text of the Bible. In studying that text Luther found the grounds for repudiating abuses in the church. And with printing now available the text could much more easily be taken with the church as it spread. Protestants, furthermore, tended to be middle-class people, among whom literacy was rapidly growing in Europe, and many of whom had enormous interest in the Book as the word of God.

The Catholic position changed dramatically, however, after the "Dogmatic Constitution on Divine Revelation" was overwhelmingly passed by the assembled bishops at Vatican Council II in 1965. In that document the Roman Catholic church officially gave up its heavy reliance on Latin for Scripture and worship in favor of promoting vernaculars worldwide, and of encouraging cooperative translation with non-Catholic Christians. It also changed from restricting lay access to the Bible to encouraging its universal use, including the use of Scripture editions for evangelizing non-Christians.[20] All over the world, Bible societies began getting overtures from Roman Catholics seeking to be incorporated into translation programs and seeking guidance from translation consultants of the United Bible Societies.

---

[19]Nida, ed., *Thousand Tongues*, 24, 25; Richie, "Aymara."

[20]Abbott, ed., *Vatican II*, 125-26, 128.

In light of such radical change, a group of representatives from the UBS met with representatives from the Catholic Secretariat for Promoting Christian Unity to discuss cooperation in translation. The meeting agreed upon a small document called "Guiding Principles for Interconfessional Cooperation in Translating the Bible," published in 1968.[21] This pamphlet outlined procedures for cooperative translation and discussed points of potential conflict, spelling out solutions to each.

Since then interconfessional cooperation in translation has increased rapidly, especially in projects guided by the Bible societies, and has been relatively free of problems in spite of noncooperating pockets on both sides. As an interconfessional translation project gets started both Catholic and Protestant participants may feel suspicious or threatened, but as the work progresses their alienation almost always disappears. Roman Catholics contribute richly to Bible society training programs and translation projects in which they participate. In the twenty years immediately after the formulation of the "Guiding Principles" more than 160 New Testaments and Bibles were translated and published on the basis of the principles therein.[22] In 1988 Roman Catholic translators were also involved in 155 of the 527 different translation projects associated with the UBS, or 29%.[23]

The Modern Era of Non-missionary Translation (1970–). Until the beginning of the modern missionary movement at the end of the eighteenth century, almost all Bible translation was done by people translating into their own language, as we have seen. Translations began to be made by nonnative speakers (assisted by native speakers) into languages like Malay, Massachuset and Formosan in the seventeenth century, and missionary translations into seven languages were published in the eighteenth century, but by the first decade of the nineteenth century translations into new languages were overwhelmingly due to missionary activity. Although native speakers usually played very important parts, missionaries normally instigated and directed the translation.

There were important exceptions to the missionary dominance, of course. Vincente Pazos-Kanki, for example, already mentioned as the translator of the first gospel published in a language of Latin America, ac-

---

[21]This was revised in 1987 as "Guidelines for Interconfessional Cooperation in Translating the Bible."

[22]Philip C. Stine, personal communication.

[23]United Bible Societies, "World Translations," v.

tually translated the complete New Testament in Aymara, but the rest was never published.[24] The most striking exception was Samuel Ajayi Crowther who had been captured as a slave in Nigeria, rescued and released in Sierra Leone by the British navy, and educated in Sierra Leone and in England, eventually to become the first African bishop of the Anglican church. First alone, then assisted by fellow Yoruba and finally supervising Yoruba translators, he produced the whole Bible in his Yoruba language by 1884.[25]

Sometimes missionary control could hardly be avoided if translation was to be done at all. In many situations native speakers did not have any or much formal education, especially in Christian theology or biblical languages. Sometimes they knew neither the original languages of the Bible nor any language into which it had already been translated. Unfortunately, however, in other situations missionary control of the translation process usually lasted longer and was more pervasive than necessary.

But as modern education improved in different parts of the world, as church leadership developed, as more native speakers became theologically trained and some became biblical scholars, as the spirit of colonialism diminished, missionary domination of the translation process lessened in the last third of the twentieth century. Translation consultants from the UBS also began looking for and training talented native speakers to fill as many translation tasks as possible.

In some parts of the world local people began translating on their own without any missionary presence at all, sometimes without much background or education, sometimes not even knowing of or seeking help from the Bible society in their country. In other countries committees of highly educated biblical scholars formed new translation teams and translated into their own languages. SIL instituted national Bible translation organizations in several countries, under which translation is done by a team of local citizens and expatriates. The local citizens sometimes translate into other languages than their own, however, and in such cases still count as missionaries.

Over all, the balance has shifted again in considerable degree back toward people translating into their own language, with or without foreign consultants or assistance. Considerably less than 25% of translators working in association with the UBS are now missionaries.[26] The trend is es-

[24]William Mitchell, personal communication.

[25]Nida, ed., *Thousand Tongues,* 463; Hargreaves, ''Yoruba''; Page, *Bishop.*

[26]Based on the incomplete list of translators in United Bible Societies, ''World Translations.''

pecially strong in revisions and new translations into languages with existing Scriptures. It also occurs sometimes where an Old Testament done largely by native speakers follows the missionary-led New Testament translation effort.

The symbolic date of 1970 used to mark the start of this modern era of non-missionary translation is the time when articles about the training of national translators began to appear[27] and when national translators were attending Bible society training programs in larger numbers. This era will be increasingly significant in the future now that the missionary movement is shifting from its nineteenth and early twentieth century form. Scripture translation continues to grow in the hands and heads of those translators who are native speakers, as well as of those who are missionaries. Translation still accompanies the spread of the church.

The Accelerating Spread into New Languages

The epochs just described highlight major forces which have strongly influenced Bible translation, and with it the spread of the church. A more statistical perspective is also revealing, showing, for example, the quantum leap in translation into new languages which has accompanied the modern missionary movement.

As may be seen in table 1, from 300 B.C. to A.D. 1499—the end of the century in which printing was invented in Europe—part or all of the Bible was translated into just thirty-five different languages. In this span of eighteen centuries, therefore, an average of 1.9 new languages were added per century. In the next three centuries, leading up to the modern missionary period, thirty-nine new languages were added, an average of 13 per century or a 569% increase per century over the average of the eighteen preceding centuries.

Then in the nineteenth century 446 new languages were added, an increase in one century of 503% over the total of the previous twenty-one centuries, 1043% over the total of the previous three centuries, and 3330% over the previous century. These new languages in the nineteenth century averaged 44.6 per *decade*.

For that part of the twentieth century shown in the table, the average increase was 154.38 new languages per decade, or a 211% increase over the average of the decades of the previous century. Figures for the last de-

---

[27]Loewen, ''Training'' and ''Bantu''; Fry, ''Training.''

First-Time Translation into New Languages

TABLE 1

	CENTURY	LANGUAGES ADDED	DECADE	LANGUAGES ADDED	CUMULATIVE TOTALS
B.C.	300	1			1
	200	0			1
	100	0			1
	-0-	1			2
A.D.	100	3			5
	200	1			6
	300	4			10
	400	2			12
	500	0			12
	600	2			14
	700	1			15
	800	2			17
	900	0			17
	1000	2			19
	1100	3			22
	1200	4			26
	1300	6			32
	1400	3			35
	1500	15			50
	1600	11			61
	1700	13			74
	1800	446	1800	7	81
			1810	26	107
			1820	42	149
			1830	26	175
			1840	29	204
			1850	51	255
			1860	71	326
			1870	38	364
			1880	59	423
			1890	97	520
	1900	1,390	1900	100	620
			1910	102	722
			1920	97	819
			1930	146	965
			1940	80	1,045
			1950	142	1,187
			1960	258	1,445
			1970	290	1,735
			1980	175	1,910

Sources: Data from North, ed., *Book of a Thousand Tongues*, 37; United Bible Societies, *Scriptures of the World*, 40-55; Nida, ed., *Book of a Thousand Tongues*, 70.

Notes: Fayumic Coptic, not dated in North's list, is included under 300 A.D. Some early translations were never printed and do not appear in United Bible Societies figures, so the cumulative total above is slightly greater than the total of 1907 listed for 1988 by the United Bible Societies.

cade or two, furthermore, are low because it sometimes takes years for publications to come to the attention of the UBS where the records used in the above calculations are maintained.[28]

This portrayal of the remarkable expansion of translation into new languages needs some explanation and qualification, however. For the earliest centuries it is not always clear just how much of the Bible was translated into any given language at the time indicated. There may also have been translation of which no record remains, or which may have been overlooked. But after 1450 the figures represent only those translations which resulted in the printing of at least one whole book of the Bible, anything from a gospel to a full Bible. Any translation which was not printed, or in which only parts of a full book of the Bible were printed, are not counted.

For example, Roman Catholics have translated the lectionary with its massive amounts of Scripture into various languages, especially since Vatican Council II, but even when that was done in new languages the work was not counted[29] because Bible society statistics are grouped under the categories of Bibles, testaments, and portions, the latter defined as complete books of the Bible, and therefore excluding lectionaries even though these contain more Scripture than any single book. The Bible societies also have a category of selections (less than a whole book of the Bible), but selections are not included in Bible society statistics on new languages.

Another important qualification of the table is that the term *language* is not rigorously defined. In some cases more than one dialect of the same language is included for various reasons which cannot be discussed here. The term *dialect* in this sense refers to any consistently distinguishable speech variety. For example, there are numerous dialects of English, and every person who is a native speaker of English speaks at least one of them. Two or more such varieties are dialects of the same language when they are readily mutually intelligible, but constitute different languages if there

---

[28]Grimes, ed., *Ethnologue*, published in 1988, e.g., lists languages with Scripture which were not yet included in the United Bible Societies "Language Report," also published in 1988. In 1987, furthermore, new languages added to the Bible society list included publications made in 1877, 1880, 1941, 1969, 1977, and each year since 1982. In fact, only seven of the thirty-six languages added were published in 1987.

[29]For a very impressive list of Catholic Bible translation, lectionaries, story books, Bible-history books, and others, see Rijks, *Guide*.

is not such mutual intelligibility.[30] This is different from what people mean when they apply "language" to politically powerful or culturally dominant varieties and "dialect" to subordinate ones, like calling Mandarin a language and Cantonese a dialect, or calling Tagalog or Cebuano languages and the lesser languages of the Philippines dialects.

Only 16.26% of the languages enumerated in the table, furthermore, have full Bibles, and another 36.44% full testaments. 47.30%, therefore, have less than a Testament. In many cases where Bibles or Testaments now exist, these came long after the initial publication recorded in table 1. Of those languages in which less than full Bibles have been published, some will eventually have more Scriptures and others not, depending on factors like the use to which the present publications are being put, the ability of the people to use other languages, and availability of people with the motivation and opportunity to translate.

Some of the languages represented in these figures, furthermore, are no longer spoken. Table 2 therefore shows languages now in use in which translations of some part of the Bible are available. Most of the numbers are necessarily smaller than those of table 1 for various reasons. Some of the languages included in table 1 but not in table 2 have evolved into other languages through normal and inevitable processes of language change; Latin into Italian, Spanish, French, and other Romance languages, for example. In a few other cases all of the descendants of the speakers of a language now speak other languages instead. The language of the Massachuset Indians, for example, is extinct.

Scriptures in Living Languages
TABLE 2

	PORTIONS	TESTAMENTS	BIBLES	TOTALS
Scriptures in living languages	924	582	262	1,768
Percent	52.26	32.92	14.82	100.00
Estimated languages in the world				6,170
Percent with Scriptures	14.98	9.43	4.25	28.65
Number probably needing Scriptures				1,047
Percent probably needing Scriptures				16.97
Additional number possibly needing Scriptures				2,494
Percent possibly needing Scriptures				40.00

Source: Grimes, ed., *Ethnologue* (1988), 741; International Information Services, *Bible Translation Needs* (1988), xix.

---

[30]There are some qualifications to this distinction, which cannot be discussed here.

Where a language is still spoken, furthermore, the translation may nevertheless not be used. Sometimes it was poorly done or the writing system was unreadable, or people may not have wanted it, or were not literate.

The languages in which translations are available, however, are spoken by an estimated ninety percent of the world's population.[31] That fact is impressive, but so also is the fact that the other ten percent speaks an estimated four thousand additional languages,[32] and the ninety percent includes many multilingual people for whom a translation in some other language might be better than the one they have. Translation is under way in many languages which lack them, but is not needed or not presently possible in others because the people are completely bilingual or translation is forbidden by the government. In addition to the estimated number of languages probably needing Scriptures (table 2), there is possible need in 2,494 other languages as well, but information is not adequate for judgment.[33]

Translations for the ninety percent of the world's population in whose languages some translation has already been published are not all finished either. Even in those languages for which full Bibles have been completed, revision or new translation is often in process or needed.

Not shown at all in these tables is the amount of such revision and retranslation which has taken place down through the centuries and continues at the present time. The UBS was cooperating with 103 such projects, 20% of its total, in 1988.[34] No other language can match the more than 450 different Scripture translations that have been made into English,[35] but most contemporary major languages in the world have had more than one, or additional ones are now being prepared for them. Such retranslation or revision is done to improve the accessibility and reduce the distortion in previous translation as language changes, or translators become more capable, or a different theory of translation prevails, or understanding of the principles of translation improves, or a different political situation emerges, or

---

[31]Estimates (educated guesses) run from 85% to 95%.

[32]Grimes, ed., *Ethnologue,* lists 6,170 ''known languages'' (table 2), but is often based on data of unknown validity and comparability.

[33]International Information Services, *Needs,* ix.

[34]United Bible Societies, ''World Translations,'' v.

[35]American Bible Society library files. This number does not include nonstandard English dialects. For brief descriptions of 159 of the English translations made from 1900 until 1982 see Kubo and Specht, *Versions,* 345-75.

there is need to reach a different audience (and so the style or level of language must be different), or a better understanding of the original text is gained through better education, or better texts from which to translate are known. Often revision or retranslation is needed on several of these grounds at once.

So the categories and the numbers in these tables are obviously not complete or fully comparable, but nevertheless the magnitude of the work they reflect is not exaggerated. Such figures provide one of the best indices available to the interrelation between translation and the spread of the church. And in light of the difficulty of the task, the different degrees of skill which different translators have, the many conflicting ideas which have governed translation, and the difficult circumstances under which much translation has been done, this history is a major manifestation of the Spirit of God working in the world and creating the church by means of and in spite of the imperfect human tools available.

CHAPTER 3

Missionaries, Translators, Scholars

Bible translators have often combined translation, general missionary work and a creative, sometimes distinguished scholarship which has frequently both grown out of their translation and affected their translation. During the modern missionary movement, for example, numerous missionary translators have written grammars which have contributed to knowledge of languages not previously described and to the development of modern linguistics.[1]

Translator scholarship has not been confined to languages, however. Cultures of the people among whom the missionary translators worked have sometimes been studied extensively also, and a few translators have written pioneering ethnographies (studies of local cultures), compiled folklore and mythology, or analyzed religion and world views. Others have translated local literature into European languages, discovered cures in tropical medicine, or described the natural world around them.[2]

The combined roles of missionary, translator and scholar constitute in themselves one important aspect of Bible translation in the modern missionary movement, deserving mention here for that reason alone. In addition, however, a look at the careers and accomplishment of some of the people who combined these contributions gives another perspective on translation itself, different from what we discussed in earlier chapters. Translators, even the scholars among them, have not always understood or approached translation in the same way. We have room here only to look briefly at two individuals, chosen for the contrasts they present and for the

---

[1]Wonderly and Nida, "Linguistics." This work deals with other missionary contributions as well as those of Bible translators.

[2]Walls, "Nineteenth Century."

Partial List of Missionary Translators Who Were Scholars TABLE 3

NAME	LANGUAGE OF TRANSLATION	COUNTRY OR AREA	DATE OF PUBLICATION	FIELD OF SCHOLARSHIP
Bartholomäus Ziegenbalg	Tamil	India	B 1727	Malabar religion
Paul Egede	Greenlandic	Greenland	NT 1766	Greenlandic language
William Carey	Bengali et al.	India, Bangladesh	B 1809 et al.	Sanskrit and Bengali languages, botany of India
Henry Martyn	Urdu Persian	Pakistan, India, Iran	NT 1814 NT 1815	Persian language
Joshua Marshman	Chinese	In India for China	B 1822	Chinese language
Robert Morrison	Chinese	China	B 1823	Chinese language
Adoniram Judson	Burmese	Burma	B 1835	Burmese, Pali languages
H. Goldie	Efik	Nigeria	NT 1862	Efik language
I. G. Krönlein	Nama	SW Africa	NT 1866	Hottentot languages
Joh. G. Christaller	Twi	Ghana	B 1871	Twi and other Akan languages and cultures
W. Holman Bentley	KiKongo	Zaïre	NT 1893	KiKongo language
Robert H. Codrington	Mota	Banks Islands	B 1902	Melanesian anthropology
Thomas J. Dennis	Igbo	Nigeria	B 1913	Igbo language
Edwin W. Smith	Chilla	Zambia	NT 1915	African anthropology
Maurice Leenhardt	Houailou	New Caledonia	NT 1922	Melanesian anthropology, missiology
Malcolm Guthrie	LiNgala	Zaïre	NT 1942	Bantu languages
Kenneth L. Pike	Mixtec	Mexico	NT 1951	Linguistics
Paul Lewis	Lahu Akha	Burma	NT 1962 NT 1968	Anthropology
Joseph E. Grimes	Huichol	Mexico	NT 1967	Linguistics
William L. Wonderly	Zoque Spanish	Mexico	NT 1967 B 1979	Linguistics, translation theory
Robert Longacre	Trique	Mexico	NT 1968	Linguistics, text analysis
Herbert Brown	Toaripi	Papua New Guinea	B 1983	Anthropology

Criteria for Selection: A major figure in the translation of at least a full testament (translator) into some other language than their own (missionary), with some other significant and recognized scholarly contribution in any field (scholar).

translational issues their work implicitly raises. The issues themselves, in turn, will be discussed again in appropriate chapters later on. Of those missionary-translator-scholars we could not describe here, an incomplete sampling is listed in table 1 as token of the much fuller account they and others deserve.

William Carey and His Associates

At the beginning of the nineteenth century the legendary William Carey[3] became the prototypical missionary-translator-scholar, writ large. He was not the first Bible translator in India, not by nearly a century back to Bartholomäus Ziegenbalg, who worked in the Tamil language of South India and published a New Testament in 1715.[4] But when he did appear on the scene at the very beginning of the modern missionary movement, William Carey, together with his associates, produced an explosion of translation and of scholarship.

Carey, of course, is notable for other scholarship than that which is in focus here. He wrote *An Enquiry into the Obligations of Christians to Use Means for the Conversion of the Heathens . . .* , published in 1792, a seminal document at the beginning of the modern missionary movement. He and his associates founded primary schools and the famous Serampore College near Calcutta, India. His research and reports to the British governor general in Calcutta contributed to the abolition of infanticide and of the cremation of wives alive on the funeral pyres with their deceased husbands.

Carey also developed his five-acre garden into one of the finest botanical collections in Asia, presented papers on agricultural problems to the Asiatic Society of Calcutta, and was instrumental in founding the Horticultural and Agricultural Society there. He edited several important botanical works published at the Serampore press he had helped establish. He was also made member of various scientific societies in England in honor of such work, as well as elected president of the Agricultural Society of India.[5]

Formative Experiences. Carey arrived in Calcutta in 1793 at the age of thirty-two. In more recent times he and his family would never have been sent to India by any responsible mission board because of his wife's emotional instability, and she eventually became insane there. An adverse side of his character was his insensitivity to her needs as he pushed ahead against all odds, where even she was part of the odds.[6]

Soon after arriving in India Carey became manager of a remote factory making indigo dye so that he could earn some money to support his family

---

[3]E. Carey, *Carey*; Marshman, *Life*; G. Smith, *Carey*; S. Carey, *Carey*; Oussoren, *Carey*. The best critical treatment seems to be Potts, *Baptist Missionaries*. Unfortunately, writing and publication schedules preclude use of A. Christopher Smith's forthcoming book, *The Mission Enterprise of Carey and His Colleagues*, which will be a companion volume in the same series with the present one.

[4]Nida, ed., *Thousand Tongues*, 418-19.

[5]G. Smith, *Carey*, 216-40. S. Carey, *Carey*, 388-402; Roxburgh, *Hortus*; Roxburgh, *Flora*.

[6]E. Carey, *Carey*, 86.

and his mission work. He believed that missionaries should support themselves, and although he received help from his mission board from time to time this was sporadic and usually in response to appeals for particular projects, not for him or for his family.

Carey studied Bengali at every opportunity, and after a few months began preaching to groups of people in the factory and in surrounding villages. Bengali was not by any means the first language Carey had learned. Although he came from an extremely poor family and had little formal education, at the age of twelve he had memorized most of a book of Latin vocabulary and had studied the brief grammar included in it. Apprenticed to a shoemaker, he had continued to learn Latin as he worked, plus Greek and Hebrew, using grammars borrowed from minister friends, seeking their help with the difficulties he found, and studying a portion of the Bible every morning in each language. On top of that he had learned on his own to read French, Dutch and Italian.

With this background, instead of borrowed books from which to learn Bengali, Carey used manuscripts of a translation of parts of the New Testament done by a colleague who had earlier worked in India. And instead of ministers who helped him with the classical languages he employed Ram Ram Basu as teacher and interpreter. He also mingled with people and talked with them, and in this respect his management of the indigo factory was an asset to his learning.

Soon Carey was able to converse, conduct his business with the factory workers, and preach in Bengali. Carey also became aware that the translation he was studying was not adequate, and began his own, working from Greek and Hebrew. By 1796, three years after his arrival in India, he had completed a draft of the New Testament, and a part of the Old Testament as well. He revised the New Testament several times in the next four years before it was published, writing each draft out by hand in Bengali script.

The British authorities were strongly opposed to missionary work in India, and Carey was able to stay there only because he was officially employed at the indigo factory. In 1799 missionary reinforcements arrived from England, but on reaching Calcutta they had to flee to the nearby Danish colony of Serampore to avoid government efforts to send them back. The indigo operation failed at about the same time, and Carey joined them at Serampore.

In the new party of missionaries was William Ward, a printer and newspaper editor who became one of Carey's two longtime associates. He also became a missionary scholar, although not a translator, producing a work on Indian culture[7] in addition to running what became a major press with its own type foundry, paper mill and bindery.

The other of Carey's two major associates was Joshua Marshman, also in the new group. He, too, became a missionary-translator-scholar producing the first published translation of the whole Bible into Chinese right there in Serampore, as well as translating some Chinese texts into English and working with Carey in other translation tasks. He was also in charge of the educational program at Serampore. Both Marshman and Ward, like Carey, were involved regularly in preaching and in other more direct forms of Christian ministry as well.

They became known as the Serampore Trio, working together for twenty-four years until Ward died in 1823, after which Carey and Marshman continued for another eleven years until Carey died in 1834. Although the account which follows focuses on Carey's contribution, he was a part of a team without which he could have done only a fraction of what he did.

Carey's Language Work and Translation. In 1801, not long after he moved to Serampore, Carey was appointed teacher of Bengali in the new Fort William College in Calcutta, founded to give junior functionaries of the East India Company more knowledge of their Indian surroundings. There he associated with well-educated Bengali speakers and was exposed to a more prestigious dialect than was spoken in the distant backwoods location of the indigo factory, both changes a great help to his literary and scholarly work. His salary from there also supported much of his translation work for many years.

Table 2 shows most of the major works which Carey and his associates produced in Bengali, the primary language among the many in which they worked. Carey's own primary responsibility as listed for each project in the table entailed other tasks as well. When he was translator he worked and reworked his manuscripts, checking with the source text and discussing wordings with Bengali assistants. He wrote out every new draft by hand and then saw the manuscript through the press by editing and proofreading it.

As author of a grammar, or compiler of a dictionary Carey performed much the same task, except that he wrote his own text rather than translate it. As editor he took someone else's writing or translation, prepared it for the press and proofread it. When he was supervisor someone else did the

---

[7]Ward, *View.*

Carey's Major Bengali Publications

TABLE 4

CAREY'S ROLE	NEW TESTAMENT	OLD TESTAMENT	BIBLE	OTHER
Translator	dr 1796			
Translator	1800 Mt			
Translator	1801			
Author				1801 Grammar
Editor				1801 Pratapiditya
Editor				1801 Buttees Sinhasan
Compiler				1801 Colloquies
Translator		1802 Pent		
Editor				1802 Ramayana
Editor				1802 Mahabharata
Translator	2r 1803	1803 Wis		
Author				2r 1805 Grammar
Translator	3r 1806	1807 Pro		
Translator		1809 Hist	Completed	
Translator	4r 1811	r 1813 Pent		
Author				3r 1815 Grammar
Translator	5r 1816			
Compiler				1818 Dictionary v1
Author				4r 1818 Bengali Grammar
Compiler				? Dialogues
Translator				3r 1818 Dialogues
Translator				b 1822 government laws
Compiler				2r 1825 Dictionary v2
Supervisor				1827 Abr Dictionary 2v
Compiler				3r 1830 Dictionary 3v
Translator	8r 1832	3–4r 1832	3r 1832	

Sources: Nida, ed., *Book of a Thousand Tongues*; United Bible Societies, *Scriptures of the World*; G. Smith, *The Life of William Carey*; Hooper and Culshaw, *Bible Translation in India, Pakistan, and Ceylon*; Wilson, "Remarks of the Character and Labors of Dr. Carey"; J. C. Marshman, *The Life and Times of Carey, Marshman, and Ward*; S. Carey, *William Carey D.D.*; some original publications of the Serampore Press, listed in references to this book. Sources differ on some dates, so dates should be taken as approximate.

Abbreviations: abr = abridged; b = began; c = change in script; dr = draft completed; Hist = Historical; Mt = Matthew; n = new translation; Pent = Pentateuch; Pro = Prophets; t = Translation completed; v = volume; Wis = Wisdom books; 2r, 3r, etc. = second edition, revised, etc.; ? = Date unknown.

first draft under his direction, and he then checked it, edited it and proof-read it.

The Bengali New Testament progressed through eight editions, each of them incorporating at least a revision, sometimes a complete retranslation. The Old Testament was published in sections, parts of it revised and republished two times, other parts three. The final page of the final revision came off the press the year before Carey died in 1833.

Carey's Bengali grammar went through three editions, with revisions, as well. His dictionary consisted of 2,260 large printed pages. The *Colloquies* and *Dialogues* were Bengali texts collected and published for students learning the Bengali language. The other publications were works which Bengalis had written or had translated from the classical Sanskrit language of India, all edited for the press and proofread by Carey.

As time went on the work of the Serampore Trio began to have an effect on Bengali literary culture. The infusion of Serampore publications became model and catalyst to the development of modern Bengali prose. Bengali writers, some of whom worked with Carey in the college, began to write prose on their own, some of which Carey encouraged and published.[8]

Linguistically, however, India has more and deeper complications than simply its enormous number of languages. Traditionally, for example, Indians believed that the only language worthy of literary production, especially religious literature, was Sanskrit, a classical language learned by the educated, which functioned much like Latin did in Europe during the Middle Ages. Sanskrit was therefore the special province of the Brahmins, and a key to their religious control. Bengali and the other major languages of north India are modern vernaculars descended from Sanskrit, like French and Italian are descended from Latin, so Carey also saw Sanskrit as a stabilizing force among the many languages and dialects.[9]

Carey realized early that if the Bible was to be taken seriously by Indian religious leaders it would therefore have to be translated into Sanskrit, even though Sanskrit was no longer anyone's mother tongue. He also believed that a Sanskrit translation could be a source text for translation into vernaculars which were derived from it, a text from which Indians who did not know Greek and Hebrew could translate. So Carey started studying Sanskrit along with Bengali, and an appointment as teacher of Sanskrit was added to his responsibilities at Fort William College.

Carey wrote a Sanskrit grammar which was much larger than his Bengali grammar, running to 1,040 pages, 9 x 12'' in size, as against less than two hundred smaller pages for the Bengali. In doing so he drew on grammars of Sanskrit previously written by Indian grammarians, and seemed to treat it as more foundational than his grammars of the vernaculars, which were briefer aids to language study.

Carey and Marshman also began to translate the *Ramayana* into English. Three volumes of this Hindu classic Sanskrit epic were published both in Sanskrit and English, but the manuscript of a fourth volume was

[8]Sen Gupta, *Missionaries,* 185-89; G. Smith, *Carey,* 202-204; Walker, *Carey,* 236.

[9]Young, *Hinduism,* 33-34.

destroyed in a disastrous fire at the press in 1812. The fire also destroyed an enormous amount of other work, including manuscripts and printed parts of books, both Scriptures in several languages and other publications. The *Ramayana* series was never finished after that catastrophe. In the meantime, translation of the Bible into Sanskrit was also proceeding regularly, the last part of the Bible published in 1822. Carey did not revise and retranslate the Sanskrit Bible, however, as he repeatedly did the Bengali.

Carey also set about to learn Marathi, a language spoken far away in the west-central part of India. He lived outside the Marathi-speaking area, but learned the language from an educated speaker while he was translating the whole Bible into it, publishing it in 1819, and revising the New Testament in 1824. Characteristically, he also wrote a grammar and dictionary while he did all that, and Marathi was added to the languages he taught at Fort William.

Carey turned to Hindi as well, one of the major languages of north-central India, and translated the Bible in much the same way by 1818, although apparently he did not write a Hindi grammar or dictionary. He also revised the New Testament in 1818, after which he undertook some further revision and new translation of the gospels, including one in a different script.

These four great languages, then, Bengali, Sanskrit, Marathi and Hindi, were the ones in which Carey was the primary translator at Serampore, but that was only the beginning. A different pattern of work was used for Oriya, Carey's fifth language, spoken to the south of Bengali. This time he entrusted the drafting to an Oriya who translated from the Bengali translation. In the meantime, Carey learned the language by studying the draft, wrote a grammar of it, and himself revised the draft, checking it with the Greek and Hebrew original texts, and consulting with the Oriya translator as he went along. The Bible was completed in 1815.

This led to a procedure where Carey supervised numerous translations done by Indian assistants. They would translate into their own languages, consulting with each other about problems as they did so. Carey would examine and revise their drafts, then edit and proofread them.[10] In this way he produced a full Bible in one additional language, a New Testament with part of the Old Testament in five more, the full New Testament (but nothing of the Old) in eighteen beyond that, and less than the New Testament in several more yet, for a total of thirty-four languages. Sometimes Carey

---

[10]E. Carey, *Carey,* 360-61.

wrote grammars to help him in his supervision and checking, especially in languages he found to be somewhat different from most of those he worked with, like Kashmiri (spoken far away) and Telugu (from a different language family).

By 1832, two years before Carey's death, 212,000 volumes in forty languages had been published by the Serampore Press. During the first decade of the modern missionary movement, 1800 to 1810, furthermore, the Serampore Press published all but one of the seven Scriptures in new languages enumerated in table 1 of chapter 2. In the seventh case, Urdu, although the Serampore Press did not publish the first portion, it did publish the 1814 New Testament. In the 1810s thirteen of the twenty-seven Scriptures in new languages were likewise printed at Serampore. In the 1820s eighteen of the forty-two Scriptures in new languages came from that press. Thus, in the first three decades of the modern missionary movement forty-nine percent of first translations into new languages anywhere in the world were published at Serampore, most of them translated by Carey or under his supervision, and virtually all of them edited and proofread by him.

Carey's Translation in Perspective. Unfortunately, however, Carey's massive language and translation program was seriously flawed.[11] If there had been competent Bible translation consultants[12] in Carey's day, they would not have approved for publication much, if any, of the translation work done by Carey and under his supervision. More than that, during Carey's own lifetime translations appeared, or were under way, which quickly supplanted ones produced at Serampore.

In eleven of the languages in which New Testaments were produced by Carey, little or no further Scripture translation was ever published because the church did not follow the translation into the language, or if it did, it followed using a more important language, usually Hindi. In another fourteen of the languages in which New Testaments were produced follow-up translation was published twenty to seventy years later. In some of these cases the Carey translation had a useful life, but in others a different translation was needed when evangelism eventually did begin and a church was established. Carey never lived to see some of the translations on which he worked distributed or used.

---

[11]Potts, *Baptist Missionaries,* 79-113.

[12]See chap. 4, below.

None of Carey's own translations were as futile, however, as the Chinese Bible on which his colleague Joshua Marshman spent fourteen years with Joannes Lassar, an Armenian raised in Macao on the coast of China and living in Calcutta. Aside from the impossibility of doing an adequate task so far from any Chinese-speaking community, the full Bible published in 1822 preceded Robert Morrison's translation, made in China itself, by only a year, and portions of Morrison's translation were coming off the press at about the same intervals as those done in Serampore. In fact, Morrison's New Testament was published eight years before that of Marshman.[13]

Carey remarked frequently that he knew the translations he made and supervised were not perfect, and he hoped that others would build on them. One of the purposes of founding Serampore College was to train Indians who could improve the translations.[14] The fact that he revised the Bengali so many times, the language he knew best, indicates a search for quality in translation. Nevertheless, most of the translations which Carey supervised lasted longer than most of the ones in which he was the primary translator.

Of the translations Carey made himself, the Sanskrit lasted longest before the publication of a translation which ultimately replaced it. The interval was thirty-three years, a very respectable period for a pioneer translation like that. Perhaps it lasted longer because Sanskrit was a classical language rather than a vernacular language, and Carey's linguistic weaknesses described below did not come into play as much. Or perhaps it lasted because other translators just did not get around to making a new translation sooner. At any rate, the translation was not very good, marked by "inelegance of expression and harshness of construct."[15]

A rival New Testament to Carey's Bengali New Testament appeared eighteen years after Carey's first edition of the New Testament was published, just two years after his final revision. The Hindi and Marathi translations were effectively supplanted after fifteen years of the first edition, thirteen years and two years, respectively, of the revised edition. Clearly

---

[13]Nida, ed., *Thousand Tongues*, 72. Coincidentally, Morrison's *Grammar of the Chinese Language* was published at Serampore one year after Marshman's *Elements of Chinese Grammar* came off the press there.

[14]Young, *Hinduism*, 35.

[15]E. Carey, *Carey*, 606-607.

other people were not content with Carey's work and began early the laborious effort of preparing alternatives. Among other problems, the dialect of his Marathi New Testament was not widely known, and the script was inappropriate.[16]

The reasons for the short lives of some of the Carey translations are easiest to see in languages like Hindi and Marathi, which were not spoken where Carey lived. Carey, who had learned to read so many languages from books, and who found he could quickly learn to communicate in another north Indian language because of its similarities to Sanskrit and Bengali, was naive in his understanding of how people use languages. He did not sense deeply enough the fact that even though particular languages are very similar in grammar and vocabulary, and even though people speaking different related languages in north India can quickly learn to understand each other, effective communication depends on subtle factors within each system, making each language significantly different from the others in more ways than obvious, automatic vocabulary and grammar differences. Nor did he sense that reliance on translation from Sanskrit made his vernacular translations heavy, wooden and bookish.

But it is Carey's translation into Bengali, on which he worked for thirty-two years, at which we must look for a deeper evaluation of his efforts. His lack of a sense of the importance and subtlety of language as it is used was true here also, so he did not pick up and incorporate the natural flow of the language. His Bengali translation lacked idiomaticity and naturalness, although these qualities improved over the years. ''Serampore Bengali'' was what some contemporary Bengalis contemptuously dubbed the language translated and written by the missionaries.[17]

Part of the reason for the poor Bengali in translated material was certainly Carey's inadequate understanding of the nature of translation, of language, and of communication.[18] Carey believed that ''accuracy'' was enhanced by as literal a translation as possible, with the wording and the grammatical structure of the translation geared to the wording and grammatical structure of the Greek or Hebrew original. Ironically, as with many other translators his overwhelming drive to make the Scriptures accessible in the languages of

---

[16]Hooper and Culshaw, *Bible Translation,* 105.

[17]Sen Gupta, *Missionaries,* 96; Das, *Prose;* Culshaw, ''Carey.''

[18]See chap. 1, above.

India and beyond was thwarted partly by the distortion he introduced through fear of distorting the Bible by making it truly accessible.

But Carey's lack of formal education also caused him trouble. Carey had learned to read the original languages of the Bible, but he did not have a disciplined classical education such as some translators who followed him had. Highly educated people like Henry Martyn, who lived in Serampore for a while and admired Carey very much, nevertheless found Carey's interpretation of the original languages strange at times, and that weakness contributed to its rejection by some users.

It is useful to note that although Carey's failure to recognize the importance of subtle language usage and to understand the nature of the translation task were common to translators of his time and for long afterwards, there were significant exceptions, even among some of his friends. Henry Martyn's work in Urdu and Persian was very durable, and Adoniram Judson, who stayed at Serampore for a short time when he was on his way to Burma, eventually produced a Burmese Bible which is still in use, and has remained more readable, better Burmese, than some of the later attempts to revise or replace it. Of course, when a translation lasts a long time the "King James version effect" begins to play a part in its continuing use. Whether understandable or not, its language becomes sacred language, which people feel should not be changed. But Judson's translation was nevertheless significant in the length of time it lasted in its own right because he used better translation principles and had a better sense of language use than Carey did.

Carey's Political Problems. There were other reasons also for the short life of some of Carey's major work, not all of them translational faults, and in fact the translations which replaced Carey's were not always much better than his. The saddest reason was ecclesiastical politics.[19] The Serampore Trio were Baptists, dissenters, part of a minority in Britain. The Protestant ecclesiastical world in Calcutta was dominated by the Anglican state-church majority. When Carey first arrived in Calcutta he went to visit one of these Anglican ministers and was received with cool condescension. "He carried himself as greatly my superior, and I left him without his having so much as asked me to take any refreshment, though he knew I had walked five miles in the heat of the sun."[20] Such attitudes diminished in time, but were never fully overcome.

---

[19]Sen Gupta, *The Christian Missionaries in Bengal,* 44-49.

[20]E. Carey, *Memoir of William Carey,* 97.

Three months after the British and Foreign Bible Society was formed in 1804 its secretary wrote a letter to one of the same Anglican leaders in Calcutta, proposing the formation of a Committee of Correspondence to coordinate Bible Society assistance to the translation and distribution of Scriptures in the area. When Carey discussed this with one of the Anglicans the latter "expressed his astonishment at the liberality and condescension of the Bible Society in thus inviting Dissenters to unite in a committee which would have to correspond with bishops, and added that 'nothing could be done at present'."[21] Eventually the Anglicans did agree to work with the Baptists in the committee, but when Anglican committee members withheld funds which the Serampore men felt had been given for their work, the Trio withdrew.

The Calcutta Auxiliary of the British and Foreign Bible Society, a branch society formed in 1811, was dominated by Anglicans, although the Baptists were also members. That auxiliary began to promote rival translations to the ones being done at Serampore.

Then in 1827 some Anglicans and others who practiced infant baptism by sprinkling began to object to Greek *baptizo* "baptize" being translated with a word meaning "immerse" in the Serampore translations, and requested the British and Foreign Bible Society to withdraw the support which it had been giving them. In vain Carey and Marshman pointed out that many of the classic translations of Europe, and some of the European translations which the Bible Society itself distributed translated the word in the same way they did. They pointed out also that their work had been extensively distributed by Anglicans in India, and that they, in turn, had gladly distributed translations by others in which the word was borrowed from the Greek rather than translated.

The Calcutta auxiliary, however, sided with those who had protested the translation and recommended that the British and Foreign Bible Society withdraw support. The Bible Society went along with the request and required that the Greek word be transliterated, carried over into each language without being translated. The Serampore men refused to capitulate. As a result of this conflict, in some languages of India and elsewhere there developed two translations, one supported by the Bible Society and the other not, because the word for "baptize" had to be different.[22]

---

[21]J. C. Marshman, *Life*, 231-32.

[22]Marshman, ibid., 441-45; E. Carey, *Carey*, 311-14; Canton, *History*, 2:114.

Sadly, also, the Serampore literary work did not last after Carey and Marshman died. These men and Ward, who had worked so unbelievably hard and accomplished so much, left no institutional framework in which their literary heritage could be directly carried on. They could not tolerate fellow missionaries working closely with them who were not as single-minded, and who did not follow their exhausting work schedules. They would not incorporate new, less experienced missionaries into their tight system of communal life at Serampore, either. The younger people also strongly disliked Marshman. After a series of policy disputes between the new missionaries and the older ones, Carey and Marshman—Ward was dead by then—were forced to withdraw from the mission and mission property in 1827, taking their work with them.[23]

Maurice Leenhardt

William Carey in the first third of the nineteenth century, for all of his vision was nevertheless very much a creature of his era. He both articulated and manifested his times in the missionary movement. Quantity aside, his translations were like those of many contemporaries, as was his approach to Bengali, his first Indian language. His non-translational scholarship, although more varied than that of most missionary-translator-scholar, was also in the same mold as others of the century and later.

Maurice Leenhardt in the first quarter of the twentieth century, on the other hand, was a translator whose ideas fit better into our present period than into his own. His approach to Houailou translation showed a viewpoint on Melanesian culture which most of his missionary contemporaries could not understand and did not accept. His type of scholarship, likewise, had few contemporary parallels among missionary-translator-scholars.[24]

Carey arrived in India and confronted Hinduism and Islam as an antagonist. His discussions on religion were argumentative.[25] He referred to Hindu culture and religion as having ''poison'' in it.[26] His letters con-

---

[23]Potts, *Baptist Missionaries*, 22-26; Oussoren, *Carey*, 111-15.

[24]The primary sources on Maurice Leenhardt used here are Clifford, *Person* and "Translation"; Crapanzano, "Preface"; Leenhardt, "Translating," *Do Kamo* and *Grande Terre*.

[25]E. Carey, *Carey*, 143-44, 296.

[26]Ibid., 150-51, 157.

stantly refer to "superstition" and "idolatry," and his attempts to learn about such things were motivated by a desire to undermine and replace them. Some Indian historians and reformers have agreed that the missionary disgust with the moral situation in Bengal at the time was warranted,[27] but that is not the point. Carey's strategy was to attack from the outside, although the Serampore missionaries were not nearly as hard on Indian culture in their magazines intended for readers in India as they were in their letters, suggesting that some of the harshness may have served to justify themselves to their supporters.[28]

There were many things Leenhardt did not like in New Caledonian culture either, but his approach was that of a learner, not a would-be conqueror. Faith could not be forced on the Melanesians, but had to take shape in them.[29] Conversion, he believed, was a process of reciprocal translation between two worlds, emerging from a conversation, not from a monologue or an argument. When asked by a skeptical university student in Paris how many people he had really converted, Leenhardt, who had worked for twenty-four years with teacher-evangelists to build a strong church replied, with a twinkle in his eye, "One," referring to himself.[30]

Carey caught the attention of the Protestant world with his dramatic accomplishments. He is on anybody's list of giant figures in the missionary movement, and there have been several biographies about him. He worked in the heart of the British empire, in a country with millions of people, and in thirty-four of its languages.

Leenhardt is little known outside French-speaking countries and the circles of specialists on Melanesia. The usual histories of mission do not mention him. Although there have been numerous articles about him in French, the first book-length biography and analysis of his work appeared in 1982. He worked on the periphery of the world, from the standpoint of Europeans and Americans, in only one language, in a tiny country where nobody not directly connected was paying any attention. But of the two, Leenhardt was the more profoundly innovative, the more creative, the one

---

[27]Potts, *Baptist Missionaries*, 7.

[28]Sen Gupta, *Missionaries*, 65-75.

[29]Clifford, *Person*, 45.

[30]Ibid., 1.

who grasped the complicated role of the receptor[31] in that form of communication which is translation.

Leenhardt as Learner. Leenhardt and his wife Jeanne were both from influential French Protestant families, his father a minister and professor. They were sent out by the Paris Missionary Society to New Caledonia in the Pacific, to lead work which had been started six years before by twenty-four or so Melanesian Christians from the Loyalty Islands, some 150 miles away, where the mission had been working for a time. These teacher-evangelists, many of them considerably older than Leenhardt, had made converts among the New Caledonians and had formed alliances with a few local chiefs in Melanesian fashion.[32] Their presence was opposed by French colonists, who were seeking their expulsion because they taught people to read, write and add, skills which helped people resist exploitation. The young Leenhardt felt intimidated and unprepared, especially as he realized the teacher-evangelists knew so much more than he did.[33]

The strategy of the missionaries supervising this work from the Loyalty Islands had been to try to control from a distance, but within the first three years Leenhardt learned another relationship. He wrote to his parents that he was "astounded at all the pathways different from ours that I've discovered in their hearts. But it's not enough to discover a country, you've got to know how to map it."[34] In coming to this realization, Leenhardt was on his way towards becoming one of the finest field ethnographers in his day, one of the most sensitive students of another culture than his own. His developing ethnographic inquiry into life and its meaning in New Caledonia was also to be the heart of his approach to Bible translation.

Leenhardt's preoccupation with understanding New Caledonian culture, its religion, world views, power structures and everything else, was the foundation of his other contributions as well. He became the supporter and defender of people who were losing their land and their lives. His knowledge of how the New Caledonians saw things and experienced them made him able, sometimes, to thwart moves of the colonists, so that he

---

[31]See chap. 1, above.

[32]Rey Lescure, *Racines.*

[33]Clifford, *Person,* 32, 55-57.

[34]Clifford, "Translation," 5.

gained their enmity and risked his life.[35] And under the Holy Spirit, this one missionary couple, together with the teacher-evangelists and the Christian village leaders, built a church that grew in twenty-four years to be almost half as big as the Catholic church with its nearly one hundred missionaries (priests and nuns), a church which had been there half a century longer, but had no leadership from among the people.[36]

Leenhardt took the traditional religion of the island very seriously. He felt strongly the relationship between New Caledonian life and the world view that supported it. He believed that God was already in New Caledonia before the gospel came,[37] and he wanted the resources of traditional religion to become an expression of Christian faith: "Something is spiritual only if it is fashioned in its own form. Outside this there is only the domain of human authority."[38]

Leenhardt learned, for example, that "gods come from men and totems from women." The term that was being used for God was identified with male ancestral lineage, and represented power, as manifest in the chief. But there was another authority as well, associated with the female ancestral lineage, the totem. It represented life, and was manifest in the authority of the maternal uncle. The chief incarnated the heritage of masculine "power" and the maternal uncle the heritage of feminine "life." These forces were complementary, in reciprocal union. The New Caledonians wanted to use the masculine term for God, and Leenhardt did not object, but he encouraged ways of combining with it the feminine, totemic meanings.[39]

For example, Leenhardt heard a Melanesian pray to "God who is wholly long . . . you stretched yourself out . . . and arrived in Monéo, and again stretching yourself you came to Paci'." "Long, fluid, stretching, spreading" was a reference to the life force coming out of the totem. In "Long God" life was linked to power, and God was androgynous. Leenhardt remarked to university students in France years later that "the concept of the 'Long God' is a moving one, touching the missionary's heart."[40]

---

[35]Clifford, *Person*, 102-103; Guiart, *Destin*, 10-13.

[36]Clifford, *Person*, 56, 60.

[37]Ibid., 81-82.

[38]Maurice Leenhardt, "President de la Société des Missions Évangéliques" (typescript, 1932), quoted in Clifford, *Person*, 121.

[39]Clifford, "Translation," 16-19.

[40]Ibid., 10.

This would have been too much pagan world view for some missionary translators, and Leenhardt was uneasy about such things for some time, too. Some translators in other situations have used a borrowed term for God, but most have rejected that solution, using a local term because they realize that people must have some way of identifying with God. Even many of those translators, however, never understood the worldview contexts of the term they used as fully as Leenhardt did. They typically checked for unwanted characteristics of the deity, ones contradictory to a Christian understanding of God, but did not thereby necessarily learn how the local religious system worked. Where they sometimes therefore accommodated to pagan contexts and pagan meanings unknowingly, Leenhardt did so knowingly, and with purpose.

Leenhardt called the New Caledonian Christians ''pagano-Protestant.'' At first he was expressing dismay when he did so, but later believed that the combination was a normal and healthy state of affairs. Other missionaries who are horrified at syncretism among converts may not look deeply enough to see that it is always present in any Christian, any church, including in themselves and in their supporters. Leenhardt sought to give the new hybrid, this product of conversation between two worlds, significant meaning.

Leenhardt as Translator. One of the teacher-evangelists had translated the Gospel of Matthew into the Houailou language. The process of conversation, and of the conversion of the translator, continued for years as Leenhardt and the Melanesians together grew a New Testament, published in 1922.

> The work of the translator is not to interrogate his native helpers, . . . but rather he must solicit their interest, awaken their thinking. . . . He does not create a language; this is composed by the native himself; it is the product and translation of his thoughts. And the translator, he who has initiated this thinking, merely transcribes the words he has aroused, overheard, seized upon—fixing them in writing.[41]

Leenhardt's procedure was to begin the translation of a passage with a single helper, Boesoou Erejisi,[42] the oldest of the teacher-evangelists and the one most knowledgeable in traditional ways. He then read and discussed draft

---

[41]Leenhardt, ''Bible,'' quoted in Clifford, *Person,* 86.

[42]R.-H. Leenhardt, *Sociologue.*

chapters with his students, and later preached on them. In the afternoon after a sermon students summarized what they had retained, sometimes phrasing something much better than anyone had thought of before. He discussed troublesome parts repeatedly with people, and would listen until someone spontaneously expressed the idea in a meaningful way.[43]

Many other translators have come upon an expression for a Biblical idea in a similar way but may have shrunk from using it, fearing that it might carry over too many associations from the traditional religion. Leenhardt, however, was especially glad when the expression came out of the people's religious experience and belief. "Propitiatory" was translated by a term which referred to a leaf used in traditional religion to heal a wound after the proper sacrifices had been made.[44] The term for "redemption" referred to "a tree planted on land that had been cursed by the blood of battle or some great misfortune." The tree absorbed the evil and misfortune and took it away from the world.[45]

For Leenhardt the process of translating the New Testament was a process of self-understanding as well as of understanding the world of the New Caledonians. It enriched his Western religious concepts as well as those of Melanesians:

> The missionary has once more experienced the power of the gospel, and the people have helped him in better understanding this power. He perceives that even though the psychological and theological terms are abstract and indefinite in European languages, the equivalent expressions as they come from the experience of the believer are concrete and definite. He realizes that religious facts expressed in abstract terms are so often without active value and constitute merely a dead formula. He has seen the danger of himself betraying the gospel, if he does not employ the living and meaningful vocabulary. Otherwise he becomes an unskillful translator, dogmatic and artificial, failing to understand the spiritual development of the believers.[46]

The mission board and other missionaries, however, began to oppose Leenhardt's work. They could not adopt his learning, consultive style, and wanted to impose their control from the outside. They wanted to transplant

---

[43]Leenhardt, "Translating," 151-52; Clifford, *Person*, 83-84.

[44]Leenhardt, "Translating," 151.

[45]Ibid., 150.

[46]Ibid., 152.

their experience from the Loyalty Islands, where a hierarchical indigenous social structure existed, to egalitarian New Caledonia, and to form a hierarchically organized church there. They expanded the number of missionaries and dominated the teacher-evangelists. Leenhardt, who had returned to France, protested in anguish, but his advice was disregarded.[47]

So in time Leenhardt began teaching at universities and research centers in Paris. He developed a distinguished academic career, reflecting on and interpreting what he had learned from the New Caledonians. He was eventually appointed to the prestigious chair of History of Primitive Religions at the École Pratique des Hautes Études. He did further important field research, writing numerous books and other works.[48]

Leenhardt's anthropological work is being revived in the 1980's through English translations and evaluations, in part apparently because it bears an implicit critique of assumptions of ''objectivity'' in anthropology, and of the anthropological tendency to abstract too much from human life.[49] His ethnological work was all of one piece with his translation, growing out of the same conversation over long periods of time, and showing up the limitations of short-term ethnological research, as much as those of monologue translation.[50]

In time Leenhardt also became an elder statesman of the French-speaking Protestant missionary world. People partially forgot what they had held against him, and times changed. He founded Le Monde Non-Chrétien, an important missionary-anthropological journal, and in other ways took intellectual leadership in missionary scholarship and practice emanating from France.[51] He died in 1954.

The Contrast

So in strikingly different ways these two men, Carey and Leenhardt, each played their respective roles as missionary-translator-scholar. Whereas

---

[47]Clifford, Person, 112-21.

[48]Clifford, Person, includes six pages of titles of publications by Leenhardt on both missionary and Melanesian topics. A few of Leenhardt's major books are listed in the reference list of the present volume.

[49]Crapanzano, ''Preface,'' xxii-xxv.

[50]Clifford, Person, 142-44.

[51]See the tributes to Leenhardt's missionary and anthropological contributions after his death in Le Journal des Océanistes 10 (Décembre 1954) and Le Monde Non-chrétien 33 (Janvrier-Mars 1955).

Carey's translation work was a mighty broadcast, speaking to India in many voices, Leenhardt's was a quiet conversation with New Caledonians. Whereas Carey gave translations to the Indian peoples, Leenhardt grew a New Testament among the New Caledonians. Whereas Carey manufactured translations in a factory, Leenhardt, the teacher-evangelists, his New Caledonian students and fellow conversationalists gave birth to theirs in the church, the school and the villages. But whatever their strategy, however different their understanding of their task, in both cases their scholarship and their translation were inextricably intertwined.

CHAPTER 4

The Translating Institutions

William Carey was a Baptist, a missionary of the Baptist Missionary Society for most of his career, a member of the Serampore mission, and at times a member of the Corresponding Committee of the British and Foreign Bible Society in Calcutta and of the Calcutta auxiliary of that society. So even right at the beginning of the modern missionary movement Carey operated within a network of institutions which helped to make his translation work possible.

Like Carey, individual Bible translators have almost always been associated with the church which spoke the language of the translation and/ or the home church in the case of missionary translators. Church and/or mission have often taken part in translation on every level. For a long time many missions even operated their own presses, of which Serampore was the greatest. The constitution of the first American mission board, the American Board of Commissioners for Foreign Missions, founded in 1810 by Congregationalists, provides "That one quarter part of the annual income from the funds of said Board shall be faithfully appropriated to defray the expense of imparting the Holy Scriptures to unevangelized nations in their own languages: . . ."[1]

As just one illustration of the variety of different churches, missions, and other institutions which can be involved in a language over time, the history of translation into Arabic since the sixteenth century includes Catholics (at least Lebanese Maronites, Dominicans, Paulists and Jesuits), Church of England, Congregationalists, Greek Orthodox, Presbyterians and Egyptian Copts. Publishers for these translations included commercial ones, Congregation for the Propagation of the Faith, Society for Promoting

---

[1]American Board, *Constitution*, 5.

Christian Knowledge, British and Foreign Bible Society, American Bible Society, Society of Jesus, Trinitarian Bible Society, Convent of S. Sauveur, Peace and Love Society, and the Bible Society in the Near East.[2]

At the present time, many institutions continue to be involved in Bible translation around the world, including such specialized groups as the Lutheran Bible Translators and the International Bible Society, for example, among Protestants. Much Catholic work is led by the Catholic Biblical Institute. But overall, the contributions of two types of institution greatly outweigh all others. They are the national Bible societies in the various countries, working together in the United Bible Societies, on the one hand, and the Summer Institute of Linguistics on the other. In the case of the Bible Societies, they incorporate and coordinate much of the widespread work being done by many churches and missions.

The Bible Societies

The founding of the British and Foreign Bible Society in 1804 was mentioned earlier as the symbolic beginning of the Bible Society era in Bible translation.[3] In the words of its original "Laws and Regulations" the "sole object" of the Society "shall be to encourage a wider circulation of the Holy Scriptures. . . . without Note or Comment."[4]

The Society had several precursors, one of which was the Society for Promoting Christian Knowledge, listed above in the discussion of Arabic. It was founded in 1698, more than a hundred years before the British and Foreign Bible Society, to operate schools and to publish and distribute Scriptures, prayer books, and Christian tracts.[5] It continued to play an important role in Scripture publication and distribution for a time after the Bible society began.

There were also several earlier institutions called "Bible societies" or similar terms as well. The most important was the Canstein Bible Institution, founded in 1710 at Halle, Germany, as an agency of the pietist movement which gave rise to the pioneering Moravian missionaries under the leadership of Count Zinzendorf. By the time of the formation of the

---

[2]Nida, ed., *Thousand Tongues,* 14-15.

[3]See chap. 2, above.

[4]*Reports,* 3.

[5]Owen, *History,* 20-21.

British and Foreign Bible Society nearly one hundred years later, it had distributed over two and one-half million Scriptures in inexpensive editions. It still exists, located in Witten, in the Ruhr.[6]

The new Bible society, however, immediately established its leadership in Scripture translation and distribution. It quickly began publishing translations in new languages as well as republishing and distributing existing ones, and within months became a model for other Bible societies, encouraging their establishment in other countries. Its immediate success and that of societies like it was due in part to factors which are still pertinent in the Bible society movement today.

Its founders, for example, were stimulated by a profound concern for Christian faith and life, and by belief that the Bible was important for sustaining these, but were distressed to know that Bibles were not always readily accessible. Some people were too poor to buy them; others were frustrated when editions were sold out; and in many languages the Bible had never even been translated at all. Although agencies like the Society for Promoting Christian Knowledge had done their best they were not able to meet the need. Even today, Bible societies are the only significant source of Scriptures in most languages, even in most countries of the world.

The movement started by the British and Foreign Bible Society was more successful than previous agencies for several reasons. First of all, it was an interdenominational movement far ahead of its time. Roman Catholics, to be sure, were not included in most Bible societies until after Vatican II, although early on the British and Foreign Bible Society did encourage and provide help to at least one Catholic Bible society in Europe and to a number of Catholic individuals interested in Scripture distribution.[7]

Except for Catholics, however, the government of the British and Foreign Bible Society was deliberately and explicitly formed to represent the range of Christian expression in England. Anglicans and non-Anglicans in equal numbers served on the governing committee of the society, and were matched in the two secretaries who carried out much of the business. Foreigners living in England were also included on the committee, and a third secretary was from that group.[8]

---

[6]Aland ''Pietismus,'' 6; Stoeffler, *Pietism*, 36.

[7]Owen, *History*, 118-24, 173-84, 441-42, 450-51.

[8]Ibid., 53-55.

One advantage of interconfessional cooperation was that greater resources from more churches and individual Christians could be applied to the Bible society task than would otherwise have been possible. The society could also serve almost the full range of Protestant and Orthodox churches, missions and ultimately translators. Thus the British and Foreign Bible Society avoided a major limitation which hampered an institution such as the Society for Promoting Christian Knowledge, members of which all belonged to the Church of England.

The provision that Scriptures would be distributed "without note or comment" was essential to keeping the movement interconfessional. Notes in other published Scriptures often advanced interpretations not acceptable to all Christians. Because Bible societies never published such editions the world has been spared many rival denominationally oriented translations. Present interpretations of this rule do permit notes about difficulties when translators are not sure of what the text means or when cultural or historical facts about the text need to be explained.

Interconfessional cooperation was greatly strained at times in the British and Foreign and other Bible societies, as when they withdrew support from Carey for translating *baptizo*.[9] The Trinitarian Bible Society (which still exists), in turn, split off from the British and Foreign Bible Society in 1831 because the latter refused to set theological requirements for membership and would not open its meetings with prayer because of theological mistrust within the membership. In time the national Bible societies outgrew the restriction on prayer but have never placed theological requirements on members, governors, or staff.

The other major national Bible societies which ultimately became extensively involved in Bible translation outside their own countries were the Netherlands Bible Society (founded 1814), the American Bible Society (founded 1816 as a coalition of several slightly older state and local Bible societies), and the National Bible Society of Scotland (founded 1861 from societies and auxiliaries which had earlier split from the British and Foreign Bible Society). The Netherlands Bible Society worked in Indonesia, and the National Bible Society of Scotland in several countries, but with small constituencies their share of the translation task was necessarily limited. Until after the middle of the present century, when translation efforts of all these societies were channeled through the United Bible Societies,

---

[9]See chap. 3, above.

the great bulk of Bible society involvement in translation was carried first by the British and Foreign Bible Society, later joined by the American Bible Society.

Preprofessional Help for Translators. By the first half of the twentieth century these two large societies had fairly standard ways of serving translators, almost all of whom were missionaries or committees of missionaries and native speakers. Each had an official in the home office responsible for dealing with translators, primarily through correspondence, and each had a subcommittee of the board responsible for decisions about translation. Each had a set of rules for translators, specifying limits on the languages and dialects into which translations should be made, which texts of the original languages should be used, and other requirements. Each offered exegetical help from biblical scholars to translators who wrote to London or New York asking about the meaning of Bible passages. Each often provided some financial support toward the cost of those translations with which it was associated.

The societies were concerned, of course, about the quality and acceptability of translations. Where more than one mission and/or church, except the Roman Catholic church, had an interest in a language the Bible societies insisted that translation be a joint effort, in keeping with the Bible society interconfessional ethos and because it wanted all groups to be able to use the Scriptures it produced. The committee which was formed would translate under the Bible society umbrella.

Bible society translation officials required translators to sign a statement that they had adhered to the rules for translators, and when manuscripts were received from translators they were examined for evidence of poor work. For example, without knowing the language but with the help of a Greek concordance, someone in the translation department would look up the various passages in which a theological term occurred in Greek, and check to see how consistently it was translated in the manuscript. An examiner who found what seemed to be inconsistencies in the wording would write to the translator, asking for an explanation, occasionally uncovering significant problems. What was consistently wrong would be overlooked in such an approach, however, and it gave the impression of favoring literal translation because the examiner could not discuss the problems at length with the translator and make sure that verbal consistency was really warranted in a given passage.

Then when a translation was finished the Bible society edited it for publication and had it printed. The printed books were sent back to where the language was spoken, and were distributed through the Bible society agent there or through the churches or missions involved. The price of a book was based on what ordinary people would be able to pay, not on the cost of this whole expensive process.

The Bible societies, in short, contributed experience, biblical scholarship, coordination and money. They made it unnecessary for each new translator or translation committee to reinvent all aspects of translation procedure each time a new project got started. Their role was greatly valued by most translators, and was a major force in the advancement of Scripture translation in the world.

There were, however, some fundamental inadequacies with this system, most dramatically manifested when a translation occasionally sat unsold on the shelves of a Bible society or missionary warehouse after publication. Nobody wanted the books because the translation was unreadable, or the writing system was not clear, or nobody knew how to read, or the translation was in a poor choice of dialect, or the people for whom the translation was intended were not ready for it in some other way.

For the Bible societies to help translators more adequately, however, they would have to develop types of knowledge which nobody had at the time. These included:

1. An adequate theory by which translators could understand their task.

2. A practical body of operational principles much more comprehensive than the societies' existing guides, geared to the theory of translation.

3. Ways of teaching the theory and practice of translation to translators all over the world.

4. Ways of helping translators develop better writing systems for unwritten languages.

5. Ways of helping translators with other technical linguistic problems such as complicated grammatical structures in the languages in which they were translating.

6. Ways of determining need for translation in a particular language or language area, and which dialect in a range of dialects should have a translation.

7. Ways of gearing the level of language in a translation to the language competence of the potential readers.

8. Ways of making the great store of scholarly knowledge about the meaning of the biblical texts more adequately accessible to translators and of focusing this knowledge on the particular needs and questions translators have.

9. Ways of enabling qualified people to work with translators, helping them learn to find and apply the kinds of information implied above, making sure that they were following good principles and knew how to apply translation theory.

10. Ways of organizing translation projects so that the best available combination of translators could be involved, sound working procedures used, and all interested churches and missions informed of what was going on, and able to comment.

11. Ways of assessing the skill of each translator and the quality of each translation project from its early stages, on the spot, before inadequate principles and procedures became fixed.

This list of what the Bible societies needed to know and to be able to do is formulated from today's perspective, of course. In the early part of this century many of these needs were only vaguely felt and were relatively unformulated if felt at all. The concept of a professional approach to translation which incorporated biblical studies but went beyond them to draw on the social sciences, had not been sufficiently articulated. Nor, for that matter, had the social sciences been sufficiently developed.

Professionalized Help for Translators. The symbolic beginning of the professional era in Bible translation was listed earlier as 1943, when Eugene A. Nida joined the American Bible Society,[10] but this era also had its precursors. One, for example, was the service of Edwin W. Smith as Editorial Superintendent for the British and Foreign Bible Society from 1933 to 1939. He had been a missionary translator in the Chilla language of Zimbabwe after preparing a writing system for it. But Smith was also an anthropologist in the tradition of missionary-translator-scholars, author of several books on African cultures,[11] a man with the stature to become president of the Royal Anthropological Institute.

Smith drew together some of the wide experience which the British and Foreign Bible Society and others had gained in working with translators, his own experience, and his anthropological sense, to focus more fully on

---

[10]Chap. 2, above.

[11]For examples, see "References" in this volume.

translation problems from the standpoint of the receptor language than did some of the biblical scholars who preceded and followed him.[12]

An essential precursor was also the emergence of modern linguistics in the United States between the two World Wars. "Descriptive linguistics" as it was called when it first began to influence translations, was born in the United States out of a marriage between anthropological investigation of nonliterate peoples and the older historical linguistics and philology of Europe.[13] Here, at last, was an academic discipline where researchers focused on determining the actual sound and grammatical structures of languages, especially languages previously unwritten and little known to Westerners, analyzing them in their own right, rather than describing them as though they conformed to classical European grammars.

Out of this study came discoveries concerning sound structures, grammar and meaning which in the 1930s were harnessed to the task of Bible translation by such people in the Summer Institute of Linguistics as Kenneth L. Pike and Eugene A. Nida, who was an early member before joining the American Bible Society staff. Both of these men made such contributions to linguistics that each was later elected president of the Linguistic Society of America for a term.

In the 1940s new theories of communication also emerged, beginning with mathematical models based on the telephone and other forms of electronic communication,[14] but leading on eventually to understanding communication as a social process, providing models which have been influential in cross-cultural communication and translation theory for Bible translators.[15]

So when Nida joined the staff of the American Bible Society at the age of 29, he brought with him unbounded energy, a flair for showmanship in public lecturing, a long-standing interest in Bible translation, a mind with the capacity to relate seemingly disparate information, an undergraduate degree in Greek, an M.A. in Greek New Testament, a Ph.D. in linguistics,

---

[12]E. Smith, *Shrine.*

[13]Bloomfield, *Language*; Sapir, *Language.*

[14]Shannon and Weaver, *Communication*; Cherry, *Communication*; E. Hall, *Silent Language* and *Hidden Dimension.*

[15]Chap. 1, above. Nida lists the influence of theoretical developments in other disciplines as well in *Science of Translating,* 5-10. Some other formative influences are also mentioned in chap. 6, below.

a short period of living and working among the Tarahumara Indians of Mexico, extensive reading in anthropology, and several summers of teaching at the Summer Institute of Linguistics. This latter program increasingly introduced translators of many missions to linguistic analysis in the field, and provided Nida with a personal tie to Bible translators who were spreading out over the world after this training.[16]

Nida immediately set out on long trips of many months, visiting translators at work, using his linguistic and anthropological skills to help them develop better alphabets, understand better the grammatical systems of the languages in which they were working, investigate meanings in the local language and find ways of translating biblical meanings. He shifted the focus of American Bible Society help radically by giving practical assistance on the spot, focused on problems created by the receptor language. He kept extensive notes as he worked, accumulating the factual base he needed for the development of a realistic theory and practice of translation grounded in the problems of translation worldwide.[17]

Concurrent with this gradual professionalization of translation was another series of events within the Bible society movement, leading to the formation of the United Bible Societies.[18] At present the United Bible Societies is a federation of 110 societies in as many countries, with its own staff of specialists to help individual societies with technical tasks like publication, distribution and translation. About fifty translation consultants and advisers serve in the United Bible Societies and an additional ten translation staff specialists serve in some of the individual Bible societies directly. These people work with churches in the selection of translators, training them, providing resources, helping them with technical problems, checking the quality of translations, and doing research on translation theory. Consultants do not usually engage directly in translation themselves.

United Bible Societies translation consultants are drawn primarily from people with a Ph.D. either in linguistics or in biblical studies, and have some exposure to the other field. Many also had field experience as missionaries, linguists or anthropologists before becoming translation con-

---

[16]For a sketch of Nida's life and accomplishments up to 1973 see North, "Nida."

[17]Data from those early trips may be found in some of Nida's books including *Morphology, Bible Translating, Learning, God's Word, Customs,* and *Message.* On the theory of dynamic equivalence translation which emerged, see chap. 6, below.

[18]Somerville, "UBS"; Daniels, ed., *UBS.*

sultants, and recruits usually served for a period under the supervision of an experienced consultant before working independently.

Published Helps for Translators. Along with the personal services provided to translators and the many training institutes and seminars conducted for them all over the world, Nida and his colleagues have produced a variety of published helps, including a quarterly periodical, *The Bible Translator,* textbooks, a series of monographs on translation and a series of translators' handbooks on individual books of the Bible.

Most of the handbooks, which by 1989 covered almost all of the New Testament and several books of the Old, are written by teams consisting of a linguist and a biblical scholar. Each summarizes conclusions from up-to-date biblical scholarship on the text but then goes on to discuss ways of translating the text into other languages. Here, for example, is one extract from the treatment of Galatians 2:19, "So far as the Law is concerned, however, I am dead—killed by the Law itself,"[19] or "For I through the Law died to the Law:"[20]

> "Dying" to something means primarily to be rescued from its domination and control. "Dying to the Law" therefore means that Paul no longer considers the Law as controlling him, as important in his life; he has given up the Law as a valid instrument through which one is put right with God. *I am dead* must be understood figuratively, and a shift from metaphor to simile may be required in some languages, for example, "I am just the same as dead," or "I am like as though I were dead." However, it is fairly possible that this figurative language, even in the form of a simile, would be completely misunderstood in the sense that it was the Law which condemned Paul to death. It may be important in this instance to indicate by a marginal note that "dying to the Law" would, in this context, mean "no longer under the control of the Law." It may also be necessary . . . that the implications of *I am dead* be included within the text, for example, "I am as it were dead and therefore not controlled by the Law. . . ."[21]

An even more fundamental kind of help for translators is the *Greek-English Lexicon of the New Testament Based on Semantic Domains.* This recent pioneering work brings some of the insights of semantic-domain theory from linguistics and anthropology to the analysis of New Testament

[19]*Good News Bible.*

[20]Revised Standard Version.

[21]Arichea and Nida, *Galatians,* 59.

vocabulary. Whereas the usual Greek-English lexicon (dictionary) is organized by Greek words in alphabetical order, this one is organized by ninety-three areas or domains of meaning, such as, 1. Geographical objects and features, 2. Natural substances, 10. Kinship terms, 12. Supernatural beings and powers, 73. Genuine, phony, 85. Existence in space, and 93. Names of persons and places.

Each of these major domains is subdivided as well. Examples of subdomains under "Geographical objects and features" are, A. Universe, creation, B. Regions above the earth, C. Regions below the surface of the earth, K. Sociopolitical areas, N. Pastures and cultivated lands, and P. Thoroughfares, roads, streets, paths.

Organization by semantic domains allows the translator to study and contrast the range of related meanings in the receptor language with the corresponding, but never identical, range or ranges in Greek. By seeing domains as wholes, translators can better judge how meanings of various terms partially overlap between the two languages, and what term would be best to use in the receptor language in a given context. Through the indices a translator can look up any term in Greek to find the domains under which its meanings are treated, or look up many of the meanings in English, or look up sample passages to find some of the more important domains within them.

An example of how meanings are treated for translators may be seen in the following entry from the "Geographical objects and features" domain, "Universe, creation" subdomain:

> **1.1** κόσμος, ου *m*: the universe as an ordered structure. . . . In many languages there is no specific word for universe. The closest equivalent may simply be 'all that exists.' In other instances one may use a phrase such as 'the world and all that is above it' or 'the sky and the earth.' The concept of the totality of the universe may be expressed in some languages only as 'everything that is on the earth and in the sky.'[22]

Another primary tool for translators is *Greek New Testament* put out by the United Bible Societies.[23] This Greek text differs from previous ones in that it was done by an international and interconfessional committee of scholars, including Catholic participation. That fact makes it much easier

---

[22]Louw et al., eds., *Lexicon*, 1:1.

[23]Aland et al., eds., *The Greek New Testament*.

for all the members of translation committees which now include Roman Catholics to use the same Greek text. The notes on the text list many variants which are found in different ancient Greek manuscripts, but differ from previous Greek New Testament texts in that they include only those variants which make some difference in translation. Translationally meaningless variations in spelling and punctuation, for example, are not included. The editors furthermore rate each variant placed in the text according to the probability that it is the original form. Translators are therefore immediately alerted to cases where the variant in a footnote has about as much probability of being the original as the one in the text. This Greek text is used in most current Bible-society-related translation projects in which translators are competent to use the Greek text at all. [24]

Along with published helps the United Bible Societies has modeled the dynamic equivalence theory of translation by producing translations based on it in English and various other major languages. [25] Although such translations as the *Good News Bible* in English were produced for widespread distribution, not as helps for translators, they do show translators what a dynamic equivalence translation can be like in contrast to more traditional approaches, and some people find them very helpful when translating into other languages.

Weaknesses in Bible Society Translation Contributions. In spite of these major achievements, however, there are weaknesses in the United Bible Societies translation program. Its size often makes it unwieldy and slow, and translation consultants are often stretched to the limit because of the many translation projects with which they work. The energy required for political maneuverings within an international federation of societies is great, as well, especially when administrators from the older societies remain reluctant to give up controlling power and engage in turf struggles. Sometimes, also, the program is hindered by personnel in the United Bible Societies or in a member national society who lack vision or competence. Occasionally Scripture publication may be delayed by a national Bible society because of overload or inadequate procedures, and may not appear until several years after the translation is finished.

---

[24]The Bible Societies seek to have translation done by the most competent people available. If knowledge of the Greek is not included among the available competencies, they seek to strengthen the exegetical competence of the committee in whatever way they can.

[25]Nida, *Good News.*

Now that solutions have been found to what have so far turned out to be the easier problems of translation theory, translation personnel do not offer stimulating new insights as often as they once did, so that the creative edge which marked the earlier years of the professionalization of translation has been dulled. Helps for translators and other works on translation sometimes give the impression of having been hurriedly prepared. Consultants are too overworked to make many significant contributions to their own academic disciplines, or even to do long-range research on translation. The opportunity to inject a cross-cultural perspective on biblical interpretation into the field of biblical studies has been only weakly pursued.

Nevertheless, the massive contribution of the Bible societies to translation continues to grow, and the world of Bible translation has been radically transformed from what it was forty years ago. In 1988 the United Bible Societies were cooperating with some 2,000 primary translators, not including review committees, belonging to 250 churches and missions, working on 527 active translation projects in 104 countries. In 424 of those languages a part of the Bible was being translated for the first time, while in the remainder an existing text is being revised or a new translation is being done.[26] The professionalization of translation, furthermore, has brought the translation of the Bible in all parts of the world into the twentieth century and has provided a base for advances in years ahead.[27]

The Summer Institute of Linguistics

Nida and the Bible societies were not alone, of course, in bringing professionalism to Bible translation. By far the most important of the other forces has been the Summer Institute of Linguistics, another "translating institution," but very different from the Bible societies.

For the Bible societies, translation feeds into their program of publication and distribution of Scriptures. The United Bible Societies translation budget was only twelve percent of its total budget in 1987. For SIL, on the other hand, production and distribution of Scripture flows out of its translation work. It does not publish many of its own translations, but usually relies on agencies like the World Home Bible League and the Inter-

---

[26]United Bible Societies, "World Translations."

[27]A sample of the broad range of recent work on the theory and practice of translation produced by United Bible Societies consultants may be seen in Stine, ed., *Issues* and *Current Trends*.

national Bible Society, both independent of the United Bible Societies, or less often on member societies of the United Bible Societies. Even when the actual printing is done by SIL on its own presses the printing is normally financed by one of these agencies.

The United Bible Societies translation program exists primarily to help other translating individuals and institutions, churches, missions, and combinations thereof, to do their work well. Hundreds of SIL workers, on the other hand, are actually engaged in translation. The organization exists to help provide the Scriptures, now usually a New Testament and an abridgement of the Old Testament where possible, in all of the functioning languages of the world where it is needed, no matter how small the population, how isolated, how insignificant, how low in prestige. Its policy is based on the belief that God wants all peoples to have the Scriptures in some language they can fully use. And since literacy is an important part of seeing that Scripture is used, SIL emphasizes teaching people to read their own language, so that development of approaches to literacy is also one of their important emphases.[28]

The SIL Contribution. SIL was started by William Cameron Townsend in 1934 as a summer training program for prospective Bible translators, with two students in attendance. He had worked first as a Bible distributor in Latin America, but when he discovered that most people in Guatemala were members of minority groups who could not read Spanish he began working as a translator among the Cakchiquel Indians. In studying and analyzing the language and translating the New Testament he came to appreciate what the new linguistics could offer.[29]

The linguistic father of SIL, however, is Pike, who shared the role with Nida for a few years before Nida left to work with the American Bible Society. His own translation was into one of the Mixtec languages of Mexico, following which his career was balanced between teaching at the University of Michigan, teaching in SIL summer programs, and research and consulting with Bible translators all over the world for SIL.[30]

By 1989 3,000 SIL members (about half of their total membership), from thirty-two countries had worked in 1,200 languages spoken in fifty-

---

[28]Larson, "Summer Institute"; Gudschinsky, "Literacy."

[29]E. Pike, "Townsend"; Hefley and Hefley, *Uncle Cam*; Cowan, *Word.*

[30]E. Pike, *Pike.* A few of Pike's major works are listed in "References," below.

three countries, and had completed or had been substantially involved in the completion of 300 New Testaments.[31] Many SIL workers fit the missionary-translator-scholar category, with about two hundred of them having earned the Ph.D., primarily but not exclusively in linguistics. Members have also published more than 12,000 books and articles ranging from technical linguistic analyses to primers and other cultural development materials, more than half of these publications written in the languages into which they had translated or were translating.[32]

High quality of practical training for beginning-level and intermediate linguistic field work has been a hallmark of SIL training for translators.[33] At the present time year-round training centers are located in the USA (Texas), England and Australia, and during the summer, courses are also taught in nine other locations around the world as well.

SIL has established a strong place in linguistics unparalleled by any other missionary organization in any secular academic discipline.[34] This is due in part to the enormous amount of accurate field data and analyses of many languages collected and published by members of SIL and on the fact that a few of its members along with Pike have made valuable theoretical contributions.

The all-important place given linguistics in SIL is not fully matched, however, by emphases on other fields essential to the multidisciplinary nature of Bible translation. Anthropology, for example, has always been included in SIL training and emphasis, but in a less exacting way than linguistics. There are, to be sure, scores of people with advanced degrees in anthropology in the group, so that the anthropological sophistication of the better translators is usually higher than that in most missions. Pike's *Language*, furthermore, is a valuable contribution to anthropological theory as well as to linguistics, and contributions by members to anthropological data are considerable.[35] But in spite of all this, the group does not give the same rigorous overall attention to culture as to language, and the

---

[31] Mildred L. Larson, personal communication.

[32] Elson, ed., *Language*, viii; *S.I.L. Bibliography*.

[33] Robbins, "Training"; Kietzman, "Field Training."

[34] Newmeyer, *Politics*, 59-61; Rensch, "Contributions."

[35] Dye and Merrifield, "Anthropology"; Taylor, "Summer Institute."

worldview challenging anthropological depth which Leenhardt found to be essential for translation is not often apparent.

Stranger yet, from some perspectives, is what seems to be minimal participation in professional level biblical studies. Of the large number of members with Ph.D. degrees, only a handful of these are in biblical studies, while some 150 have Master's level degrees in fields related to the study of the Bible. All members are required to demonstrate a knowledge of the Bible, and in each field situation consultants with greater biblical knowledge do oversee the exegetical quality of translations. A few members also do sophisticated linguistic research on biblical texts. But this organization of highly educated and academically oriented people created expressly to translate the New Testament does not have the same standards for academic competence in biblical studies that it has in linguistics.

In its earliest years, people in SIL were preoccupied with the linguistic analysis of unknown languages in preparation for translation, and did not give concerted and systematic thought to translation theory as such, looking to the Bible Society staff for workshops and other translational help. Then in the 1960s they began to develop their own translation workshops, exploring translation theory and preparing helps for translators.[36] Now their primary textbook on translation[37] is superior to the pioneering but older Bible societies textbook.[38] Some SIL members are now also breaking more new ground than are Bible society consultants in some areas of linguistic analysis necessary for the further development of translation theory and practice.

One such type of contribution which SIL is making with increasing sophistication is in sociolinguistic surveys of language areas.[39] It is often difficult to determine in which of a series of rather similar dialects, for example, a translation should be made, or to know if the nearly universal multilingualism in an area means that translation into some of the languages is not necessary. SIL has teams of people conducting surveys in a

---

[36]Moore, "Translation"; Beekman and Callow, *Translating.*

[37]Larson, *Translation.*

[38]Nida and Taber, *Translation.*

[39]Blair, *Survey.*

few of the linguistically complex areas of the world, and some of their members are developing the theory and methodology of such surveys.[40]

Another area of advance is the study of structures in larger units of text in different languages, how sentences are combined smoothly, and how larger units like paragraph and episode can be handled effectively in translation. Some members have also been developing "semantic structure analyses" of different books of the New Testament in which such sets of relationships between larger and larger pieces of the Biblical text are described and visually portrayed.[41]

SIL has also produced other helps for translators which are different from those published by the Bible societies. Its periodical for translators, *Notes on Translation,* for example, is less formal, more of an "in house" publication than *The Bible Translator,* published by the United Bible Societies, whereas a new SIL periodical called *Occasional Papers in Translation and Text Linguistics* is more academic and technical than either, geared to scholars interested in the development of translation theory.

For many years SIL worked primarily in previously unwritten languages where the people were largely monolingual. They saw translation, therefore, as a task which could only be done adequately by expatriates with linguistic training working with "language helpers." But with a changing world, and as SIL is now working in countries where people have more education, their approach to translation by native speakers has also broadened. Especially in Africa their members frequently serve as advisers or consultants to people translating into their own languages. Considerable effort also goes into training national translators in some areas. SIL also encourages the development of national Bible translating organizations in various Asian and African countries,[42] in addition to its long-standing internationalization of expatriate personnel.

In some respects SIL is organized like many independent parachurch missions of a more conventional sort. Potential members apply for admission, and if accepted raise their own support in pledges from individuals and churches. This is one source of strength, as the size of SIL is not limited by what funds the organization itself can raise. It can grow as long as

---

[40]Grimes, ed., *Ethnologue* encapsulates this information and other like information from a variety of sources.

[41]E.g., Johnson, *2 Peter*; Banker, *Titus.*

[42]Larson, "Indigenizing."

approved candidates can find individuals and churches to support them. It may also be a source of weakness, because SIL people are sometimes available and eager to step in to do the work themselves rather than holding back and encouraging qualified local people to do it.

Conflicting Views on SIL. SIL has a sister organization called the Wycliffe Bible Translators. The two are separate corporations, with separate functions relating to separate constituencies, but with the same membership. The role of WBT is to receive financial support from the outside Christian community in the home countries of the members, promote prayer support for the work of SIL, and care for personal needs of its members. SIL, in turn, provides academic training, receives money not only from WBT but also from grants, relates to governments, universities, or other local sponsors, and provides a range of services, along with translating the Scriptures.

This organizational split has been criticized by some outsiders because money is given to WBT for religious purposes so far as church contributors are concerned, but spent by SIL for scientific and developmental purposes so far as the host countries are concerned. The dual arrangement has never been concealed, and for members the purpose of the two organization is identical, with each organization having a separate role. Many observers, however, even sympathetic ones, see it as doublespeak. It seems doubtful to them that church people would give to something called the Summer Institute of Linguistics, the original organization, as freely as they give to something called the Wycliffe Bible Translators, or that governments would sign contracts with an organization called Wycliffe Bible Translators as readily as with one called Summer Institute of Linguistics.

In spite of its impressive accomplishments, SIL has been touched by other controversy as well. Townsend's founding vision, for example, included signing contracts with the governments of the countries in which SIL would work, authorizing it to study the languages and cultures of the minority peoples, conduct literacy programs and engage in other forms of community development. It would be understood that Scripture translation would be part of the program as well. This policy has come under criticism both from some fellow Christians who have seen linkage with sometimes repressive governments as inhibiting a prophetic stance against injustice and from other observers who have accused the organization of being a tool of United States foreign policy in these countries, destroying local cultures in support of national regimes.

SIL specializes in Bible translation, but its contracts with governments are stated in secular terms. It has therefore been accused by some of being too missionary because significant churches have emerged in some places as a result of its presence and work, and because members cooperate with a church where a church already exists. But it has also been accused by others of not being missionary enough because it does not have a stated goal of church planting.

In some countries where SIL works, minority groups live in places which can be reached only by long and dangerous trips by trail or river. SIL therefore has its own large networks of aircraft and airstrips to transport people and supplies. Such facilities are also made available to other organizations and to local citizens. Some people, however, find the aviation program at odds with the culturally sensitive stance the group claims to take.

Translators belonging to SIL often work under very difficult field conditions for years, many living in accommodations far below their home-country standards because it is locally appropriate when working in remote villages. To give such workers some relief and to provide for administrative and support services, SIL has therefore established centers in rural areas of some countries, where members can rest, do concentrated academic work, prepare materials for printing, etc. In some cases the centers also serve as training centers for members of minority groups who become teachers, health promoters or community leaders in their home villages. These centers however, give some observers the impression of Western "company towns," where several hundred translators and support workers live in isolation from the peoples and cultures around.

In spite of the fact that it was opposed and attacked by Roman Catholics in its early days in Latin America, SIL extended some of its services to the Roman Catholic church long before Vatican II, as it also did to everyone else. The use of SIL planes to transport priests brought criticism from some groups in the United States, and rather than change its policy of service to all, the organization withdrew from the Interdenominational Foreign Missions Association.[43]

The heaviest published attacks on SIL have come from a few anthropologists who portray the translators as lying and scheming agents of the United States government, leaving a swath of cultural destruction behind

---

[43]Hefley and Hefley, *Uncle Cam,* 186-92.

them as they establish their religious empire all over the world.[44] These attacks are not anthropological studies, however, but sectarian political journalism. The authors show no understanding of the ethos of SIL or of missions in general.[45] However, although the overall caricature they draw is nonsense,[46] there is enough documentation of troublesome issues in these writings to make them painful to SIL and to others interested in Scripture translation.

Some of the range of criticism to which SIL has been subjected from many quarters has implications for what the organization seeks to do in translation, while other criticism shows the narrowness of the critics. One indication of the maturity of the leadership is that it is grappling with the problems which do appear significant to them.

Complementary Visions

For the first thirty-five years of this two-hundred-year span we call the modern missionary movement William Carey and his Serampore colleagues and the Indians translating under his supervision constituted a little "institute of linguistics," producing Scripture translations, grammars and dictionaries in Indian languages. During the last more than thirty-five years of this same two-hundred-year period we have seen a big "Serampore" emerge, producing Scripture translations, grammars and dictionaries in languages of the Americas, parts of Africa and Asia, and the Pacific. There is a fascinating similarity in outlook, purpose and vision between "institute" and Institute, between Serampore and "Serampore." And spanning both of those periods and the time between them stretches the Bible society movement, involved with both Serampore and Institute and sometimes in tension with both.

---

[44]Stoll, *Fishers* and "Wycliffe"; some of the papers in Hvalkof and Aaby, eds., *God*.

[45]In contrast, Clifford, *Person*, is not only critical but also informed, sensitive and perceptive in its treatment of Leenhardt and of missionaries in general. See also Whiteman, ed., *Missionaries*; Salamone, ed., *Missionaries*; Beidelman, *Colonial Evangelism*; Boutilier et al., eds., *Mission*.

[46]Corrective reviews of and replies to these books include Canfield, "Accusation"; Kornfield, "Fishers"; Yost, "Mandate"; and Stipe, "Perspective." For a self-assessment of the group's academic contribution see Brend and Pike, eds., *Summer Institute*. The scholarly reports included there have a very different flavor from many fund-raising "prayer letters" which SIL members send to church constituencies, some of which are quoted with ridicule by detractors. A sober but uncritical popular presentation to the Christian public is Cowan, *Word*.

Both Serampore and Institute were/are concerned with the need to translate for the first time into all the languages possible, a goal which the United Bible Societies presently qualifies. Although 65 to 70% of current translation projects with which the United Bible Societies are associated are also in languages with no previous Scriptures,[47] such translation is part of a somewhat larger Bible society concern to insure availability of Scriptures in languages with significant populations or with promising, growing churches, to see that the Scriptures in such languages are adequate and remain so with dynamic equivalence translations, and to insure that translations everywhere change in response to changing language and cultural development. The Serampore/Institute and Bible society visions are generally complementary, and there are times when SIL and Bible societies collaborate directly. A joint statement in 1988 formally recognized this complementary relationship for Africa.[48] Occasionally the two institutions also disagree, but certainly translation of the Scriptures in the past generation has been far more greatly advanced because both exist than it would have been if either one existed alone.

The Serampore/Institute mandate as presently stated could conceivably end in the next few decades as the first New Testament translations are completed in all the remaining languages where they are needed according to SIL criteria. But the Bible Society mandate will go on because language and culture never stop changing. People will regularly need new translations or revised translations in languages which already have the Scriptures as long as the centrality of translation to the Christian faith and the making of books do not end.

---

[47]United Bible Societies, *Annual Report*, 20, records 65%, whereas United Bible Societies, "World Translations," v, indicates 70%.

[48]Belete and Robbins, "The United Bible Societies in Africa and the Africa Area of the Summer Institute of Linguistics."

CHAPTER 5
Theology in Translation

A translation consultant was once trying to help inexperienced translators express idiomatically what they had drafted in a relatively mechanical, literal way. As he did so, however, he sensed uneasiness and resistance, until finally one of the pastors in the group turned to the end of his English Bible and read:

> I warn every one who hears the words of the prophecy of this book: if any one adds to them, God will add to him the plagues described in this book, and if any one takes away from the words of the book of this prophecy, God will take away his share in the tree of life and in the holy city, which are described in this book.[1]

"Aren't you suggesting we do these prohibited things?" was the implication of his unspoken inquiry.

The kind of problem these translators were concerned about can be illustrated with the use of five translations of the first part of Romans 1:17 into English:

> a righteousness For of God in it is revealed. . . .
> (Marshall, *The Interlinear Greek-English New Testament*)

> For in it the righteousness of God is revealed. . . .
> (Revised Standard Version)

> For in the gospel a righteousness from God is revealed. . . .
> (New International Version)

> For the gospel reveals how God puts people right with himself. . . .
> (*Good News Bible*)

---

[1] Revelation 22:18, Revised Standard Version.

> This Good News tells us that God makes us ready for heaven—makes us right in God's sight. . . .
>
> (*The Living Bible*)

The first translation is about as literal a translation of the Greek as is possible in English, but even there the English has nine words while the Greek has six. Greek has no article before the word for "righteousness," nor is there a separate word for "of," and a single Greek word is translated as "is revealed." The larger number of English words is required to cover the literal meaning of the Greek because of the difference in the grammatical systems of the two languages.

The Revised Standard Version has arranged the same English words in more normal English order and has used a different article before *righteousness*, indicating that they understand the meaning to be a definite, particular kind of "righteousness of God" rather than some general, maybe multiple kinds of righteousness.

The New International Version makes explicit that the *it* refers to the gospel, getting this information by interpreting the context. In so doing it has not changed any meaning, but simply made the meaning more unmistakable to the reader of English. Unlike the Revised Standard Version, it has also translated with the indefinite article before *righteousness*, sounding like one of many righteousnesses, or some kind of indefinite righteousness. It also translates with *righteousness from God* rather than *righteousness of God* believing that the Greek does not mean "righteousness which is characteristic of God," as the Revised Standard Version seems to say, but "righteousness which God gives." The literal "righteousness of God" in Greek and Latin misled Luther for a long time[2] and still contributes to distortion of the message in any translation which uses it.

The *Good News Bible* makes the sentence active rather than passive, and it translates "righteousness of God" more fully and clearly as "God puts people right with himself." These differences make the passage considerably more accessible as well as reduce the possibility of distortion through misunderstanding. The number of words is increased but the meaning is not changed.

The Living Bible is also clear, modern English, but it contains the words *makes us ready for heaven* which introduce a distortion because God put-

---

[2]Kooiman, *Luther*, 43.

ting people right with himself does not refer to heaven in the passage but to delivering people from the power of sin. *The Living Bible* is thus the only one of these translations which significantly adds to the meaning of the original in this passage. The Revised Standard Version and the New International Version, on the other hand, both take away some of the meaning for the ordinary reader.

As discussion of this kind continued between the translation consultant and the translators who were nervous about adding and taking away from the words of Scripture, it was clear that important assumptions were involved, assumptions about the nature of language, how a message from God is expressed in language, the nature of communication, Scripture as communication, and the nature of the Bible. The consultant used samples of their translation to make the point that by translating literally they themselves had been "taking away from the words of this book" in a different sense from what they had considered before. By definition translation results in difference between the source text and the translation. The significant issue is the nature of that difference.

Bible translators necessarily come to their task with theological assumptions about what translation is and how translation of the Bible should be done, some of those assumptions explicit and others not even clearly realized.[3] Such assumptions, along with others drawn from nontheological currents in their lives, serve to provide an often unformulated folk theory of translation, directing aspects of their work. Their translational decisions are therefore often governed in important measure by their theology.

Bible readers (including potential readers and hearers of translations read aloud) also have their theological assumptions which establish what they expect of translations and what they will accept in new ones. Even with new converts or in cases where the Scriptures are being translated for the first time, translations are heard, read, received or rejected in part because of preconceptions. A new translation in a new language, for example, may be rejected because it does not literally match the translation in the dominant language of the area, even though it may be much clearer and more accurate.

Some people's theology of translation is extremely naive, as when people ask if a particular translation into a language of Papua New Guinea

---

[3]Arichea, "Theology," "Taking Theology Seriously, "Old Testament"; Newman, "Theology"; Ellingworth, "Presuppositions."

is a "King James translation," or even a "Saint James" translation. Dorothy Sayers quotes a newspaper editor writing in opposition to her using her own translations of Scripture in contemporary English in dramatizing Bible stories: "In quoting the Bible we must take the Authorized Version, and not the interpretations of scholars, however wise."[4] The editor overlooks the fact that the translators of the King James version were also scholars, and that their translations came from their interpretations, however wise, and that by his criterion anyone who does not know English is barred from using the Bible.

On the other hand, theologies of translation may be very sophisticated; they may draw from a wide range of biblical and other knowledge. Theologians have struggled with some of the issues, and have differed profoundly.

There are, of course, some theological assumptions which virtually all Bible translators hold in common. The long association between the Bible and translation and the drive to translate the Bible down through the centuries have been supported by at least four common theological assumptions:

1. *God communicates with people through language.* This communication has taken place in many forms in Jewish and Christian experience, and its various canonical manifestations have been compiled in the Old and New Testaments (and some other books, for some people).

2. *People perceive/experience God through language.* People read or hear the Bible and study it, and learn about God in other ways involving language, ways in which they participate actively.

3. *People communicate with each other about God through language.* This human communication about God takes place in conversation, or through sermons and classes, or through the works of professional theologians who write their thoughts about God.

4. *Such communicative events may take place across time, language and cultural differences.* The missionary movement has existed to pass along communication events involving God and about God to people of other languages and cultures. New churches in different parts of the world have learned or developed ways of participating in some of these communication events. The Scriptures have been translated to extend the scope of the first two of these assumptions and to provide a basis for the third.

---

[4]Sayers, *Born*, 18-19.

But although these four assumptions are widely shared, the process of communication and the nature of language and cultural differences are so complex, and are so differently understood by translators, that working out their implications in a theology of translation varies widely, and is sometimes highly controversial.

Brief descriptions follow, touching on a few widely differing assumptions among translators and readers of the Bible. They will generally be presented as polarities, views in tension, with only positions near the extremes normally mentioned. Actual translators and readers are more often found at many points between, and a given translator or reader may take a different position along each of the different continua.

Theological Assumptions about Language

Sometimes theological assumptions about language itself underlie the ways in which translators approach their task, or readers react.

Sacred or Natural Language. At one end of one set of polar opposites, for example, are those translators and users of the Bible who see the language of Scripture as sacred and to some degree supernatural, while at the other end are those who believe it to be fully normal human language. Late in the last century the discovery of nonbiblical Greek manuscripts of many types showed that the New Testament was written in the everyday language of the first century, called Koine Greek.[5] Before that many people thought that the Greek in the New Testament and the Septuagint was different from more learned Greek because of direct action by the Holy Spirit. This Greek was sometimes even called "the language of the Holy Ghost."[6] Hebrew was also assumed to be the language of heaven by many people, and to be the language of the Garden of Eden.

But sacred language assumptions are not dead yet, and even extend to the language of some translations. They are generally associated with strongly entrenched church languages or church dialects, language reserved for religious use.[7] Latin was a church language from the Middle Ages on. Church dialects like King James English have not existed as long, but are nevertheless distinct from nonchurch vernaculars, as can be illustrated when King James version English is used to discuss a modern subject:

---

[5]Deissmann, *Light.*

[6]Colwell, "Greek," 486; Barr, *Semantics,* 239-41.

[7]See chap. 9, below.

Now the mistress of the household did send unto the repairer of the television, and commanded him, saying, "Behold, this my television set which was purchased with the two score and nine pounds which my father did give me on the day of my marriage. This same television set is broken, and the picture doth not appear unto me in my chamber at even. Wilt thou, I beseech thee, cast thine eye upon it, and see wherein it faileth, and if it be pleasing in thy sight, restore unto me this my picture again.[8]

Theological assumptions about the sacredness of language sometimes also exist even where the sacredness does not derive from an ancient Christian liturgy or a classical translation of the Bible. Resistance to translating the Bible into everyday Arabic has been strong, for example, because Christians have felt that the classical Arabic in which the Qur'an was written, the Muslim holy book, was more appropriate.

And even when there are no sacred texts to give a sacred aura to a dialect, people may believe that the Bible should not be translated into ordinary speech. The language of the elite or of the priests or of the highly educated would be more worthy, even though the New Testament writers did not use the contemporary high-level literary Greek of their day, but wrote in the widespread colloquial dialect which ordinary people used for ordinary purposes.

The sacred language/natural language polarity shows up in translation during the modern missionary movement in different ways. One of these is in resistance to contemporary language translations. People speaking many languages feel that the familiar wordings of the older translations should not be "tampered with" through revision or new translation. The *Good News Bible* has been condemned because, among many other things, Mary was said to be "pregnant" rather than "with child."

In many languages a sacred aura derives in part from archaic terms like "with child" and from artificial terms constructed on the analogy of Latinized theological vocabulary in English. English *justification*, for example, is derived from Latin translated from Greek. Its theological meaning has to be explained to an ordinary English-speaking congregation whenever it is an important term in a sermon, and even educated English-speaking people cannot be assumed to understand the Bible when the term is there. (Compare the non-Latinized "put right with God" in the *Good News Bible*). Correspondingly, many translators all over the world have labored

---

[8]From a twentieth-century manuscript.

to construct a single-word artificial theological term to translate *justification* in other languages rather than express the meaning in a short phrase, or in some other natural way. In fact, some have resisted more natural expressions precisely because they do sound natural and ordinary, and therefore not sacred enough.

At the other end of this polarity, however, are people who believe that the language of the Bible at all stages and at all times is normal human language. To them church languages and dialects are also normal, although specialized, human languages, and any sacredness is imputed to them by the believer. The subject may be God but the language which is used comes right out of human culture.

Absolute or Relative Language. The second polarity of theological presuppositions about language ranges from belief that language (or at least sacred language) can be absolute, fixed, rigid, unaffected by context and circumstance, to the opposite belief that it is always relative, changing, fluid, dependent in considerable degree on context and circumstance.

Christians have not normally subscribed to the most extreme absolutist position, which is exemplified in the Muslim belief that the Qur'an was dictated by God in classical Arabic. Orthodox Muslims hold[9] that only this dictated Arabic text (including the spoken sounds) is the true Qur'an, and that any translation of the Qur'an is therefore an interpretation or a representation of the content, not the Qur'an itself. The true Qur'an should be memorized in Arabic even if the person who memorizes does not understand Arabic.[10]

Some Christians who believe that the Bible can and should be translated nevertheless also believe that any word of the original should always be translated the same way into another language, particularly if the word is of theological importance. This, too, tends toward an absolutist position, even if not as extreme. They may believe, for example, that the Greek word *sarx* should always be translated with the same word in any language, even when it is being used in a secondary or figurative way. In English that translation would be ''flesh'' or ''meat,'' depending on whether the translator wanted an older word or a contemporary one. Other, more figurative meanings for *sarx,* however, include ''physical body,'' ''hu-

---

[9]Daniel C. Arichea, Jr., reports that this position is not as strongly maintained by Muslims in Indonesia (personal communication).

[10]Sanneh, *Translating,* 212, 224.

man being," "descendants," "human nature," "sinful nature," "sexual desire," and "sexual immorality."

At the other end of the polarity Christians typically believe that the translation of *sarx* should depend on what it means in context. For them, "He burned the meat [or flesh] and the skin outside the camp"[11] is an appropriate translation, but "The Word became a human being" is more accessible and less distorted than "The Word became flesh [or meat],"[12] and "the people of my own race" or "my fellow Jews" more accessible and less distorted than "them which are my flesh [or meat]."[13]

Sometimes language absolutists even project a distinction from a biblical language onto the English. In Revelation 5:9, for example, the *Good News Bible* has "you were killed . . . " where more traditional translations have "thou wast slain," and one critic with absolutist assumptions commented, "The Greek uses a verb meaning 'slain' and not 'killed'."[14] The criticism implies that there is a significant difference in meaning between the two words in modern English, but the primary distinction is that *slain* has an archaic or poetic flavor to it, nothing to do with the behavior to which they both refer. The difference imputed to the English words by the critic is not English, but Greek, where *sphazo* often means "slaughter (of animals)" as well as "kill" (of human beings), one among many words meaning "kill."

People who have an absolutist view of language may also express it by making the sentence structure of the translation match the original language (or the language of a sacred translation) as much as they can. They think that they can carry over the original text in an almost fixed or absolute way into the translation. One translation, for example, sounds like this:

> I write to you in the epistle not to commingle with paramours. And undoubtedly it is not as to the paramours of this world, or the greedy and extortionate, or idolaters, else as a consequence you ought to come out of the world. Yet now I write to you not to commingle with anyone who is named

---

[11]Leviticus 9:11, *Good News Bible.*

[12]John 1:14, *Good News Bible* and Revised Standard Version. An example like this illustrates the translational matching described in the chapter, but the assumptions lying behind the particular translation may well be something different, as literal translation is a symptom of several of the assumptions under discussion.

[13]Romans 11:14, *Good News Bible,* Revised Standard Version, King James Version.

[14]Van Bruggen, *Future,* 191.

a brother, should he be a paramour, or greedy, or an idolater, or a reviler, or a drunkard, or an extortioner. With such a one you are not even to be eating.[15]

Compare this with a more meaningful translation:

In the letter that I wrote you I told you not to associate with immoral people. Now I did not mean pagans who are immoral or greedy or are thieves, or who worship idols. To avoid them you would have to get out of the world completely. What I meant was that you should not associate with a person who calls himself a brother but is immoral or greedy or worships idols or is a slanderer or a drunkard or a thief. Don't even sit down to eat with such a person.[16]

There is a tendency for people who believe in the infallibility of the Scriptures or in their inerrancy (however they define these terms) to hold to relatively absolutist assumptions about language, but not all do so. For some such people inerrancy and/or infallibility applies to the content of what was written rather than to the language in which it was written, and they are therefore happy to translate without the need to make an absolute match of linguistic forms.

Theological Assumptions about Communication

How translating the Bible involves communication processes beyond the four shared assumptions listed above provides other areas of theological difference.

Traditional or Nontraditional Terminology. Some people believe that a translation into a language where there is no established Christian terminology should carry as little as possible of the overtones of pre-Christian religion, while others believe that traditional religious language often communicates the message of the Bible best. The first group often includes those who would borrow the word for "God" or "Holy Spirit" from Greek or Latin or from the dominant language of the area rather than use terms from the language of the translation. The second group includes those who would expect to use existing terms and expressions from the language of the translation unless it is impossible to do so.

The first group assumes that indigenous religious terms will reinforce the traditional religion and distort the message of the Bible. The second

---

[15] 1 Corinthians 5:9-11, *Concordant Version of the Sacred Scriptures.*

[16] *Good News Bible.*

group believes that local religious language, judiciously used, brings richer meaning to the Christian message than is possible with exotic and meaningless borrowed terms, and that any overtones from traditional religion which may be contrary to the gospel will be modified by Christian context and usage. They feel that the term for God is especially crucial, as a borrowed term implies that God is alien, unconnected with the people's past, while a term from the people's own tradition means that God has been present, even if people knew God less perfectly before they could read the Bible. God is rooted in a people's past through God's name.[17]

The issue is complicated by the fact that religious systems and religious terminology vary a great deal, as do attitudes toward them. Opposition both by Christians and by Muslims to using Islamic terms in a Christian context can be very strong, for example. In Malaysia the government has prohibited their use by non-Muslims, and in parts of Indonesia Christians do not want to use them because using them could be interpreted as a form of surrender to a Muslim viewpoint.[18]

Propositional or Holistic Communication. In another major polarity of theological assumptions some people believe that they are translating a text which is to be understood primarily in propositional ways, as statements of fact, as against others who find theological propositions to be only a part of many different communication levels and media within the Bible. For the person who believes that the message of the Bible is primarily propositional almost everything in it can be reduced to statements or commands. Stories have a moral. Poems have a theme. Figures of speech have a corresponding nonfigurative form of expression. All is very analytical and Western.

The following is an extreme case of treating a poetic passage propositionally.

> God's laws are perfect. They protect us, make us wise, and give us joy and light. God's laws are pure, eternal and just.[19]

This is given as a translation of

---

[17]Observation by Lamin Sanneh. See also above, chap. 3. There is a large literature on translating the names for God. For a recent example see Ugang, "Translating 'God'."

[18]Daniel C. Arichea, Jr., personal communication.

[19]Psalms 19:7-9, *The Living Bible.*

The law of the LORD is perfect,
    reviving the soul;
the testimony of the LORD is sure,
    making wise the simple.

The passage then goes on with "the precepts of the LORD," "the commandment of the LORD," "the fear of the LORD," and "the ordinances of the LORD."[20] The powerful poetic rhythm and symmetry of the original has been disregarded, distorting the nature of the message.

People who believe that the Bible is a more holistic form of communication resist reducing everything to propositions. They believe that the Bible communicates not only ideas but also feelings, not only propositional truth but also intuitive truth, not only straightforward command and assertion but also subtle structures and interrelationships. They feel that too much emphasis on the propositional side strips the Bible of its overtones, its harmonics, its emotion, and its imperative.

One criticism of dynamic equivalence translation is that it is too propositional, not holistic enough. But that discussion will have to wait for another chapter.

Theological Assumptions about Translation

Some assumptions about the translation process itself have also influenced translators and readers of translations almost from the beginning of the Christian era, long before the missionary movement.[21]

Divine or Human. One legend from the first century about how the first five books of the Hebrew Old Testament were translated into Greek to produce a part of the Septuagint translation illustrates ancient belief in divine inspiration of translation. According to this legend a number of isolated translators were inspired by God so that each translated the same texts with exactly the same words, as though the translation was dictated to them simultaneously.[22] The view that translations are divinely inspired, of course,

---

[20]Ibid., Revised Standard Version.

[21]This section is indebted to Schwarz, *Principles,* but some of the terminology used here and the organization into polarities is different.

[22]Yonge, *Philo,* 81-82. This is a different legend from the one about seventy-two translators in seventy-two different rooms each translating the Pentateuch in exactly seventy-two days.

is not the same as the more common view that the original texts were divinely inspired.

At the other end of this polarity people assume that translation is strictly a human activity, no different *as translation* from translating anything else of similar complexity, no matter how sacred the document or subject matter may be. Between the extremes lie various forms of theological assumption that the Holy Spirit works through translators, or through the church when the church is brought into decisions about translation.[23]

People do not usually begin to assume an extreme form of inspired translation until that translation has been used for a long time, and the translators are no longer living. The idea of inspired translation often emerges most strongly when people feel the need to strengthen the authority of an existing translation and to rule against anyone making other translations. In the fourth century, for example, Augustine argued that the Septuagint was an inspired translation when Jerome decided to translate the Old Testament into Latin from the original Hebrew instead of from the Septuagint.

Authorized Translation or Original Languages as Source. Jerome's case illustrates another contrasting pair of assumptions concerning whether the translation should be based on an older translation authorized by church tradition (whether assumed to be inspired or not) or on texts in the original Greek and Hebrew. Over time Jerome himself changed from translating the Old Testament from the Greek Septuagint, as authorized by tradition, to translating directly from the original Hebrew.

Ironically, Jerome's Vulgate translation from the Hebrew later became the traditional, authorized translation in the Western church for a long period, so that by the Middle Ages it had superseded texts in the original languages as the usual source text for translation. Then during the Reformation, when the place of the Vulgate was threatened by people who translated from the original languages once more, theories of inspired translation were sometimes invoked to protect it.

In the modern missionary movement many people have translated from languages other than the original languages, but except for some Catholic translations from the Vulgate, they have usually done so only because they did not know the original languages, not because they wanted to translate from translations dictated by tradition. Most have felt their responsibility

---

[23]Loewen, "Inspiration."

to the original even when they could not read it, and have consulted commentaries and other helps to get closer to it.

Exegetically or Theologically Based. Two people in particular helped arouse interest in Biblical interpretation and translation based on the original languages in the late fifteenth and early sixteenth centuries. Johannes Reuchlin resurrected the study of Hebrew and the Hebrew Old Testament, and Desiderius Erasmus did the same for the Greek New Testament. In addition to that, both Reuchlin and Erasmus assumed that translation should be exegetically based, that translators should determine the meaning of the original as best they could, and should translate that meaning regardless of traditional translations, established interpretations, theological presuppositions, or other factors.

Martin Luther, however, partially disagreed. Although he used the exegetical work of Reuchlin and Erasmus, he concluded that all of the Bible should be interpreted in light of his understanding of justification by faith and of Paul's writings in general. This illustrates a belief that translation should be based on a theological position rather than only on exegesis of the passage being translated.

Responsible translators since Luther's time have usually drawn back from conscious theologically based translation. There have been exceptions, however, as when Roman Catholics requested changes in one Catholic edition of the Revised Standard Version.[24] In Luke 1:28, for example, the Catholic edition the salutation was changed from ''O favored one'' to the traditional Vulgate-based ''full of grace,'' and references to Jesus ''brothers'' elsewhere were changed to ''brethren.'' Both types of changes made the translation fit better with Catholic teaching about Mary.

However, one year before publication of this Catholic edition another edition of the Revised Standard Version was approved for Catholics without such changes.[25] *The Jerusalem Bible,* moreover, translated by Catholics and published the same year as the Catholic edition, did not have these wordings either. Catholics, furthermore, have made no attempt to maintain traditional wordings not supported by sound exegesis of the oldest and best Greek texts in any of the many interconfessional translations in which they have participated since Vatican II.

---

[24]Revised Standard Version, Catholic Edition.

[25]Revised Standard Version, *The Oxford Annotated Bible with the Apocrypha.*

But although deliberate translation for theological reasons against convincing exegetical evidence is not very common, unconscious theological effect is always present, even when translators seek rigorously to base their work on biblical exegesis. And what is convincing exegetical evidence to one person may not be to another with different presuppositions.

Translation or "Paraphrase." Contemporary discussion of translation is often centered on another pair of terms, "paraphrase" and "translation," which seem to sum up many people's understanding of the topic, including that of many biblical scholars. In this usage a "translation" is rather literal, and to be commended, while a "paraphrase" is not to be trusted, not as truly the Bible.

In more technical terms, however, the meaning of *paraphrase* has nothing to do with translation at all, but refers to a restatement of meaning in other words in the same language. It means rewording. "He fell into bed exhausted" is a paraphrase of "He went to bed extremely tired," and vice versa.

If *paraphrase* in this general usage were logically extended to translation, all accurate translations would be paraphrases as the meaning is always stated in other words, the words of another language. But the way in which the "translation" and "paraphrase" polarity is usually used reflects an inadequate theory of translation that renders the terms useless for serious discussion. It is far more useful, as we have seen, to think of translations according to the interplay between the accessibility they provide and the distortion they create.[26] The best translations are those in which the accessibility of the meaning of the original is highest and the distortion lowest. The poorest are those in which the accessibility is lowest and the distortion highest.

The Living Bible seems anomalous here because it is also called a "paraphrase" by its translator and publisher although they obviously do not intend that term to be pejorative. Procedurally *The Living Bible* is a paraphrase made by rewording the American Standard Version, an English language translation. But that does not make it any less a translation, because the person who paraphrased the English intended to make the meaning follow the meaning of the original Greek and Hebrew.[27]

---

[26]Chap. 1.

[27]*The Living Bible,* 1st ed. preface.

But *The Living Bible* was made to communicate well in modern idiomatic English, and therefore does not match the definition of "translation" with which "paraphrase" is usually contrasted. The self-applied "paraphrase" label for *The Living Bible* therefore points up part of the problem with the pair of terms because although the translation is usually idiomatic, at times it is far from accurate, too often not conveying the meaning of the original. Linguistic accessibility is high, but the meaning is distorted to an unacceptably high degree, and the term "paraphrase" does not distinguish between the two. "Everything is ready and the roast is in the oven," [28] for example, is idiomatic and clear, but is not equivalent in meaning to "I have made ready my dinner, my oxen and my fat calves are killed, and everything is ready." [29]

In a more complex example, *The Living Bible* has

> Look up into the heavens! Who created all these stars? As a shepherd leads his sheep, calling each by its pet name, and counts them to see that none are lost or strayed, so God does with stars and planets! [30]

This is an unnecessary misrepresentation of the original military figure, as made explicit in the following translation:

> Look up at the sky!
> Who created the stars you see?
> > The one who leads them out like an army,
> > he knows how many there are
> > and calls each one by name!
> His power is so great—
> > not one of them is ever missing! [31]

Theological Assumptions about the Bible

Theological views of the nature of the Bible also have bearing on how the translator and reader understand the task of translation. Although all Bible translators believe in the importance and authority of the Scriptures

---

[28] Matthew 22: 4, *The Living Bible.*

[29] Revised Standard Version.

[30] Isaiah 40:26, *The Living Bible.*

[31] *Good News Bible.*

in some sense, and that the Bible is a document in which God is communicating with people, from there assumptions vary widely.

Inspired or Human Language. Some translators approach their task believing that the words and grammatical structures of the Bible in the original language are inspired by God. This belief sometimes leads to sacred language assumptions which were discussed earlier, but not necessarily, as people may believe that the language used for the biblical message is inspired even if the words and grammatical forms are not considered sacred.

Such belief is especially common for theologically charged words. The translators of the *Good News Bible* were accused of "taking the blood out of the Bible" when they translated "For by the death of Christ we are set free" where the more literal Revised Standard Version has "In him we have redemption through his blood."[32] The accusation implies a denial of something essential, a betrayal of the gospel in some way. Translators have been accused of deliberately violating the word of God in some such cases.

For these translators, however, "blood" in this context obviously means "death," so that what is lost is primarily the English word *blood,* plus a prevailing biblical image rooted in Old Testament culture. There is, however, no loss of idea or implication. The translators of the *Good News Bible* felt that the gain in accessibility, in clarity, in modern expression, outweighed the loss of the figure. They were even less concerned about the loss of the English word, wanting to provide clear accessibility to the meaning of the Greek instead.

At the other end of the polarity from belief in inspired language are people who believe that the Bible is written by human beings, that divine involvement comes in the insight which the Holy Spirit brought to the writers in their experience with God, and brings to the reader. The words are human words, the grammatical structures human structures, the types of literature human types, the thought structures human thought structures.

Belief in inspired language can lead to literal translation, to a feeling that even though the Hebrew and Greek words should be individually matched as closely as possible. But it does not inevitably do so. Many translators who believe in the verbal inspiration of the original texts do not believe that translations are inspired in the same way, so that some have adopted with enthusiasm less literal ways of translating.

---

[32]Ephesians 1:7.

And translators whose understanding of the importance of the Bible is not tied to a theory of verbal inspiration do not necessarily avoid literal translation, either. Such people may want to reflect the variety of sources which they see in the text.[33] Or they may want to preserve formal literary characteristics of the original languages. Or they may want to display their knowledge of issues which scholars are debating. Such purposes may hinder accessibility or introduce distortion for the reader, so that biblical scholars who are very insightful in interpreting the text may not be at all creative when translating it, sometimes producing translations which are rather wooden.[34]

With Apocrypha or Without. Alongside such differences in theories of the language of the Bible go divergent views on its composition, including different beliefs about the apocrypha or deuterocanonical books. These are books which were not in the Hebrew canon, the Hebrew collection of sacred Scriptures, but were included in the Septuagint translation and were therefore part of the Bible of the early Greek-speaking church. For that reason they were included in the Latin Vulgate (against Jerome's wishes), and from there they were translated into European languages, including the King James version in English, from which they were later removed in many published editions. Today they are used by Roman Catholics, Anglicans, Lutherans, the Orthodox churches and others. In Protestant churches which use them they do not usually have the full status of the books which come from the Hebrew Old Testament, but have an important secondary place.[35]

Whether or not to translate and distribute the apocrypha has been severely controversial at times for the Bible societies in Britain and America. Because of intense opposition from financial supporters in 1827 both societies refused to use any more money for printing or distributing Bibles which included these books, even though this hindered Scripture distribution in Europe and in Latin America, where the books were considered to be part of the Bible.[36]

On the one hand people who did not believe the apocrypha to be authentic Scripture were unwilling to support a Bible society which pub-

---

[33]Chap. 1.

[34]Observation by Daniel C. Arichea, Jr.

[35]Metzger, *Apocrypha.*

[36]Dwight, *Centennial,* 100.

lished them, and on the other hand churches which did use the deuterocanonical books felt that the societies were forcing a theological point of view on them. In present-day interconfessional translation projects the books are translated, and two editions of the Bible are normally published, one with these books and one without.

Uniformity or Diversity of Content. The diversity of the Bible and the integrity of the different books within their historical setting has been another very controversial issue. Some translators who believe that the documents come from God in some supernatural sense also believe that this entails full harmony among them, so that apparent contradictions must be resolved in translation. And because they believe the New Testament contains the ultimate revelation, the Old Testament must be translated in light of it, a form of theologically based translation again. In this view, because Matthew quotes Isaiah in the context of the virgin birth of Jesus, Isaiah must be translated as "virgin" in its own context in spite of the awkward fact that the Hebrew of Isaiah does not mean virgin, and that in Isaiah's context he was obviously talking about immediate local problems and the birth of a contemporary child.[37]

Other translators believe that there is discontinuity as well as continuity in Scripture, and that harmonization of the discontinuity brings an artificial flatness which distorts the message, obscuring the diversity of historical development and points of view. For them, to do justice to the Bible means that its diversity, its contradictions and the different values it expresses must be allowed to stand and speak for themselves. Each part should be translated according to its meaning in its own setting.

What Greek Text to Use. In light of the many mostly minor differences among Greek manuscripts of books of the New Testament, the problem of just what Greek text a translator should follow involves another set of polarities.

On one end are those people who believe that the group of texts represented in the King James version of the New Testament are the best, texts deriving from relatively late Greek manuscripts dating from the Middle Ages. They now often call these texts the "majority text" because more manuscript copies of that type exist than do copies of types seen only in older manuscripts. This is because the majority text type was widely re-

---

[37]Isaiah 7:14. This reasoning is explicit in a footnote to this passage in, e.g., *The Living Bible.*

produced in monasteries in the Middle Ages, long after the earliest centuries of the Christian era. All translations of the New Testament from Greek were made from that type of text from the Middle Ages until late in the nineteenth century because it was effectively the only type available in Europe. People who hold that such a text should still be used often believe that God preserved the New Testament in that form through the centuries and made it the text of the church.

On the other end of this polarity people believe that New Testament texts should be reconstructed from the oldest available manuscripts and manuscript fragments going back to the first centuries, in some cases hundreds of years before some of the "majority text" manuscripts. They also believe that manuscript variants should be analyzed for evidence of their authenticity and compiled into a text more likely to be closer to the original form of the New Testament writings.[38] As an example of differences which show up, in Colossians 1:14 the King James version reads, "In whom we have redemption through his blood, even the forgiveness of sins." The oldest Greek manuscripts, on the other hand, do not contain the words "through his blood." Presumably a copyist was reminded of Ephesians 1:7 (where it does occur in the old manuscripts) as he copied Colossians, and wrote it into the text there as well. Then his copy was copied by others.[39]

At present the majority of translators use the United Bible Societies' Greek New Testament text, the product of an attempt to reconstruct the most authentic possible text from the oldest and most reliable sources.[40]

Theological Distortion in Translation

Inevitable as theological assumptions are, and important as they may be, distortion does enter into translations through them, usually in small ways, in spite of the fact that responsible translators seek to be as fair as possible with the evidence as they translate. One very great advantage of a translation committee over against a single translator, or of extensive checks by people in

---

[38]Aland, "The Text of the Church?"

[39]Beegle, *God's Word*, 29. This book argues that texts based on the older manuscripts are most likely to reflect the original. A book on translation into English which argues for the majority text is Van Bruggen, *Future*.

[40]Chap. 4.

addition to the translator(s) is the likelihood that some theological distortion will be lessened through group scrutiny and discussion.

At the same time, evaluation and acceptance of translation is often based on the reader's perception of the theology of the translators even more than on the translation itself. Nonacceptance of the Revised Standard Version in its early years by some Christians was often based in considerable measure on belief that the translators did not have acceptable assumptions about the nature of the Bible. The New International Version was later organized as a countertranslation, to be translated by people who did have acceptable assumptions, from their point of view. Ironically, as it turned out, the two translations are remarkably alike, but some people still trust the New International Version and not the Revised Standard Version.

The accusation of theological distortion is normally made only when the theological positions imputed to the translators or perceived in the translation are different from those held by the critic. As one put it, "There is a difference between the NIV and the TEV: At points the TEV is influenced by doctrinal considerations."[41] This critic apparently has much the same theological assumptions as the translators of the New International Version, and apparently cannot see those translators as "influenced by doctrinal considerations."

Literalism as a way of distorting the message was the common solution to fear of distortion at various points in this chapter, common among people from different theological positions. Variations on the following comment, for example, are frequently to be heard as people discuss the translation of the Bible:

> I would rather have a literal translation, even if the meaning is not so clear, than that the translator should give us what he thinks the original writer might have said. Otherwise the book is no longer a trustworthy version of the best text available, but a version interspersed with the translator's concealed emendations and comments.[42]

This statement reveals part of the dilemma of those who would translate in ways which are accessible, but do not know how to judge distortion, or how to control it. They believe that translation can be done without "interpretation," which is nonsense, because interpretation is required for un-

---

[41]Van Bruggen, *Future*, 192.

[42]Ritson, *World*, 64.

derstanding the text, and understanding is the first requirement of translation. Every translation, even the most literal, consists of what the translator "thinks the original writer might have said." It is impossible to translate otherwise.

A serious discussion of the problem of literalism cannot take place, however, in reference to translating the biblical languages into English alone because the long historical and cultural relationship blurs the problem, and because students of the Bible in English are so used to literalism in biblical translation that they often cannot hear what it sounds like to the uninitiated.

Often literal translation gives a wrong meaning. In Bariba, a language of West Africa, to translate literally as "Jesus said, 'I am the light of the world'" would mean that Jesus said the reader of the Scripture is the light of the world. The translation has to read, "Jesus said that he is the light of the world."[43]

Often literal translation is grammatically impossible as well. In the Chulup language of Paraguay every proper name must have one of sixteen articles which distinguish not only masculine, feminine, plural, and non-human, but also indicate whether the bearer of the name is present, absent but known, absent but not known, or dead. For every proper name in the Bible the translator has to decide whether the writer or the person speaking knew the person named or not, and whether or not the person named was present or absent.[44]

A literal translation is not a finished translation, but leaves the reader to guess at "what the original writer might have said." Perhaps the following advertisement for another religion will make the point:

GOSWAMI SHRIMUKUNDJI MISRA VYAS has come in Bangkok on the cordial invitation of Hindu Samaj Devmandir and Vishnu Mandir, Bangkok, Thailand. He is an eminent pupil of GOSWAMI SHRI BINDUJI MAHARAJ and unique preacher of "SHRIRAM CHARIT MANAS" the most genuine epic of Veda, Puran and many Shastra etc.

. . . It is therefore suggested to all the ambitious Ladies and Gentlemen of Bangkok to come at Hindu Samaj Devmandir as well as Vishnu Mandir and to be advantageous by this lecture because Goswamiji will soon travel for Malaysia, Singapore, Penang and Hongkong etc.[45]

[43]John 8:12, Beekman and Callow, *Translating*, 43.

[44]Omanson, "Problems," 606.

[45]Singh, "Notice."

People who try to avoid making a literal translation, however, do not necessarily know how to do so, often do not know how to judge equivalence, and so may also end up with a misleading translation. Thus either literal translation or a mistaken nonliteral translation may result from lack of a theory of translation which deals adequately with the all-important dimensions of accessibility and distortion.

CHAPTER 6

Dynamic Equivalence Translation

Some theological and other assumptions which translators bring to their task have been rather stable down through the years of the modern missionary movement, as have been some kinds of knowledge and skills which translators have had. Other assumptions, as well as some knowledge and skills available to translators have changed in important ways over time.

For example, many missionary translators of the nineteenth and early twentieth centuries had at least one significant advantage over most present-day Bible translators, whether missionary or not, in that they knew the original languages of the Bible better. Many had strong classical educations in the style of the times, with years of Latin and Greek study in high school, university and seminary, and considerably more Hebrew than most modern seminary graduates have studied. Present-day translators, on the other hand, have access to anthropological and linguistic kinds of knowledge which did not exist in the last century, although they often have to exert considerable effort to seek it out, as it is not part of the typical Western curriculum.

Unlike earlier years also, knowledge relevant to translation can now be integrated within the theory and practice of dynamic equivalence translation. Theological assumptions, the Greek and Hebrew languages, biblical exegesis, hermeneutics, understanding of the nature and significance of language and culture, realization of the differences between languages and between cultures, perspectives on the process of communication, and understanding of specific receptor languages and cultures can all intersect, enabling translators both to gain greater insight into their task and to do it better.

Dynamic equivalence translation[1] is the name of a theory, a set of ideas about what translation is and how it should be done. Certainly people can translate without a formulated theory, but without one they cannot tell anyone else systematically what it was they did, or what the problems are with a translation, or teach anyone to translate, or compare differences between translations. A theory provides the conceptual framework and defines the terminology needed. It does not create talent or aptitude, but gives direction and awareness to the translator.

Bible translators did not use the term "theory" for their ideas about translation until the middle of this century, when the professionalization of Bible translation was well under way.[2] Earlier translators did have folk theories of translation, however, unsystematic ideas about how translation should be done, and loose ways of talking about it, using terms like "literal," "free" and "paraphrase," for example.

One source of such translation folk theory throughout the two hundred years of the modern missionary movement has been language instruction, in which professors often tested students by requiring them to translate a passage from the language they were studying. What students were supposed to do under the name of translation was to show in their own language as much as they could of the grammatical structure and of the meanings of the words in the text from which they were translating. They were to provide a fairly close receptor language match for each source language word and for each grammatical structure, so that the professor could see that they knew the word, and that they recognized the grammatical structures of the text.[3]

Some grammar books for seminary students still sport translational gems reflecting this point of view, like "you are being loosed by the apostles,"[4] "the woman who is believing on the Lord is being saved by him," and "take up your bed and go on walking. . . . and he took up his bed and

---

[1]Nida has changed the name he uses for this theory to "functional equivalence translation," trying to avoid misunderstanding of the term "dynamic equivalence" (de Waard and Nida, *One Language*, vii). Larson uses "meaning-based translation" for much the same body of theory in her book by that title. Beekman and Callow use "idiomatic translation" in *Translating*.

[2]See chaps. 2 and 4, above.

[3]Torre, "Attempts."

[4]Goetchius, *Language*, 96.

was walking.'''[5] Some Bible translators have believed that they should translate the Bible into other languages the same way. Others have seen the artificiality of such translation, and have sought ways of doing something else, but were often uncertain about what they should do.

Formative Developments Leading toward Dynamic Equivalence

Dynamic equivalence translation has brought a much higher degree of sophistication to Bible translation than was possible with the folk theories, incorporating many elements from previous and contemporary thought and experience. We will mention only a few of these elements which have also exerted direct influence on Bible translation even independently of their place in dynamic equivalence translation.

One was philology, the historical study of a few literary languages of Europe and the Middle East, particularly as they were recorded in ancient documents. With skills developed especially during the nineteenth century, philologists restored and deciphered ancient inscriptions and manuscripts, and the New Testament scholars among them compared ancient manuscripts to reconstruct older and better New Testament texts than were previously available.[6] Philologists also studied ancient texts in extinct languages to determine what they meant. This involved analyzing and comparing ancient languages of the same language family, like such Semitic languages as Hebrew, Arabic and Ugaritic, to learn more about each. Cumulatively such processes have contributed importantly to what translators of the Bible can know as they translate.

As philological studies of biblical texts moved along, some nineteenth century biblical scholars became increasingly dissatisfied with the King James translation.[7] They therefore undertook a revision,[8] published as the (English) Revised Version in 1885, and then further revised as the American Standard Version of 1901.

---

[5]Kaufman, *Grammar*, 77, 123.

[6]Chap. 5.

[7]One of many discussions of unsatisfactory features in the King James version is Beegle, *God's Word*.

[8]The distinction between a revision and a new translation is not always easy to maintain. In this case the work was a revision which stayed within the tradition of the King James and kept some of its archaic language, but had elements of a new translation because it followed an improved text and somewhat different translation principles.

However, from the standpoint of the need for a better translation of the Bible for common use, the results were disastrous. The Greek text base was much better than was that of the King James, to be sure, and in some passages the translators understood the Greek and Hebrew better than had those who had translated the King James, but the theory of translation they followed led to a combination of archaic vocabulary and literalism which made their translation even less accessible than the King James version, and unpleasant to read. Of the two versions, the American Standard was a little better, and has been used more widely, but even there accessibility is low. The strangeness of the language may be seen in the following examples.

And they shall be abhorring unto all flesh.

. . . bonds and afflictions abide me.

The abjects gathered themselves together against me.

And all they that cast angle into the Nile shall mourn.[9]

Although these two revised versions did not often replace the King James version in English-speaking churches they did begin to replace it as a model for many English-speaking translators. Because these translations had been made by prestigious scholars, skilled in philological ways of understanding the Bible, some other translators assumed that translations like these should be made all over the world. A whole generation of revisions was therefore produced in different languages, revisions in which the text and exegesis were better than in earlier versions, but accessibility was often worse. Christians therefore frequently stayed with their older translations, easier to understand and more natural in language, in spite of their imperfections.

Fortunately, counterforces were also at work as some people realized that the King James version had not only become obsolete textually and exegetically, but that the Bible message was also no longer sufficiently accessible to many people in it and in the revisions. Different pioneer versions were therefore produced between 1889 and 1935, each experimenting with the modern English of its time.[10] Such translations encouraged some English-speaking Christians to believe that translations could have good textual bases, be exegetically sound, and still be clearer than what people

---

[9]Isaiah 66:24; Acts 20:23; Psalms 35:15; Isaiah 19:8; Kubo and Specht, *Versions*, 41-43.

[10]Esp. *The Twentieth Century New Testament*; Weymouth, *Testament*; Moffatt, *Bible*; Smith and Goodspeed, *Bible*.

were used to reading. More people began to realize that good alternatives to the King James Bible and to the Revised and American Standard Versions were possible.

These translations, therefore, helped prepare the way for two other English translations, which appeared in mid century, at the same time as the professionalization of translation was getting under way. The first was the Revised Standard Version, with New Testament published in 1946, Old Testament in 1952, and Apocrypha in 1957. It was designed to be a revision of the American Standard Version, staying within the King James tradition in its wording where possible, but following the best text and exegesis, as judged by the translators. It is somewhat literal, rather difficult in some places, often dull, but immeasurably more accessible and less distorted for most modern readers than either the revised versions or the King James version. It replaced the latter for many English-speaking Christians.

The other influential mid-century translation was J. B. Phillips's *Letters to Young Churches,* published in 1947.[11] Much of that translation was prepared during World War II, when Phillips was dealing with British young people to whom the King James version was a closed book. His translation opened up the epistles, making accessible the books which readers of the King James had always found to be the hardest to read in the New Testament.[12] He wrote in genuine modern English, often with an idiomatic lilt which was captivating and powerful:

> With eyes wide open to the mercies of God, I beg you, my brothers, as an act of intelligent worship, to give him your bodies, as a living sacrifice, consecrated to him and acceptable by him. Don't let the world around you squeeze you into its own mold, but let God remold your minds from within. . . .[13]

In their different ways, both the Revised Standard Version and the J. B. Phillips translation were radical departures from what the English-speaking world was used to in its Scriptures. The more obvious influence on other Bible translation was from the translationally more conservative

---

[11]Three books which provide simple but sound evaluations of English translations are Kubo and Specht, *Versions*; Lewis, *Bible*; and Duthie, *Translations*.

[12]Phillips went on to translate the full New Testament (1958), and then revised it (1972). He also translated four of the Old Testament prophets.

[13]Romans 12:1-2a, *Letters to Young Churches.*

Revised Standard Version. It became, for a time, the new and much improved model for translators, generally replacing the American Standard and the King James versions in that role. The influence of Phillips's work was more limited, but it awakened some translators in different parts of the world to the possibility of translating in lively modern language.

Some other twentieth-century influences contributing to the development of dynamic equivalence translation were mentioned earlier.[14] These linguistics-anthropology-communication influences brought attention to the receptor side of translation, balancing philology, which had concentrated on the source text. A social science perspective also led a few people to think in terms of formulating a theory of translation which would be as explicit and as universal as possible. Thus dynamic equivalence translation was formed out of many different concepts in many different fields of knowledge.

Outside of Bible translation, translation issues have long been a subject of discussion by some students of literature, but such people did not begin to systematize their knowledge of translation until recently. Except for attempts at machine translation, translation likewise did not become a focus of theory for linguists or other social scientists unrelated to Bible translation until years after the professionalization of Bible translation began. Fortunately, such theoretic discussion has become more widespread in the past few years,[15] but most of it is limited by involvement only with closely related languages, or languages of Europe and the Middle East, a parochial outlook which is characteristic of almost all discussion of translation outside of dynamic equivalence translation, and of some criticism of dynamic equivalence as well.

Some Fundamentals of Dynamic Equivalence Translation

We will explain and illustrate here only a few of the ideas which drive dynamic equivalence translation,[16] to give an impression of what it in-

---

[14]Chap. 4.

[15]Bassnett-McGuire, *Translation*, and Snell-Hornby, *Translation*, are critical surveys of some of the work done outside the Bible-translation field.

[16]The best basic textbook is Larson, *Translation*. Some of the progression of Nida's thinking may be seen in four books: *Bible Translating, Science of Translating,* (with Taber) *Translation,* (with Reyburn) *Meaning,* and (with de Waard) *One Language.*

volves. A few other aspects are discussed in various other chapters in this book.

Eugene A. Nida, the most important person in the formulation of dynamic equivalence translation contrasts it, or functional equivalence, to "formal correspondence,"[17] by which he means literal translation. He uses formal *correspondence* rather than formal *equivalence*[18] because a literal translation is not equivalent to the original text, as we have illustrated repeatedly. It matches or corresponds to the original in various formal, surface ways, but gives the wrong meaning, or obscures the meaning or renders the communication awkward and unnatural. Dynamic equivalence translation, however, is not necessarily the same as a "free" translation, with which literal translation is typically contrasted, because that term is often used for translation which is only an approximation of the source.

In a dynamic equivalence translation meaning and impact on the receptor, the reader or hearer of the translation, should be as close as possible to the meaning and impact which the message had for the original receptors. This principle, like everything else, requires qualification and adaptation. When Jesus' or Paul's words made opponents angry, the translation should not therefore make modern readers angry. Rather, they should be able to sense the reason for the anger in the language of the translation. The same would apply if evidence were found that one of Paul's letters made the Corinthian church angry.[19]

Just whom to count as "original receptors," furthermore, when there are layers of oral and written tradition is not easy to establish. We can only reconstruct through exegesis what the impact on the hypothetical readers may have been at a stage when the book was written or edited much in its present form, or became part of the canon of Scripture.

From one perspective, formal correspondent and dynamic equivalent translation are polar opposites, with all translations scattered along many intermediary positions. They differ in more dimensions than that, however, because they have different goals, are useful for different purposes,

---

[17]In this discussion we will use the terminology and emphases of United Bible Societies' people, which differ at times in terminology and emphasis from usage of members of the Summer Institute of Linguistics.

[18]Actually, Nida used "formal equivalence" in *Science of Translating,* 165-66, 171-76. He later changed it as inaccurate.

[19]Carson, "Limits," 205.

and manifest different kinds and degrees of distortion. Formal correspondence translations seek to match the form, the wording and syntax, of the original text as much as possible. In doing so, translators make differing degrees of concession in the direction of equivalent meaning where they cannot match the form and still have what they consider an acceptable translation, however they define acceptability. Dynamic equivalence translations, on the other hand, are intended to match the response and impact of the original.

The essential technique in formal correspondence translation is to make a consistent match between linguistic units in the source text and corresponding units in the receptor text on one or many levels. If the corresponding units are words the result is word-for-word translation, *sarx* always translated as "flesh," as illustrated earlier.[20] If the corresponding units are phrases then each phrase in the receptor language should match a phrase in the source, whether the phrases fit together in the receptor language or not:

> Now about virgins: . . .I think it is good for you to remain as you are. Are you married?[21]

Married virgins? Or then again:

> There came a man who was sent from God; his name was John. . . . He was in the world, and though the world was made through him, the world did not recognize him.[22]

The correct meaning, of course, is that the Word was in the world, not John, as seems to be implied here.

> By faith he was commended as a righteous man, when God spoke well of his offerings. And by faith he still speaks, even though he is dead.[23]

Note that according to this translation God is dead if the phrases are read: "God *spoke well* of his offerings. And by faith he *still* speaks, even though he is dead."

---

[20] Chap. 5.

[21] 1 Corinthians 7:25-28, New International Version.

[22] John 1:6, 10, New International Version.

[23] Hebrews 11:4, New International Version.

Instead of matching form for form as much as possible, the essential technique in dynamic equivalence translation is to search for the meaning of the text and then to use the resources of the receptor language to the best advantage in expressing that meaning. The translator needs to imagine the original writer in the original setting, but writing in the receptor language rather than in the original one. To achieve this effect, translators engage in three processes: (1) *analysis,* or figuring out just what the text means, (2) *transfer,* or sensing that meaning in receptor language terms, and (3) *restructuring,* or expressing that meaning in the best possible way for a specific audience in the receptor language.

To show a little of what these processes entail, we will apply them to a few examples in Amos 2:1–3.[24] An extremely formal correspondent translation of the Hebrew passage is presented first:

> this he-says Yahweh for three sins-of Moab even-for four not I-will-turn-back-him because to-burn-him bones-of king-of Edom to-the-lime so-I-will-send fire upon-Moab that-she-will-consume fortress-of the-Kerioth and-he-will-go-down in-tumult Moab amid-war-cry with-blast-of trumpet and I-will-destroy one-ruling from-midst-of-her and-all-of officials-of-her I-will-kill with-him he-says Yahweh[25]

This is a nearly morpheme-for-morpheme interlinear translation. A *morpheme* is a linguistic unit the size of a word or a meaningful part of a word, like the elements separated by hyphens in un-like-ly, boy-s, walk-ed, mak-er. The hyphens in the text example separate English words which are literal translations of Hebrew morphemes within individual Hebrew words, or in some instances English words required when a Hebrew morpheme must be translated by more than one English word. This translation is one of the legitimate uses of formal correspondence, from the viewpoint of dynamic equivalence translation. It is not intended for evangelism or the nurture of the church, but serves the restricted purpose of helping the reader who does not know the original language learn something of the structure of the original under those limited circumstances when such knowledge may be helpful.

But even this unusually formal-correspondent translation fudges a bit toward making the meaning clearer. The morphemes within each Hebrew

---

[24]For a more complete presentation see de Waard and Smalley, *Amos.*

[25]Amos 2:1-3; Kohlenberger, *NIV Interlinear,* 509.

word, for one thing, are represented by English words in English order, not necessarily the order of the Hebrew morphemes. In its choice of words, furthermore, the translation sometimes follows the word selection of the New International Version which is printed in the margin beside it, not necessarily the most literal possible match.

Analysis. To establish what this text means in Hebrew, translators first use the tools which philologists and other biblical scholars have provided, to the extent they know how. For example, if there are different possible original wordings, as shown in different ancient manuscripts or ancient translations, they choose between them. They analyze the text grammatically and from the standpoint of the meanings of the words. They consider the time, place and situation of its writing, and the purpose of the author.

For many such problems of text and interpretation, however, most translators simply accept a standard published Hebrew text or a reliable translation in another language as making their choices for them, without deciding each detail for themselves. A great deal of the information translators need for analysis is already reflected in good translations and is contained in Hebrew grammars and dictionaries, and in commentaries on the book of Amos.

For example, commentaries will suggest that one of the sins of which the people of Moab are accused in the passage above is desecrating the royal tomb and burning the king's bones, perhaps even mixing the ashes of the bones in the lime with which they whitewashed their houses. Also, "not I-will-turn-back-him" implies "I will not hold back my wrath," which means "I will punish," and "and-he-will-go-down" means "he will be defeated" or "he will die."

Sometimes there are differences of opinion about interpretation among scholars; and sometimes commentaries do not deal at all with some of the problems translators face, partly because they only discuss problems apparent from a Western viewpoint. Translators who work in non-Western languages therefore need more than what is readily available in such sources to decide questions of analysis. The United Bible Societies handbooks for translators, with their cross-cultural perspective, are intended to help in some of these situations, but do not cover all possibilities either, of course.

Some problems of analysis, therefore, have to be worked out by translators on their own, using techniques which stem from dynamic equivalence theory. For example, such translators know that meaning and grammar frequently do not completely match in any given language, that a noun does not necessarily represent a thing or entity, but may represent an event, and that events may be difficult to translate into other languages as nouns.[26]

In the Amos passage "sins," "tumult," "war cry," "blast," "one ruling" and "official (= leader)" are or include events. They are done, they happen, even though they are grammatically expressed as nouns in Hebrew. Events are translatable idiomatically as verbs more often than as nouns: "the people of Moab have sinned" instead of "the sins of Moab," and "the people who lead" rather than "the leaders." Elsewhere in the Bible theological terms which cause trouble when translators try to find equivalent nouns are often easier to translate as verb phrases because they represent events: "when God saves us" rather than "our salvation." Analysis therefore includes identifying the nouns which have event components.

On another level, translators have to understand how the parts of the texts fit together, particularly the clauses, sentences and paragraphs. Some of this relationship is explicit in the source text, as expressed by "because" and "so" in the Hebrew text of the Amos example. Other relationships are implicit in the source but cannot all be left implicit in the receptor without distortion. In the latter part of the Amos passage there are several events which implicitly occur simultaneously: fire consuming, Moab going down to defeat, tumult, war cries, blasts of trumpets, destruction of the ruler and leaders. In some languages such a string of events translated literally may be understood sequentially, or partially so: first there was fire consuming, then Moab went down to defeat, then there was tumult, etc. The problem of semantic relationships of many kinds is sometimes so difficult and always so important that the Summer Institute of Linguistics has a program of analyzing those in the Greek New Testament as a help to translators.[27]

On still another level translators should analyze how the whole passage is organized. For example, they note that the Amos passage is introduced by a statement that God is speaking. Such statements are frequent in the prophetic books of the Bible, emphasizing the authority of the message. Then at the end of this passage there is an additional "he-says Yahweh," which at first seems redundant from an English point of view. In Hebrew

---

[26]Nida, "Methodology." For a more up-to-date discussion see Larson, *Translation*, 26-42, 55-75, and other locations.

[27]E.g., Johnson, *2 Peter*.

such repetition is very common and in this occurrence accentuates the authority of the intervening statement even more. These two quotation formulae also strongly mark the beginning and end of the section.

Translators also need to look at a passage in light of the what is said before and after it, and decide how it fits into the whole book. The very similar passages around the illustrative Amos passage contribute to a powerful rhythm of words and ideas. In fact, rhythm and repetition are major stylistic devices in the Hebrew text of the whole book of Amos. They serve to focus attention, to emphasize and to create mood.[28]

Then again, the emotional tone of the passage must be analyzed. Our sample passage is clearly a pronouncement of wrath and punishment. Other passages have other moods, and in some cases it is difficult to decide what the feeling in the Hebrew is.

Translators working on these and other problems of understanding the source do not complete their analysis before engaging in transfer or restructuring, but follow the processes in a spiral pattern. The first analysis is done with transfer and restructuring in mind. Then when translators are thinking about transfer they may find that something in the original is still not clear, perhaps some exegetical question not noticed from a Western perspective alone has to be analyzed.[29] Then they transfer the results of their additional analysis to the receptor language. Likewise, when they are restructuring they are forced back to analysis and transfer from time to time.

Transfer. The process of transfer is required because the source and receptor languages and cultures are different. Whereas analysis is the task of understanding the source text in all of its intricate detail, transfer is the process of understanding that same meaning from within the thought and language of another culture.

Actually, as we were sampling the process of analysis above, we were also sampling transfer into English because we were working in English, our discussion was in English, and our helps, commentaries, grammars, dictionaries, etc., were in English. We saw the Hebrew meaning through English. Because we are not native speakers of Hebrew, or highly competent bilinguals, we cannot do such analysis without transfer into our language.

For most other languages, in which published helps to analysis are not available, there may be an important difference in transfer procedures be-

---

[28]De Waard and Smalley, *Amos.*

[29]Ellingworth, "Exegesis," 397.

tween people translating into their own language and expatriates translating into a third language. People who are foreign to the receptor language may first have to go through the process of transfer into whatever their native language is, and then transfer again into the terms and categories of the language of the translation. Their intermediary language thus becomes another source of distortion. People who are translating into their own language sometimes make the transfer directly into their own language, but even they may also have to make a two-step transfer if they use biblical helps written in English or some other major language. They first analyze and transfer in the major language and then (or simultaneously) make the additional transfer into their own language.

Transfer is necessary in part because a biblical passage may look very different when seen from the perspective of radically different languages and cultures. From the viewpoint of the Tonga people of Zambia reading a literal translation, for example, the woman who speaks in the first chapter of the Song of Songs must certainly be a prostitute. No one else could ever be imagined to talk like that in any of the cultures with which they have direct experience:

> O that you would kiss me with the kisses of your mouth! For your love is better than wine, . . .[30]

Literal translations of some of the descriptions of the woman's beauty in chapter 4 of the same book, furthermore, suggest Tonga meanings very different from the Hebrew meanings. "Your eyes are doves" makes people think of the red eyes of local domesticated doves, and red eyes are considered characteristic either of drunkenness or of a witch. "Your hair is like a flock of goats" is misleading, among other reasons, because goats are a strong male symbol. The image of a "flowing stream" used of the woman may be taken for an infection of the urogenital tract.[31] Transfer requires finding analogous images which give the correct meaning in the receptor language, or otherwise forestall misinterpretation.

One obvious but often difficult part of transfer is selecting the words to use. Do we transliterate the divine name Yahweh, as was done in the formal correspondence translation of the Amos passage, or do we use a term meaning something like "Lord," as is done in most English trans-

---

[30]Song of Solomon 1:2, Revised Standard Version.

[31]Wendland, *Cultural Factor*, 1-4.

lations? "Consume" is used to mean both "eat" and "burn up, use up, destroy" in Hebrew and English. The receptor language may not have a word with both of these areas of meaning. Here the meaning "completely burn up" is required.

More than simple word equivalence is necessary however. To readers without background, "Moab" may sound like the name of a person in literal translations like "sins of Moab" and "Moab will die." The geographical name is used in this passage to mean the people who lived in the area. That meaning will have to be made explicit in some languages: "people of Moab." Note that in such a transfer nothing is being added to the meaning conveyed by the original. The meaning of "people" is present in the Hebrew text, although not explicit in the Hebrew words.

'For three sins of Moab, even for four' often has to be translated "because the people of Moab have repeatedly sinned." It does not mean "for only three or four sins" as it sounds in some languages when translated literally. "I will send fire" may not make sense in some languages, unless fire is understood to be some kind of God or spirit. "I will set fire to," or "I will cause to burn" may be the natural equivalents.

We have mentioned that "not I-will-turn-back-him" is an idiom meaning "I will punish." For idioms translators explore a number of kinds of solutions. In a few cases the idiom will make correct and clear sense when translated literally. If so, the translator has to decide whether or not it will be suitable in spite of its newness to the language. Sometimes a new idiom which is understood correctly adds freshness and vividness, which would be valuable in this passage. At other times its strangeness may be distracting.

More frequently, the translator will look for an equivalent idiom already in use in the receptor language. "I won't hold back from punishing them" might be one in English. Otherwise, the meaning of the idiom has to be translated directly, without an equivalent idiom: "I will punish them." This is the weakest solution because it makes the translation less forceful than the original, but is better than distorting the meaning in cases where a more colorful expression which is clear and correct is not to be found.

To illustrate the process of transfer when events are expressed as nouns, here is a different passage:

> We also boast of our troubles, because we know that trouble produces endurance, endurance brings God's approval, and his approval creates hope.

This hope does not disappoint us, for God has poured out his love into our hearts by means of the Holy Spirit, who is God's gift to us.[32]

"Troubles" are those events which caused the writer to suffer; "endurance" is a way of behaving. Other events expressed as nouns are "hope," "love" and "gift." "Gift," in fact, is more complicated than the others because it includes both an event and a thing: "something which is given."

For many languages some of these events (perhaps even all of them) cannot be expressed as nouns, or are awkward as nouns, but have to be transferred as verbs. The following example expresses the events as verbs in a way which is characteristic of such languages, although awkward in English:

We also boast about what we have suffered because we know that when we suffer we become better able to endure. And so God approves of us because we have learned to endure more, so that makes us hope. If we hope in this way we are never disappointed, for by means of the Holy Spirit, whom he has given to us, God has shown how much he loves us.[33]

This kind of transfer of source language nouns into receptor language verb structures may create other problems which have to be solved as well. In some languages "to hope" may require an explicit statement of what is hoped for, for example. That drives the translator back to analysis again. There may not be a word as generic as "approve," so the translation may have to read something like, "Thus God has tested us and has seen that we are able to do what God wants."

Restructuring. As the processes of analysis and transfer move along, translators are also at work restructuring, writing the meaning in idiomatic style suitable to the audience for which it is intended. A translation for educated people is restructured differently from one for uneducated people, one for children differently from one for adults.[34] Problems in restructuring will send translators back to analysis and transfer, asking what the emphasis of the text really is, and how it can be expressed.

Here is the *Good News Bible* restructuring of the Amos passage:

---

[32]Romans 5:7-8, *Good News Bible.*

[33]Romans 5:3-5, adapted from Newman and Nida, *Romans,* 94-96.

[34]Arichea, "New Testament" and "Old Testament for Children"; Newman, "Child."

> The LORD says, "The people of Moab have sinned again and again, and for this I will certainly punish them. They dishonored the bones of the king of Edom by burning them to ashes. I will send fire upon the land of Moab and burn down the fortresses of Kerioth. The people of Moab will die in the noise of battle while soldiers are shouting and trumpets are sounding. I will kill the ruler of Moab and all the leaders of the land."

Many of the problems have been handled much as they were discussed above, but one difference from the form of the source text deserves comment. The translation of "he-says Yahweh" has not been repeated at the end of this restructuring. No information was omitted by not repeating it, of course, because the fact that God is speaking is still clear from the beginning sentence. The translators probably judged repetition of the information to be unnatural English style.

Nevertheless, there is other meaning in these quotation formulae, as mentioned above, which seems not adequately conveyed in this restructuring. As it stands, the phrase "The LORD says" sounds like a statement of fact, not a statement of authority. Note, by way of comparison,

> Thus says the LORD: (Revised Standard Version)
>
> Yahweh says this: (*The Jerusalem Bible*)
>
> This is what the LORD says: (New International Version).
>
> These are the words of the LORD: (*The New English Bible*)

All of these translations have a more authoritative tone than does the *Good News Bible*. Of the four, "Thus says the LORD:" is archaic, not suitable for dynamic equivalence. "Yahweh says this:" is the weakest. "These are the words of the LORD:" seems less natural than "This is what the LORD says:" Other natural possibilities would include "Here is what the LORD says:" or "Listen to what the LORD says!"

Here, also, are some of the ways in which translators have restructured the final "he-says Yahweh":

> . . . says the LORD. (Revised Standard Version)
>
> . . . says Yahweh. (*The Jerusalem Bible*)
>
> By order of the Lord! (Phillips, *Four Prophets*)
>
> The Lord has spoken. (*The Living Bible*)

The first two sound colloquial, almost substandard, as if written "sez de Lawd." The other two both sound authoritative, but "The Lord has spoken." ties in best with the opening phrase.

A somewhat different restructuring of the passage, modifying that of the *Good News Bible,* illustrates how this and other problems might be handled.

> Listen to what the LORD says:
> "The people of Moab have sinned and sinned, so I'll surely punish them. They even dishonored the dead king of Edom by burning his bones to make lime!
> "I'll set fire to the land of Moab, and burn down its great fortress of Kerioth. The people will die in the noise of battle, with the soldiers shouting and trumpets sounding their defeat. I will kill the ruler of Moab, and all the leaders of that land."
> That is what the LORD says![35]

In this restructuring "Listen to what the LORD says:" expresses Amos's prophetic role of carrying a message from God, not just the abstract statement that a quotation follows. "That is what the LORD says!" then closes off the passage with a further emphatic note of authority. Printing the quotation formulae as separate lines also accentuates their force and visually marks the sharp beginning and end of the passage.

In addition to that, "They even" unites the example of sinning with the general statement about it in the previous sentence. The paragraph division marks the shift in topic from sin to punishment. This restructuring is also smoother at points, more rhythmic than the earlier one in keeping with the strongly rhythmic quality of the original. It is not poetry, however, in spite of the fact that the original is poetry. The translators of the *Good News Bible* rightly decided that poetry is not a natural or convincing medium for prophetic oracles of this kind in English.[36]

Such a brief discussion can only give a rough idea of the nature and principles of dynamic equivalence translation. Nida has defined it as seeking "the closest natural equivalent to the source-language message."[37] All of the terms in this definition represent very complex reality. Translators juggle innumerable variables as they seek to find the closest natural equivalent. There is no one correct dynamic equivalence translation, but only the constant search by analysis, transfer and restructuring, to reach maximum accessibility and minimum distortion.

---

[35]Adapted from de Waard and Smalley, *Amos,* 18.

[36]Crim, "Poetry," 106.

[37]Nida, *Science of Translating,* 166.

Perhaps the primary way in which dynamic equivalence translation is misinterpreted by some translators is in the scope of its application. Ideally, dynamic equivalence refers to language, not to culture and worldview, although these are not easy to separate from language. In principle, worldviews of the receptor culture ought not to be substituted for the worldviews to be found in the Bible, but the translator seeks to make those expressed in the text as clear to the modern reader as possible. Although the purpose of translation is to recapture what the original writers might have written if they had used modern language, it is not to guess what they would have written if they were writing today from within the worldviews of another culture. They should be left within their own perspective as much as possible.[38] In actual practice, however, some worldview distortion cannot be avoided; biblical worldviews can never be seen except through the reader's own worldviews, for example. Some cultural substitution is also unavoidable;[39] but the sky remains a dome with windows in it in the first chapter of Genesis, and people are troubled by evil spirits, not psychological problems, in the gospels.

This is not to disparage attempts to extend nontranslational dynamic equivalence to tasks of interpreting the Bible for present-day situations. All Christians must do that. Some writers explicitly use dynamic equivalence translation as a metaphor for this additional process of "transculturation."[40] The tensions between biblical worldviews and those of the reader sometimes come to a head in indigenous theology.[41] The requirements of translation, however, are to make the original text so accessible that such application is possible and appropriate, not to make the application itself.

---

[38]Nida and Reyburn, *Meaning*.

[39]Mundhenk, "Subjectivity."

[40]Kraft, *Christianity*. Shaw, who uses the term as the title of a book, does not seem to make as much difference between translation and other forms of communication.

[41]Chap. 10.

CHAPTER 7

Problems
in Dynamic Equivalence Translation

Dynamic equivalence translation has been criticized on various grounds.[1] Some critics disagree with its theological assumptions.[2] Others have not understood the theory, or have chosen not to take its objectives seriously. One seems to assume that all nonliteral translation is dynamic equivalence translation.[3] Another even writes as though all readers of the Bible are (or should be) literary critics. He seems to have no sense of a translation of the Bible for evangelism or the nurture of the church. Even so, some of his points are valid when reinterpreted within the objectives of dynamic equivalence translation.[4]

Other critics do understand dynamic equivalence translation in principle, but reject all of it or various aspects of it on one basis or another. One points out correctly, for example, that the linguistic underpinning of the theory has been flimsy, with little overall solid linguistic theoretical integration. Different problems are treated linguistically in a spotty, somewhat ad hoc manner.[5] An analysis from a Jewish point of view emphasizes the importance of various forms in the Hebrew Old Testament which are lost when the form of the original is discounted.[6]

---

[1]Often the criticism comes in the form of a review of the *Good News Bible*. An extensive bibliography of such reviews is included in Lewis, *Bible*, 400-404.

[2]E.g., Van Bruggen, *Future*.

[3]Walsh, "Translations."

[4]Prickett, *Words*.

[5]Nichols, "Translation."

[6]Greenstein, "Theories."

Almost invariably such critics opposed to dynamic equivalence translation point out loss which occurs in translations which follow such principles. Almost never do they recognize that translating as they would do would also involve loss, usually of intelligibility. Most of the critics are Biblical scholars who are so attuned to eavesdropping on the Bible[7] that they do not seem to understand the missiological concept of the Bible speaking to the present generation. One such critic takes almost a page to explain each of several subtle literary devices which he sees in the original, and points to their loss. The long explanations of the literary devices is necessary because they are not even apparent in literal translations, although the reader can find them there after reading the lengthy explanation first.[8]

Other critics see value in dynamic equivalence translation, but point out weaknesses in conception or application. Judging equivalence by similarity of receptor reaction to the reactions of original receptors can only be done subjectively, even speculatively, for example.[9]

There is constant debate on some such issues among people involved with dynamic equivalence translation as well, part of the process of learning. In the remainder of this chapter I will describe certain areas in which I think further growth is needed, as I perceive them from within the theory.[10] Essentially, they boil down to uneven application of the theory to different aspects of language and incomplete attention to prioritizing issues of accessibility and distortion for different kinds of audiences.

Kinds of Meaning to be Translated

There are certain biases in the way in which dynamic equivalence translation has been developed and applied in many languages so that translators who follow it tend to do some things better than others. To assess some of the weaknesses we need to distinguish between three kinds of meaning: *ideational* (meaning as information), *interpersonal*, or *interactional* (meaning as relationship between the people involved in the communication, the kind of communication they are involved in, the feelings and attitudes they display) and *textual* (meaning as the way in which the

---

[7]Chap. 1.

[8]Walsh, "Translations."

[9]House, *Model*.

[10]See also Peacock, "Current Trends."

communication is structured, the meaning which lies in the form itself).[11]
All three kinds of meaning are to be found both in the source texts and in
any translation. Almost all texts have them all simultaneously, but different kinds of meaning are more prominent in one text or another.

By way of illustration, "The LORD says" in the Amos passage from
the *Good News Bible*, discussed in the previous chapter, not only provides
the information that God is being quoted (ideational), but also implies a
simple statement of fact, which is its interactional meaning. However,
"Listen to what the LORD says," while providing the same information,
makes an imperative call to the listener, highlighting the prophetic nature
of the utterance, a different interactional meaning. That, in combination
with "That is what the LORD says!" at the end also gives the utterance
greater authority, another interactional meaning. The authoritative statements at the beginning and the end also provide strong boundaries to the
passage, a textual meaning.

The decision to translate the Amos passage as prose rather than as poetry (textual) is made for interactional reasons. We do not normally make
strong prophetic-type English utterances in poetry, where poetry is for
songs, commercials, greeting cards and other jingles, or for abstruse poems
which ordinary people cannot understand and do not care about.

Of the three kinds of meaning, dynamic equivalence translation has focused most heavily on ideational meaning and thus tends to be monodi-
mensional rather than tridimensional for several reasons. Theologically,
the goal has been to make the Bible which was written in a different culture
and different age understandable by people of today in their different cultures. Such understanding is most obviously ideational. It is clear also that
the form of the original usually cannot be carried over into the translation
without distorting the meaning, and form is textual. Many translators have
not been as aware that in sacrificing the textual form for the ideational
meaning, important textual meaning may also be lost.

Westerners, furthermore, tend to think of meaning in ideational terms.
They find it more difficult to think of interactional and textual meaning as
"meaning." It tends to get overlooked in the search for the meaning of the
text.

---

[11]Halliday, *Explorations*. Beekman and Callow, *Translating*, and Larson, *Translation*,
use the terms *referential, situational,* and *organizational.*

Then again, advances in linguistics which stimulated discoveries of ways to translate ideational meaning have not been as helpful for interactional and textual meaning. The core of concepts clustering around componential analysis, much more than we illustrated in Chapter 6, has provided tools for judging ideational equivalence, for example, but is not as readily adaptable to the other kinds of meaning.

Translating Interactional Meaning. Scholars have discussed the ideational meaning of individual words of the Bible for generations, but only sporadically do they pay much attention to the interactional meaning, to the degrees of forcefulness or politeness or anger or sadness in a passage, or to how such interactional meanings are indicated in the biblical text.

Translations also vary widely in the interactional meanings they manifest. The King James version is unintentionally hilarious (interactional) nonsense (ideational) in 2 Corinthians 6:11-12:

> O *ye* Corinthians, our mouth is open unto you, our heart is enlarged. Ye are not straitened [= "constricted"] in us, but ye are straightened in your own bowels. Now for a recompense in the same, (I speak as unto my children,) be ye also enlarged.

The Revised Standard Version translators removed the constipation (ideational), but leave Paul trying to lecture (interactional) the Corinthians with his mouth open:

> Our mouth is open to you, Corinthians; our heart is wide. You are not restricted by us, but you are restricted in your own affections. In return—I speak as to children—widen your hearts also.

The *Good News Bible,* on the other hand, provides an encouraging pep talk (interactional) which makes everything perfectly clear (ideational):

> Dear friends in Corinth! We have spoken frankly to you; we have opened our hearts wide. It is not we who have closed our hearts to you; it is you who have closed your hearts to us. I speak now as though you were my children: show us the same feelings that we have for you. Open your hearts wide!

J. B. Phillips's New Testament starts out the passage by expressing the feeling of a father hurt by the hostility of his children (interactional), but ends up with a sentence which seems to me to be too stiff to maintain that mood (interactional):

Oh, our dear friends in Corinth, we are hiding nothing from you and our hearts are absolutely open to you. Any restraint between us must be on your side, for we assure you there is none on ours. Do reward me (I talk to you as though you were my own children) with the same complete candour!

The New English Bible has a last sentence appropriate to the feeling of being hurt, but starts out like a general haranguing the troops (interactional):

Men of Corinth, we have spoken very frankly to you; we have opened our heart wide to you all. On our part there is no constraint; any constraint there may be is in yourselves. In fair exchange then (may a father speak so to his children?) open wide your hearts to us.

To my ears, a combination of Phillips and *The New English Bible* would give an excellent equivalent of the interactional meaning which I assume to be that of the original.[12]

But note the "I assume" in the previous paragraph. One of the great difficulties in translating interactional meaning is the lack of exegetical analysis. There is no consensus of scholars because they have neglected interactional meanings for generations while they focused primarily on ideational meaning. Not even the biblical scholars among translation consultants seem to work much on this problem. Take, for example, two passages which come from similar emotional situations, in each case a father learning of the (real or presumed) violent death of his son:

O my son Absolom, my son, my son Absolom! Would I had died instead of you, O Absolom, my son, my son![13]

It is my son's robe; a wild beast has devoured him; Joseph is without doubt torn to pieces.[14]

The anguish is obvious in the English translation of the father's verbal reaction in the first instance, while in the second the reactions sounds very matter of fact: "Ho hum! So the animals must have eaten my son!" We know by the context, however, that the father was overcome with grief.

Exegetically we need to know if the second passage really sounds as uncaring in Hebrew as it does in English. In the ChiChewa translation of Malawi the translators have included a mournful wail, an equivalent of

---

[12]Smalley, "Phillips."

[13]2 Samuel 18:33, Revised Standard Version.

[14]Genesis 37:33, Revised Standard Version.

"Woe is meee!" in the passage, believing that such a feeling is conveyed in the Hebrew sound play: *tarof toraf Yosef!*[15] Because biblical scholars have not worked out adequate exegetical principles in this area, translators generally take the easy way out and translate literally, which means that the translation sounds strange to anyone who really listens to the text. Other translators may take the emotional meaning from the context.

Perhaps another reason for weak or erroneous interactional (and textual) meaning in dynamic equivalence translations is that the people who work with this theory do not always have enough literary orientation. Some biblical scholars point out that the Bible is theological *literature,* with pervasive characteristics of literary writing.[16] Literature sometimes implies evocativeness, subtlety and indirection, but the purpose of dynamic equivalence translation is to make things clear. Thus we have conflicting objectives.

Literature implies vivid imagery, but the vivid imagery of the original does not necessarily carry over into another language unless equivalent imagery is taken from the resources of that language. Dynamic equivalence translators sometimes have to reduce imagery to its ideational meaning and translate that, but the result is loss in interactional and textual power. Translators must learn to use the subtlety, the indirection, the evocativeness, the imagery of the receptor language if they are to do justice to the Bible.

The importance of interactional meaning has always been supported in principle but then generally ignored in the active development of dynamic equivalence theory and its application. Nida mentioned "expressive function" in his writing from early on, but it was only briefly alluded to, between long discussions of how to handle ideational meaning.[17] Recently there has been more study and discussion of it under various names, but it remains conceptually marginal in the field as a whole.[18]

---

[15]Wendland, *Language,* 40-41.

[16]E.g., Alter and Kermode, eds., *Literary Guide.*

[17]Nida and Taber, *Translation,* 25-28, with occasional brief comments elsewhere about its importance, in a book of 218 pages.

[18]Wendland, *Language* and *Cultural Factor,* 83-165, seem to be the most extensive treatments of at least part of the field of interactional meaning within dynamic equivalence theory. See also Smalley, "Poetry." Larson devotes only sixteen pages (of 503) to "the communication situation" in *Translation,* 421-37.

Translating Textual Meaning. Slightly more attention has been paid by people in dynamic equivalence circles to some kinds of textual meaning in the Bible.[19] Such study does not necessarily carry over into finding effective textual equivalents in receptor languages, however. Poetry still remains the most difficult and the weakest area in translation under any theory because it requires ideational, interactional and textual equivalence, with particular focus on textual equivalence. At present qualified people translating under dynamic equivalence normally do well at ideational equivalence; interactional equivalence is possible but sporadic, its principles and procedures not thoroughly worked out; but to have textual equivalence as well simply seems beyond reach for many translators.

To have an equivalent poem, meeting the requirements of acceptable poetry in a receptor language, may mean that the ideational components of the original have to be radically rearranged. Even some of the most ardent proponents of dynamic equivalence draw back from a restructuring like the following experiment, for example:

The subject nations are planning rebellion. . . .
   Their people are plotting. . . .
      Their kings and rulers join in revolt. . . .
         "Freedom!" they say,
         "Freedom from rule!"
         "Off with control
            of the LORD
            and the king he has chosen."
   Plotting
   Useless plots
   Why?
The LORD laughs on his throne.
   Mocks them in heaven.
Furious, he terrifies them,
Speaks to them, angry.
      "I have installed the king,
      Placed him on Zion,
         My holy hill."[20]

[19]E.g., Clark, "Parallelism"; de Waard and Smalley, *Amos,* 1-19, 189-214; Callow, *Discourse*; Nida et al., *Style*; de Waard and Nida, *One Language,* 86-120; several articles in Stine, ed., *Issues;* Mundhenk, "Form." A new journal, *OPTAT: Occasional Papers in Translation and Textlinguistics,* published by the Summer Institute of Linguistics, may help to stimulate more thought, especially on problems of textual meaning.

[20]Psalms 2:1-6, Smalley, "Poetry," 341-42.

Compare a more nearly formal correspondent translation of the same passage:

> Why do the nations conspire,
> and the peoples plot in vain?
> The kings of the earth set themselves,
>   and the rulers take counsel together,
>   against the LORD and his anointed, saying,
> "Let us burst their bonds asunder,
>   and cast their cords from us."
> He who sits in the heavens laughs;
>   the LORD has them in derision.
> Then he will speak to them in his wrath,
>   and terrify them in his fury, saying
> "I have set my king on Zion, my holy hill."[21]

It is ludicrous to think of people plotting rebellion in English with the words, "Let us burst their bonds asunder, and cast their cords from us."

Among those who have wrestled with the translation of poetry, Jacob A. Loewen has studied samples of West African praise poems to see how African translators might use that genre for the translation of some Old Testament poetry. One requirement of such poems is that they must have the rhythms of the drum tunes by which they are traditionally sung. In the example below an extra syllable -la is inserted as one of the conventional ways of providing a needed beat, for example. Wording and sentence structure also reflect that limitation, as does some of the repetition. The example is a literal back-translation into English of two verses of David's lament over the death of Jonathan:

> There on those there Gilboa mountains
> Israel-people's soldiers good disappeared,
> Israel-people's soldiers good bit the earth,
> Israel-people's soldiers brave bit the earth.
> You, Israel-people's soldiers who are brave and good
> There you disappeared, poof.
> There you bit the earth.
> All you who know about this word,
>   do not tell its news in Askelon town,
>   do not tell its news in Gath-la town.
> If you go gong-gong it in their streets
>   the Philistine women will rejoice,

---

[21]Psalms 2:1-6, Revised Standard Version.

the Philistine women will dance.
Hu, those foreigners who don't obey God
    will dance themselves.[22]

On the other hand, the Revised Standard Version renders the verses as follows, and many translators around the world follow this textual form rather closely, regardless of poetic conventions in the receptor language:

Thy glory, O Israel, is slain upon thy high places!
    How are the mighty fallen!
Tell it not in Gath,
    publish it not in the streets of Ashkelon;
lest the daughters of the Philistines rejoice,
    lest the daughters of the uncircumcised exult.

Priorities in Dynamic Equivalence Translation

Although it certainly will eventually be possible to reflect interactional and textual meaning with less distortion than is common in much dynamic equivalence translation now, there remains the fundamental question of priorities. A typical ordering of theoretical priorities is (1) fidelity to the meaning of the original, (2) intelligibility in the receptor language (3) naturalness of receptor language, and (4) closeness in form to the original text.[23] The theoretical basis for priority 4 has never been made clear in dynamic equivalence translation, however. In practice what often happens is that closeness of form is the default position. When the translator does not know what else to do the fourth priority is allowed to take over for any of the others. Perhaps in an ideal translational world there would be no need for priority four.[24] The definition would then be ''the most natural equivalent'' rather than ''the closest natural equivalent.''

These priorities, however, have normally applied only to ideational meaning in translators' work. There has been little theoretical consideration given to where accessibility should be preserved and distortion allowed when fidelity to the ideational meaning conflicts with fidelity to the

---

[22]Cf. 2 Samuel 1:19-20. Loewen, ''Poetry,'' language not specified. The article gives information about transfer and restructuring, which provides rationale for some of the wording.

[23]After Wendland, *Language*, 218.

[24]Mundhenk, ''Form,'' 34.

interactional or textual meaning. If something interactional or textual strikes translators as not acceptable when they restructure, they normally reconsider it, but otherwise they fall back on of formal correspondence with respect to these types of meaning. The more they do so, the more the unnatural sound and implication of the text seems natural to them. The resulting translationese then often provides a basis for the development of a special church dialect.[25]

On the other hand, skillful translators following dynamic equivalence theory work with sections of text, not with individual words, phrases, or sentences. This can give them more sense of interactional and textual meaning than is true of people who translate more literally. They also keep the relationship between source and receptor in mind. Both of these techniques may help sometimes to give them some sense of the larger interactional and textual meanings, and they may therefore reflect them into their translation on a somewhat intuitive basis, which may sometimes compensate for the lack of clear treatment in the theory.

So there is still a long way to go. By presenting this unresolved area in the theory we simply illustrate that people are still at work trying to find solutions to old and significant problems. Translators are still experimenting; consultants are still probing; theorists are still proposing models for consideration.

In spite of unfinished agenda and clear weaknesses, dynamic equivalence translation has made an enormous contribution. In some aspects of the task it has shown how to do what needs to be done. Elsewhere it has opened up more precisely to researchers and translators the issues on which more thought and experimentation must be expended.[26] It makes the teaching of translation principles possible, and the discussion of strengths and weaknesses of translations more pointed.

But most of all, dynamic equivalence translation has resulted in a whole new generation of Bible translations around the world, translations which are much more accessible than most earlier ones, often with significantly less distortion. In some situations it has helped rescue the Bible from being a dusty sacred relic to being the "living oracles" of God.[27]

---

[25]Chap. 9.

[26]Peacock, "Current Trends."

[27]Acts 7:38, Revised Standard Verison.

CHAPTER 8

Translation Strategy under Language Diversity

We have seen that the world is multilingual, with more than six thousand languages (see chapter 2, table 2). It is also multilingual in the sense that a considerable proportion of its people could not live normal lives without knowing two or more languages, sometimes without using them daily. Most languages, furthermore, have more than one dialect, and within languages there are often numerous levels or styles which people use in different situations. Multiplicity of languages and dialects, multilingualism, and multiple levels of language usage are all potentially severe problems for people who seek to determine what Bible translation should be done.

Language diversity, in turn, has been affected by decisions made down through the history of translation, beginning with some of the great ancient translations and continuing in the modern missionary movement. The selection of a language or dialect for translation sometimes directly changes its history. Other aspects of life, including ethnic identification, social structures, modernization and indigenous theology, have also been affected by the interplay between translation and language diversity, as we shall see in chapters which follow. Here we look at the nature of language diversity as it impinges on translation strategy.

At times, of course, translation strategy decisions seem obvious and straightforward, as when William Carey went to Bengal and started translating the Bible. He was in a subcontinent with many languages, but he did not doubt that he should translate first into Bengali, the language of the area where he worked, a language spoken by a large population, a written language, and an important language of India. But then Carey soon came to realize that

"Bengali" covered a range of different dialects,[1] different varieties of speech, and that in the hinterland where he first settled he was learning and using a rural and localized dialect which had no prestige. Eventually he moved to Serampore, and began to teach in Calcutta, where people spoke what was considered better Bengali, and he translated into that.

Carey's preference for translation into a more prestigious dialect reflected attitudes toward language differences expressed by Indian people, but no doubt also corresponded rather closely to ones he had brought from England. Translating into the rural dialect may have seemed analogous to translating into a local dialect of English like Yorkshire. The dialect of the educated speakers in Calcutta may have seemed like upper-class English.

What translation strategy to use was less self-évident, on the other hand, when missionaries contemplated translating Scriptures in a section of the Vietnamese highlands in the middle of this century. The six minority ethnic groups in the area called themselves by different names like Cil, Srê and Ma, and spoke somewhat different but mutually intelligible dialects. From the missionary point of view it was all one language, but there was not yet any generally used common name for such a language nor was there any common ethnic name at the time for this collection of peoples as a whole. None of the dialects, furthermore, had a written form, and none of the people had much formal education in any language. Populations of the various groups were not large, ranging from 3,000 to 40,000.[2]

Decisions about translation strategy should never be made lightly, of course. and the commitments implied in beginning translating into a language of this Srê-Cil-Ma type and under these circumstances, are formidable. Any missionaries involved have to learn to speak the language well. A writing system must be devised, a painstaking and often difficult task. Translation of the Scriptures may take years of part-time work by several people including both missionaries and native speakers, often requiring payment of salaries and expenses. Then there must be literacy instruction if people are to read the trans-

---

[1]As was mentioned before, *dialect* in this book refers to recognizably different forms of speech which are mutually or unidirectionally intelligible because they are closely related, and each is identified with a particular geographic area. Upper-class British English, Boston English, Southern American English and Standard American English, various forms of Australian English, Indian English and Philippine English, e.g., are all different dialects of English by this definition.

[2]Manley, *Srê*.

lation. Other literature should also be written or translated to nourish reading skills, support the translation and build on it.

With limited resources, translation into all of these mutually intelligible dialects in Vietnam was impossible in the viewpoint of the mission. Besides, since the people of the different dialects could understand each other, they could all learn to read the same material and there should be no need for multiple translations, all of which would be intelligible to readers of all of the dialects.

So the missionaries chose the Srê dialect as the one in which to translate, partly for their own convenience, because of the availability of a Srê-speaking convert and the relative accessibility of the group. Fortunately the decision also reflected an aspect of cultural reality, as the Srê were agriculturally more advanced and their culture therefore carried slightly more prestige than the other groups. More of the Christians were Cil, to be sure, but for the Cil to read the Scriptures in Srê was acceptable, while the reverse might not have been.[3] In their decisions the missionaries were again reflecting, at least in part, attitudes which they had learned from some of the people concerned, as well as attitudes they brought from their homeland.

Such a solution does not always come that easily, however. Many Christians who speak the Mong Leng dialect in Laos, and now in the United States, rejected using Scriptures translated into the mutually intelligible Hmong Daw dialect even though speakers of the two dialects all call themselves Hmong (or Mong) and recognize a common identity for most purposes. Many Mong Leng insist that their language is not the same as Hmong Daw, even though the two groups understand each other. This attitude has forced the publication of parallel translations, although a committee with members from both groups is now (1989) trying to prouce a common translation acceptable to both.

The Srê and related dialects, furthermore, are concentrated in an area small enough so that one set of missionaries could contact all of them, whereas the dialects of Inuit (Eskimo) are scattered over an enormous area from Greenland across Canada and Alaska into Siberia. Intelligibility is fairly high among many of these dialects except at the westernmost end,[4] but different mission groups working among Inuit peoples in relative iso-

---

[3] Ansre, "Unify or Dialectize?" discusses some of the issues in cases like this in African languages.

[4] Bergsland, "Eskimo-Aleut."

lation from each other have had different language policies,[5] and produced Scripture translations in at least ten of the dialects.[6]

Mission language policy extremes in working with Inuit peoples can be illustrated from two areas. Christianity first came to the Inuit of Norton Sound, Alaska, in the 1880s, through missionaries who did not bother much with the Inuit language. They preached, taught and conducted services in English, as did the Inuit preachers whom they trained. They had no thought of translating the Bible into Inuit. Several hundred miles away in central Canada, on the other hand, missionaries often learned Inuit well. They adapted a syllabic writing system to the language, and the first Scripture translation was published in 1881. Such differences in translation strategy were to be found in other parts of the world as well. Some of their ramifications will be seen in later chapters.

Selecting a Vernacular for Translation

When people plan translation, trying to decide whether or not to translate, or into which language, or into which dialect of a language, or how to convince people of the need for translation, an intelligent decision is influenced by many factors, of which those to be discussed in this chapter are often central. Consciousness of these factors has varied widely throughout the modern missionary movement, and some of them are only beginning to be articulated systematically,[7] although most of them have been implicitly present since the Septuagint was translated before the time of Christ. Availability of personnel and resources, often a dominating factor, is not considered here.

Local Attitudes toward Language and Translation. Often the most critical element affecting the acceptance of translation is the attitude of local populations toward their own languages and the other languages of the area. In some societies people have an intense desire for the Bible in their language. Some independent churches, for example, have split off from mission-founded churches in part because the missions had not provided them with vernacular Scriptures. Some native speakers have undertaken Scrip-

---

[5]Correll, ''Eskimo.''

[6]Nida, ed., *Thousand Tongues,* 128; United Bible Societies, *Scriptures.*

[7]Blair, *Survey.*

ture translation on their own without training or resources.[8] Such efforts show not only an attitude toward Scripture, but also an attitude toward their language.

Some other people, however, even Christian people, see no need at all for the Bible in their own language, rather finding the idea strange and troubling, or feeling indifferent to it. For many years, for example, Haitians resisted writing Haitian, a creole language with roots both in French and in African languages, and the suggestion of Bible translation into Haitian seemed preposterous. Educated people knew French, and although they spoke Haitian almost exclusively in informal situations they were embarrassed to see it in written form, considering it to be debased French in spite of the fact that it is rich and colorful in its own right. These attitudes carried over to uneducated people as well, people who knew no French at all.

Various ingredients contribute to language attitudes, in addition to theological presuppositions.[9] An important one is the way people perceive the boundaries between languages and dialects and between the ethnic groups which are partly defined by language. Some perceive such boundaries to be strong and fixed, while others perceive them to be loose and variable. Languages and dialects, in other words, may be bounded cultural categories or centered ones in the meaning systems of different cultures.[10]

To illustrate these perspectives from other parts of culture, for most Americans the sexes are sharply bounded categories. They perceive people as either male or female, not both, and not changing from one to the other, not male part of the time and female the rest of the time. They are therefore uncomfortable with bisexual people, homosexuals, transvestites, and people who change sex. They perceive the boundary between sexes as sharp, in other words, in spite of their scientific knowledge that sexual division is not always clear-cut.

Colors, however, are centered categories with indeterminate boundaries. People in any culture agree rather well in identifying colors at their centers on a color chart, but disagree as to where one color changes to another in the spectrum. The same people will not identify the color of the same object the same way every time they see it if it lies in a border area.[11]

---

[8] Barrett, *Schism*, 127.

[9] Chap. 5.

[10] Hiebert, "Conversion."

[11] Berlin and Kay, *Color Terms*, 13.

Boundaries between the same languages or dialects and between the same ethnic groupings may seem fixed from the perspective of people in one culture, but fluid for people of another. In northeastern Thailand, for example, people born in a Kuy village typically speak Kuy there and in other Kuy villages. From the point of view of some outsiders that makes them "Kuy people," a separate "tribe" from the people around them. And from Kuy perspective also they are Kuy people, up to a point.

But the Kuy do not consider themselves to be exclusively Kuy. Many of them also speak the unrelated Lao language, the regional language of the Northeast, whenever they are in contact with Lao-speaking people, or the Khmer language whenever they are in contact with Khmer-speaking people. If they move into a Lao-speaking area they talk Lao, live like Lao; they are Lao. They do the same with Khmer in a Khmer-speaking area. Furthermore, they are also Thai, and if they have the education to do so they speak Thai to people from outside the region. If they move out of the region they may talk Thai and live like Thai. They may be Kuy, Khmer, Lao and Thai simultaneously, with one or another identity more salient according to their situation at a given time, but without sharp boundaries from their point of view or from that of their neighbors.[12] If a Kuy person learns English, however, that person does not gain any American or British identity. English remains a "foreign" language, with a sharp boundary separating it from Kuy.

For most middle-class Americans, on the other hand, languages have fixed boundaries, and their American identity is welded to English. People may be Swedish-American or African-American, but that simply means that they are American with ancestors who were different, and that they may retain a few symbols of that origin. From the perspective of their bounded categories, Americans cannot be both African and American or sometimes African and sometimes American. The present drive to make English the only official language in the United States reflects the perception that to be Spanish-speaking is not to be American.

Once people are attracted by the Christian message, whether or not they want to have Scriptures in their own language is often influenced by whether they perceive themselves and others in bounded or centered terms. If their identity requires sharp language boundaries and they do not have too negative a linguistic self-image, they generally want a translation into their own

---

[12]Smalley, "Hierarchy."

language, or even into their own dialect. The Mong Leng mentioned above would not accept Scriptures translated into Hmong Daw, even though it is the same language, but perceived the dialect boundary as a sharp one, and wanted their own translation.

When identity is perceived as having loose boundaries the sense of need for Scriptures may not be as great. Scriptures have been translated and are used in Kuy, but there is no burning sense of need for them, or even for writing Kuy at all. After all, if people want to read or write they are supposed to do it in Thai, which is one of their identities, although many of them cannot understand Thai well, especially the Scriptures in Thai, and some of them cannot read or write Thai at all.

In India some social boundaries are rigid, as evidenced by the caste system. Some language boundaries in the northern part of the country, on the other hand, tend to be quite loose, as shown in successive census returns. Between 1951 and 1961, for example, the number of people in the state of Bihar claiming Bhojpuri as their language jumped from under 1,900 to 7,842,700, a 412,674% increase. At the same time, those claiming Magadhi rose from 3,700 to 2,818,500, a 76,076% increase, while those claiming Hindi dropped 54%.[13] People had not changed their speech, nor were they lying in either census, but for various reasons their lower-level identity in the hierarchy of languages was more salient to them at the time of the second census. The boundary between the Indo-Aryan languages of the north and the Dravidian languages of the south, on the other hand, is sharply fixed, and many people who speak Dravidian languages resent the dominance of Hindi.

Loose boundaries occur most frequently between closely related languages or otherwise rather similar languages, where it is fairly easy for the person speaking the lower language in the hierarchy to learn the higher one. Bhojpuri and Hindi are of the this type, as are Kuy and Khmer, and Lao and Thai. Kuy and Lao, however, together with Kuy and Thai, are not as closely related, and being closely related or highly similar does not insure loose boundaries, as we saw in the case of Mong Leng and Hmong Daw.

A second major factor which contributes to language attitude consists in how languages and dialects are socially structured. Some languages are perceived as approximately equal, while others appear as higher or lower

---

[13]Khubchandani, *Plural Languages*, 92, 98.

in rank. For the Kuy the ordering of languages up the scale is Kuy, Khmer, Lao and Thai.

There is a very loose boundary between French and Haitian, with educated individuals slipping back and forth across it all day long for different purposes, but French is perceived to be the higher language. French has always been considered appropriate for writing and for Scriptures in Haiti, but Haitian was not considered worthy until recently, even by people who could not understand French.

Lao spoken in Thailand shows how complicated such relationships can get. It is the same spoken language as the national language of Laos, across the border, where it occupies a higher position in the hierarchy than it does in Thailand, although there are several times fewer speakers in Laos. In Thailand Lao is subordinate to Thai, without any sharp boundary perceived between them. Lao in Thailand has been written in various scripts, but writing Lao arouses no great popular enthusiasm, for Thai usually seems more appropriate for writing. The language of education is also Thai, even in Lao-speaking areas.

In Laos, on the other hand, the same spoken language is a national language, is written in a script which looks somewhat different from Thai, and is regularly taught in the schools. People in Thailand who speak Lao as their mother tongue feel more of a boundary between their Lao and this written Lao of Laos, which they understand perfectly, than they do between their Lao and Thai, which many of them do not understand as well. The Lao of Laos occupies a different place in a different hierarchy.[14]

Lao-speaking Christians in Thailand therefore do not usually use the Lao Scriptures from Laos, but the Thai Scriptures. There have been recent experiments in translating the Scriptures into Lao in northeastern Thailand, using Thai script, and they may be successful, but at present the need for such Scriptures may be felt more by missionaries than by local people.

Language hierarchy is the outcome of major patterns of language learning and use. It is not involved when miscellaneous individuals like students in school learn miscellaneous other languages for miscellaneous reasons, but is manifest when significant proportions of the native speakers of one language regularly need to use the same one or more other languages for some aspect of their life. They need the other language to live, to work, to get ahead in the world, and even sometimes for religion.[15]

[14]Smalley, "Hierarchy"; and *Diversity.*

[15]Smalley, "Strategies."

This need, furthermore, is not reciprocal. Millions of people in the world whose mother tongue is other than English feel a need for English but there is no corresponding mass sense of need by native speakers of English for any of their languages.[16] Even when English-speaking Americans are living in areas of the United States where Spanish is the majority language most of them do not feel any need for Spanish, but believe that the Spanish-speaking people should use English. American government officials and business people abroad typically do not learn local languages although they are put at a diplomatic and business disadvantage by their parochialism.

Language hierarchies differ somewhat in their composition from one area to another, but there is nevertheless a general worldwide pattern, at least parts of which will apply almost everywhere, and which is often highly relevant to translation decisions. These rankings of language as "higher" or "lower" have nothing to do with intrinsic language quality, but arise out of differences in the collective power of their speakers.

At the top is English, the nearest thing to a world language which exists. Below it are several international languages, most of them important in areas where they once were, or still are, colonial languages: English, which operates on this level as well as on the world level, Russian, Spanish, French, Mandarin and Arabic. Only one of them is usually significant in any given area, except that English in its role of world language may be significant along with another international language of the area. In addition to these major international languages there are a few other more regional multinational languages like Swahili in East Africa, Urdu, Hindi, Bengali and Tamil in South Asia, and German in Europe, for example. The same multinational language may even have different names in different countries, like Malay and Indonesian.

Then below the international and multinational languages are often national languages, which include most of the international languages in their "home" countries, plus languages of other countries like Indonesian, Thai, Filipino, or Persian. Under these are sometimes regional languages within the country, like Javanese (Indonesia), Lao (Thailand) or Cebuano (Philippines). And finally, there are the languages of the towns and villages,

---

[16]This statement does not apply in cases such as sometimes occur in such countries as India and the Philippines, where people grow up as bilingual native speakers of English and a local language in an area where most people are not native speakers of English but nevertheless use English extensively as a higher language.

the languages which nobody from outside usually learns unless there is more than one level of village languages, or unless the language also functions on a higher level in the hierarchy of languages.[17]

One of the implications of hierarchy for translation strategy is that the higher the level on which the language occurs, the larger the number of people who can speak and read it. Languages of upper and middle ranges in a hierarchy, down through national languages and the larger regional languages have usually been candidates for Bible translation without question because of their size or cultural, political or economic importance. The more difficult questions are normally raised concerning languages at lower levels in the language hierarchy, as they are less likely to have a written form, are not likely to be standardized, and often have smaller populations. The speakers of such languages are often multilingual as well, and sometimes lack linguistic self-esteem.

This multilingualism, however, is usually not uniform. It ranges in degree from people who are nearly native speakers of more than one language to those who simply have enough to get by in the marketplace or other simple situations. It ranges in location, also, often more extensive in and near urban areas than in isolated rural ones. It often varies also with sex, education, age and generation.[18]

Linguistic confidence or self-esteem is the third major component in language attitudes as they affect translation strategy, interacting both with hierarchy and with perception of boundary. A low position in a linguistic hierarchy does not necessarily correlate with negative self-esteem. Because of their multiple identities people with loose language boundaries may accept the low place of their village language, content to use it where it is considered appropriate. They shift to their other languages for more prestigious purposes like education, writing or public expression without resentment or threat to their identity as speakers of the lower language in the hierarchy for local, informal situations. Speakers of Swiss German are one example. So are speakers of some colloquial forms of Arabic across North Africa and the Middle East.

In other cases, especially where people perceive sharp linguistic boundaries, low rank does coincide with negative self-esteem. This may

---

[17]This classification is not exhaustive, but includes the translationally most relevant categories.

[18]Smalley, "Multilingualism."

often be true in cultures which are in decline because of the encroachment of a more powerful people, especially a people which also has bounded language categories and negative perception of the lower-level language. Some Indian peoples in the Americas, for example, have caved in under the linguistic attitudes of English and Spanish-speaking people, becoming ashamed of their own languages.

Dominant people sometimes tell subordinate ones that they are stupid and ignorant, that their language is not really a language, that it is incapable of subtle expression. Those who say these things rarely speak the despised language, of course, but they have prestige associated with their power and what they say seems to be corroborated to native speakers who cannot find word-for-word equivalents in their language for some words they learn in the higher language of the language hierarchy. It does not occur to them that the reverse is also true, that their language has words not matched literally in the other language, and that vocabulary is a reflection of cultural experience, so that new expressions are added to any language when significant new cultural experience takes place.

Missionaries or Christian leaders from higher-level languages in a hierarchy sometimes contribute to negative linguistic self-esteem among speakers of lower-level languages. They may believe that a particular language is incapable of expressing Christian concepts, and act accordingly. Sometimes missionaries have been so overwhelmed by the number of languages around them that they have insisted the church use a higher-level language in the hierarchy. Or they simply have used it themselves, ignoring the lower-level languages, leading speakers of the vernaculars to conclude that their languages are not worthy of the Scriptures.[19]

On the other hand, hierarchical subordination with bounded categories may also intensify desire for Scriptures, especially if people maintain positive linguistic self-esteem and resent the dominance of other languages. So when they perceive the international, national or regional languages in which Scriptures already exist to be alien they are frequently motivated to seek for writing and Scriptures in their own language. In Northeast India groups often want the Bible in the local languages not only for its intrinsic value, but also because it brings prestige, recognition of the language by

---

[19]Loving, ''Scripture Use,'' 13.

the government, and the hope of standing against domination by Assamese and Hindi.[20]

But local attitudes toward language can and sometimes do change, and translation of the Scriptures may contribute to the change, which further complicates making rational decisions about translation strategy. Motivated by strong theological presuppositions, some translators have gone ahead with their translation in spite of lack of local interest, even in spite of opposition. Some of the resulting translations have ultimately been useful, others abortive. Frequently interest has grown as the translation progressed.

One of the most significant changes in attitude occurs when people gain more positive self-esteem as one of the byproducts of translation and related work. The Paez people of Colombia were evangelized in Spanish, and Paez Christian leaders used the Spanish Bible, but with difficulty. The image which the Paez people had of their own language, furthermore, was negative. Young people aspired to learn Spanish, not just to enhance their use of a higher level language in the hierarchy but also because they were ashamed to be heard speaking Paez. And when the New Testament was being translated into Paez, although it was much needed from a communications standpoint nobody could read Paez, and few wanted to.

Translator Marianna C. Slocum and her colleagues worked systematically to overcome these attitudes which stood in the way of the use of the Paez Scriptures. They undertook an extensive program to give people a feeling that their language was worthwhile, as well as to help them to learn the Spanish they needed. They produced a Paez-Spanish and Spanish-Paez dictionary, a bilingual grammar for learning Paez which Paez people also found useful in learning Spanish, and a more technical grammar. When government officials and school teachers in the area began buying these materials it boosted the prestige of Paez in the Spanish-speaking community, and the linguistic self-esteem of Paez people became more positive as well. This helped make it possible for people to accept the Paez Scriptures which they could understand much better than they could the Spanish.[21]

Missionary Attitudes toward Language and Translation. Usually in the past and frequently even now in some missions, missionaries have controlled translation strategy decisions, whatever local attitudes may have

---

[20]Other attitudes toward language and translation are tied in with the process of modernization (see below, chap. 11).

[21]Slocum, "Vernacular Scriptures," 11.

been. Like everyone else, of course, missionaries have perceptions of languages as bounded or centered categories, and of language hierarchy. They also place positive and negative values both on their own language and on the languages of others. All of these perceptions affect their translation decisions, along with their theological assumptions about language and translation. Some missionary perceptions of language they bring with them from their homelands, but then they frequently modify some of them in light of what they learn in the local situation.

The overall missionary population, to be sure, has always had a very wide range of language attitudes and policies. On the one hand are those hundreds of missionaries who have given their lives to analyzing, recording, mastering, using, promoting, describing and sometimes translating into one or more difficult languages, some of them doing so brilliantly. Theirs is one of the great intellectual legacies of the missionary movement.[22] The tradition of missionary language learning, furthermore, the level of language learning by ordinary missionaries who did not become language specialists, has sometimes been distinguished.

At the other extreme, however, some missionaries have been contemptuous of local languages, considering them limited, primitive, inferior to the languages of the West. Or they may have been thwarted by a vernacular because it seemed too difficult to learn.

Most truly pioneer missionaries were forced by their situation to listen to the local languages, to struggle with them, to learn them from native speakers. They had no alternative except failure, or even death. They needed the languages to eat, to work, to travel, to have social relationships, as well as to minister, and they had few other people but native speakers of those languages to whom to turn.[23] Their successors, however, were often partially buffered from the same languages by communities of missionaries who spoke their own foreign distortions of these languages, by churches accustomed to hearing foreign ways of speaking them, and by local Christians in close contact with the missionaries who sometimes even adapted their own speech to missionary limitations.

Inaccurate grammar books written by older missionaries sometimes became the norm for new missionaries learning languages instead of the

---

[22]Chapter 3.

[23]A dramatic picture of this process in the experience of one missionary translator is to be found in Slocum and Watkins, *Good Seed.*

usage of native speakers. Some missionaries even corrected native speakers, telling them how to speak their own language according to some missionary held notion. Such missionaries sometimes dominated translation teams, pushing the language of the translation into a stilted, unnatural mode, and implicitly or explicitly teaching native speakers that this mode was the proper language for the Bible.

Other missionaries insisted on the use of some higher-level language rather than the vernacular. Missionaries to Indians in the United States were often very weak in use of the Indian languages, for example, in spite of some brilliant exceptions. In addition to the contempt which many felt for Indian culture, they found Indian languages difficult to learn if they tried to learn them at all, and were often convinced that these languages were debased forms of speech incapable of expressing Christian theology or abstract ideas. Among the Cherokee Indians in the first half of the nineteenth century, for example, none of the Moravian missionaries succeeded in learning Cherokee, even after twenty-five years of ministry.[24] Missionaries of the American Board of Commissioners were much the same, except for Daniel S. Butrick, who lived in a Cherokee home and learned to speak the language, finding it to be rich and expressive.[25]

At least three important developments in the middle of the twentieth century helped to reduce such harmful missionary attitudes toward language and culture, where they existed in various parts of the world. One was the rise of independent nations and of national churches which in some cases insisted on the value of their own languages. Another consisted of ideas from linguistics and anthropology, often mediated through institutions like the Bible societies, the Summer Institute of Linguistics, the Kennedy School of Missions, the Toronto Institute of Linguistics, and some books and journals, especially the journal *Practical Anthropology*. The third was an increasing general respect for cultural diversity among educated Westerners. It is significant, of course, that the modern missionary movement itself and translation work contributed strongly to each of these forces which helped to moderate, if only for a generation, the demeaning attitude where it was to be found among missionaries.[26]

---

[24]McLoughlin, *Cherokees*, 68.

[25]Ibid., 136-37.

[26]Sanneh, *Translating*.

But even when missionaries did not appreciate the local culture, overwhelming sociolinguistic realities forced most of them, even ones with adverse attitudes, to learn some vernacular language anyhow. More than that, as a group missionaries of all types have learned more African, Asian and American Indian languages and learned them better than have any other sizable expatriate class of Europeans or Americans.

So it is that translation policy differed from mission to mission, area to area. The higher the language in the hierarchy, the more likelihood missionaries would agree on the need for translation; the lower the language in the language hierarchy the greater the chance that individual and corporate missionary attitudes would differ.

Assessment of Communication Need. Decisions about translation into the vernacular obviously also require some assessment of what translation is needed. Such assessments are founded first on the theological assumptions of the people doing the assessing, and if these are favorable to translation they are then further based upon factors like size of population and the ability of people who speak the language to use Scriptures in other languages.

Occasionally an assessment is based on nothing but ignorance or wishful thinking, as when leaders of the dominant church or the mission assume that because they can converse in a higher language of the hierarchy with some people who speak a lower language in the language hierarchy, people in the lower-language community can understand the Bible in the higher language.

On the contrary, even people who say that they understand the Scriptures in another language may not be able to do so adequately. People may get the drift of the translation some of the time, and not expect greater understanding because they may believe that religion is supposed to be obscure. Or they may simply be unwilling to admit their lack of skill in the higher language.

At other times the need or the lack of need for translation may be quite apparent to realistic observers. Most typically, the situation is complicated because some people are more adequately multilingual than others.

Ability to understand the Scriptures intellectually in another language is not necessarily enough, however. Native speakers of the lower language in the hierarchy may have adequate or even excellent knowledge of the higher language for commerce and education, but may not be at home in it for religion and the expression of emotion. The Scriptures need to be in language appropriate to the deepest parts of a people's psyche.

Often bilingualism is pervasive but shallow. Preachers among the bilingual Blaan people in the Philippines used to read the Scriptures in Cebuano, the regional language of the area, and then retold the content of the reading in Blaan, so that people could understand. After Scriptures were translated into Blaan, one Blaan leader visited the different churches and introduced the new Blaan translation by reading a passage in Cebuano, and asking the congregation what it meant. When nobody could reply, he would read the passage in Blaan. The emotional response was so great that sometimes Christians would cry as they understood the Scriptures directly for the first time.[27]

Occasionally an accurate assessment of great need for Scriptures in the vernacular plus translation done to demonstrate how it can meet that need may be what helps to stimulate positive language attitudes. Before the middle of this century some people in both the Catholic and Protestant churches in Haiti saw that Haitians were simply unable to understand the Scriptures or anything else in French unless they had considerable education, a privilege which was characteristic of only a small minority. A conviction that Haitian should be written in spite of Haitian resistance was strengthened by the work of a linguist who demonstrated that Haitian was a language in its own right, not a formless and debased French, as missionaries and Haitians had typically thought.[28]

A few other people sensed a need to write Haitian also, at least for some purposes, as when some Haitian intellectuals experimented with writing folklore. Finally, in 1975 the government legitimized Haitian as a language of education, removing some of the pressure against it.

Over these years, steady efforts by a few Christians toward writing the Haitian language and translating into it were among the forces influencing the change of attitude. Catholics experimented with translating the catechism and other materials into Haitian and the Bible societies worked to encourage Bible translation and to help the church see the need for it. A New Testament and Psalms was published in 1951, another in 1960. These paved the way for two new translations of the New Testament, one by the Catholic church in 1974, the other by the Bible society in 1975. A Bible society edition of the whole Bible then appeared in 1985,[29] and has had

---

[27]Larson and Rhea, "Blaan."

[28]See, e.g., Hall, "Le créole Haïtien," and *Haitian Creole.*

[29]Conus, "Le créole, une langue pour l'Église en Haïti"; Nida, ed., *Thousand Tongues,* 173-74.

good success. Those who believe that the Scriptures should be read in Haitian are slowly winning out.

This success may also be making it easier to advance Scripture translation in other Creole languages of the Caribbean basin, like Jamaican and Papiamentu, the latter spoken in the Netherlands Antilles, off the coast of Venezuela. On the other hand, educated Haitians do not take immediately to the Scriptures in Haiti. Individuals who look at the book sometimes say they cannot read it. Only a little bit of effort would be required to get used to the writing system, but attitudes concerning the relative places of French and Haitian still interfere.[30]

Translation strategists face a different set of problems where numerous similar dialects exist. The critical questions then concern how many different translations are needed and in which dialect or dialects. Such dialects usually form a network spread out across an area. People of adjacent dialects typically understand each other very well, but people in widely separated dialects may not. The stretch of Germanic dialects from Belgium and Holland across Germany and Austria and into Switzerland is like that, with the additional complication that Dutch and German, part of that continuum, have become national languages, have been standardized, are taught in schools, and have been developed for literature and science. Similarly, all across north India the language hierarchy with its written regional languages like Bengali, Hindi, Gujarati and Marathi masks the extensive and diverse dialect network manifested in the villages.

On the other hand, many minority languages in the Americas, Africa, Asia, and some of the Pacific Islands extend in dialect networks without much hierarchical differentiation, like the Inuit network described earlier. Sometimes people arbitrarily select one or more such dialects for translation, depending on the translators' convenience. Translators who follow a more thoughtful and systematic strategy usually seek to translate into as few dialects as will meet the needs of the most people, recognizing that location, cultural and linguistic factors may make one dialect more suitable than others, like Srê over Cil, Ma and the others.

Common Language Translation

So far in this chapter we have discussed how the multiplicity of languages and dialects which exists in many areas complicates decisions which

[30]Philip C. Stine, personal communication.

translation strategists have to make before translators begin their work. A different kind of complication arises from levels of usage within particular languages. Such levels include differences between the speech of upper class and lower class, educated and uneducated, older and younger, written style and spoken, formal style and informal, literary language and everyday language, church language and everyday language.

The higher a language in a hierarchy, the more likely there will be significant differences in levels of usage; the more complex the society, the more numerous such differences; the more tightly structured the society, the more fixed the boundaries between the levels are likely to be. In a society with nobody but farmers, where the headman of the village is also a farmer with some extra responsibilities, there is not much difference in language levels based on class or rank. In England, with its more overtly class-oriented society, differences in level have stronger class implications than they do in the United States, where class consciousness is not as overt, and where levels of usage are more likely to be identified with education.

William Carey ended up using the Bengali of educated, literary people, which was only natural at the time.[31] The same pattern was followed by most earlier translators in languages where such levels existed, and at a time when nobody but the educated could read, and educated people were in the upper class. It did not occur to many translators that this was a problem. Where a literary level of language exists, however, it tends to have vocabulary and even grammatical usage which does not occur in spoken language, especially not the spoken language of uneducated people. Sometimes the literary level is even based on an older, classical form of the language which nobody speaks any more.

So when most of the converts in many languages with higher linguistic levels actually came from lower classes the level of language found in the Scriptures was often too difficult for them even if they did learn to read. In modern times, furthermore, mass literacy campaigns have been conducted among the uneducated or minimally educated in many countries. The Scriptures translated at higher levels are not easily accessible to this large potential audience, either.

On the other hand, attempts to translate into the lower levels of language which many Christians spoke, or which was spoken by less educated people among whom evangelism was undertaken, were not usually

---

[31]Chap. 3.

successful because the language of the translation did not sound dignified enough even for the people who actually talked that way, people who knew their speech was looked down upon. Imagine reactions to a translation in English which had Jesus saying "I ain't" and "he don't," for example.

The partial solution to this problem which the Bible societies have sponsored in recent years is called common language translation, "common" in the sense that it incorporates only those elements of the language which are common to different relevant levels. A common language translation is a dynamic equivalence translation in which a limited range of language usage is employed, avoiding both that which is too difficult for people on the lower levels, and that which is unacceptable to people on the higher levels. The language of the translation should therefore be understood by all and offensive to none, although it sometimes seems weak or flat to people with literary sensibilities. In the last twenty years or so several new translations promoted by the Bible societies in major languages spoken in stratified societies have had something of this character, although they sometimes differed in the degree of restriction on usage which was manifested. The restrictions on language range imposed by common language translation are not necessary, of course, where the differences between levels are not severe. Dynamic equivalence translations in such cases are often called popular language translations.

The first common language translation to be started was the Spanish *Versión Popular,* with New Testament published in 1966 after years of experimental work led by William L. Wonderly. The full Bible was published in 1979. Many of the principles of common language translation which would also be applied to other languages were worked out in this project.[32] In the years since the New Testament was published this translation has become the major one used by the poor, lower-class, marginally educated Spanish-speaking people of Latin America, especially in the Catholic church, but has also been warmly adopted by many well-educated people as well.

Translation of the *Good News Bible* (Today's English Version), the Bible societies' common language version in English, began a little later than the *Versión Popular,* but the New Testament was published the same year under the title *Good News for Modern Man.* This translation by Robert G. Bratcher was immediately welcomed by many people around the

---

[32]Wonderly, *Bible Translations.*

world who wanted greater accessibility to the meaning of Scripture in English. Other translators then joined Bratcher in making two successive revisions. The Old Testament, translated by a committee under Bratcher's leadership, was published in 1976 as part of the whole Bible.

Since then common language translations of the New Testament or of the whole Bible have been extremely important in increasing the accessibility of the Scriptures in some other languages as well. In most cases they have been published in addition to existing translations, giving readers a choice as to what translation to use. Promoting both translations together is a way of educating believers in the rudiments of translation principles so that they can understand why there are differences between the translations and be less inclined to assume that the common language translation is wrong when it differs from the more traditional one.[33]

Some of the later common language translations are somewhat superior to the *Good News Bible* in conveying interactional and textual meaning.[34] All common language translations, however, by their very nature use less than the full resources of the language precisely because in stratified societies not everyone can understand or appreciate everything on all of the levels. Here, once again, is manifest the tension between accessibility and loss in translation. Whereas the purpose of all dynamic equivalence translation is to maximize accessibility and minimize loss, in common language translation the strategy is to do this for the widest possible range of people living in the linguistic diversity of complex sociolinguistic structures.

---

[33]Arichea and Sembiring, "Promoting."

[34]Chap. 7.

CHAPTER 9

Translation and Christian Community

Vernaculars are the ultimate carriers and symbols of cultural particularity, of ethnic diversity. There is also truth, although not the whole truth, in the statement by linguist Edward Sapir:

> No two languages are ever sufficiently similar to be considered as representing the same social reality. The worlds in which different societies live are distinct worlds, not merely the same world with different labels attached.[1]

At the same time, no two languages are wholly different, and no "distinct worlds" are ever fully separate. Over against the particularity of the vernacular is the universality of humanity and of the people of God, and the process of translation.

When a church is established in a new vernacular much more happens than the addition of a few more individuals to the number of Christian people in the world. Existing culture, community and language are all affected as well. A new social group is established, but one with ties or potential ties to fellow Christians around the world as well as local ones. It never exists in isolation.

Translation of the Bible brings the gospel which is for all to the unique local people who speak a unique local vernacular, and yet simultaneously contributes toward uniting them with the highly diverse body of believers all over the world and down through several thousand years of history.[2] In

---

[1]Sapir, *Culture,* 69.

[2]On the themes in this chapter I have particularly benefited from discussion with Donald N. Larson and Andrew F. Walls, and from Sanneh, *Translating.* See also Walls, "Gospel."

this chapter we will touch on only a few aspects of the interrelationship between translation and communities of believers, on the tension between particularity and universality within them, on division and unity in the church.

Particularity and Universality through Translation

Ever since the conflict concerning Jewish and Gentile Christians which was background to a substantial part of the New Testament, the missionary issue has not been whether or not the gospel should be translated, but which translated language to use. Once the church moved out from Jerusalem in the first century the gospel was almost never expressed except in translated form. Within a generation of the resurrection most Christians were not using the language of Jesus.[3] The use of Greek in the early church involved translation of the message from Hebrew and Aramaic, although the New Testament documents themselves were written in Greek. The way was paved for that translated use of Greek by the Septuagint, the existing Greek translation of the Old Testament, the Bible of the early Christians.[4]

In more modern times the church was in fact using translation even when Latin was the language of Roman Catholic liturgy in such diverse places as Tahiti, Canton, Kinshasa or anywhere else, for the Latin was translated Latin. In promoting Latin for generalized churchwide communication rather than restricting itself to a localized vernacular the church was elevating one translation over others. It chose the language and translation of the older church over that of the younger church, of the more powerful church over that of the less powerful church, of the more inclusive church over the less inclusive church. It was emphasizing the universality of the church over its local particularity. The dominance of universality or of particularity in church policy have very different implications for Christian community, but the church always needs both.

Translation and the Language of the Church. Inevitably, everywhere, the church has its own local, particular ways of talking, just as does any other specialized group of people. Church varieties or levels of language arise in part because the faith is partially different from the general culture, giving church people something different to talk about. Church varieties

[3]Sanneh, *Translating*, 31.

[4]Chaps. 1 and 2.

also have different historical and cultural roots going back to Hebrew and Greek cultures, mediated through a series of European cultures, and frequently through higher-level local ones like the national language of the country or the language through which the first converts were made. Probably almost all Christian groups even use a few words derived from Hebrew, for example, like local pronunciations and spellings of *hallelujah* and *amen*.

Some of the ways church people use language result directly from wordings in their translated Bible. An American pastor, for example, talked about "he-asses" and "she-asses" in a serious conversation, influenced by King James English.[5] Christian theological terminology is especially notable as specialized usage. The words for "God," "spirit" and "grace" may be the same words that everyone else uses in a particular language, for example, but they are generally also used by Christians in church contexts in ways partially different from non-Christian usage because the biblical perspective gives them partially different meanings.

The church variety of any vernacular may simply be another jargon, a specialized way of talking like the speech of farmers or pottery makers or taxi drivers; or it may develop over time into one of the hierarchical levels characteristic of stratified societies.[6] In some cases it ultimately becomes entirely separate and exclusively a church language, unintelligible except to people with special education. These various stages occurred over the centuries in Greek, Latin, Syriac, Coptic, and Church Slavonic, for example. The earlier part of this sequence was also followed in the development of King James English, and there are degrees of it in many church varieties of languages like Mandarin, Korean and Malayalam. High-level church varieties of language may also take on a sacred character, so that misuse of them is perceived as sacrilege, as some people perceived the use of "you" instead of "thee" and "thou" in talking to God in English a generation ago.

Some degree of church variety of language is not only inevitable, but also desirable. It symbolizes membership, of being part of a community of faith and ideas. It encodes Sapir's "distinct world" of the believing group. It facilitates talking to other Christians about the faith and the

---

[5]Genesis 12:16, among other places.

[6]Chap. 8.

Christian life. It is a vernacular within the vernacular, part of the bond within the Christian community.

When Christians are unwilling or unable to translate their talk into the usage of people outside the church community, however, what is bond for them can become barrier to others. What symbolizes inclusion in the one case may result in exclusion in the other. The greater the degree of difference between church and everyday usage, and the more feeling that the church variety is sacred, the more linguistic idolatry can develop. Ways of talking sometimes replace Christ as the measure of life and faith. "In union with Christ" is replaced by "in union with the way my church talks." You have to sound like me for me to acknowledge you as a fellow Christian.

Translators of dynamic equivalence translations generally try to avoid church varieties of language, one of the things for which they sometimes get sharply criticized.[7] They seek to translate into a more universal form of the vernacular, although they do not always fully succeed if the church variety is well established. Translators working in languages in which no church variety has yet developed, on the other hand, are creating the basis for such church usage, and in the future somebody may have to lead that church away from their wording by translating into a more universal form of that vernacular as it will then exist.

Not as universal as a church variety of the vernacular, but sometimes existing along with it, may be a separate church language. In the European churches this more widespread language for centuries was Greek, Latin, or Slavonic. Of these, only the Slavonic started as a church language;[8] the others were already established in the existing hierarchy of languages. The forms of Greek and Latin first used in the church were not lower-level vernaculars, nor the home or village languages of many of the people in the church who first used them. Rather, they were higher-level, more universal languages in the hierarchy.

However, the Koine Greek used by the early church was neither the classical Greek of the ancient Greek poets and philosophers nor the contemporary literary Greek, and was considered of poor quality by purists. Instead it was a widespread variety of Greek which had developed for

---

[7]Not all criticism, of course, is an expression of language idolatry. It may represent disagreement with interpretations or wordings on other grounds.

[8]Chap. 2.

commerce and communication throughout the eastern Mediterranean, with which people overcame the limitations of local vernaculars.

The variety of Koine Greek which the church naturally adopted was the synagogue variety. Christian converts from among Greek-speaking Jews and from among Gentiles who had previously been attracted by the Jewish faith already used it. Some of its differences from the Greek of people without Jewish background came from literal translations of the Hebrew in the Septuagint, with further modifications by Christians as they used it. The Greek-speaking church used this variety until roughly the sixth century, and it survives now in written form in the Septuagint, the New Testament and the writings of some of the church fathers.

All languages change over time, and in the Byzantine period a different form of Greek became the high-level language promoted by the government and used in business, becoming the language of liturgy and the church. And now that more modern forms of Greek have developed in the rest of the Greek-speaking world since the fifteenth century this Byzantine Greek, in turn, has survived primarily as the language of liturgy in the Greek Orthodox liturgy. Any speaker of contemporary Greek who wants to understand it fully needs considerable exposure to it first.[9]

Latin[10] also developed a church variety early on, and with changes it continued to be used in the western church for centuries. It had enormous unifying power in the Middle Ages in western Europe where it held something of the position, although not all of the same functions, that English occupies today in the world hierarchy of languages. It was the ultimate language to learn if you wanted power, wealth, education, travel, literature or contact of any kind with people who spoke other vernaculars than your own.

The Slavic churches broke away from the use of Greek and Latin under the leadership of Cyril and Methodius in the ninth century. Some other churches in Asia and Africa also broke away in other directions in early times, but the more general undermining of the use of Latin as a universal language in the western church did not begin until the Reformation in the sixteenth century.

---

[9]Meyendorff, ''Eastern Orthodoxy.''

[10]Further details on developments mentioned in this and subsequent paragraphs are briefly discussed in chap. 2.

But Luther and other reformers translated the Bible into European vernaculars, among the other revolutionary things they did. Universality began to give way to particularity in the sense that many vernaculars now took on some of the earlier functions of Latin. Latin hung on for a few more centuries as church language in the Roman Catholic church, its proponents fighting the rise of other languages in liturgy and Bible translation. Then in more recent times, especially since Vatican II pronouncements in 1965, even the special religious place of Latin has shrunk as the Catholic church has been vigorously pursuing vernacular liturgy and the translation of the Scriptures into vernaculars in many parts of the world.

Although the power and place of Latin has faded, the same spirit that made Latin the universal language of the western church is still alive and well, most notably now in some Protestant churches. The Christian missionary imperative which pushed toward use of the vernacular has generally been dominant in the modern missionary movement,[11] but simultaneous institutional pressures and individual missionary inability or unwillingness to cope with language multiplicity and difficulty have also exerted counterpressure toward reducing the number of languages which the church or missionaries must use. Today, for example, increasing numbers of Protestant missionaries use English exclusively. English is the primary language of power in the world, and such missionaries symbolically work through that power rather than through the vernacular, the language of the "distinct world," the language of incarnation in the local situation.

This is not only a missionary problem, however. For some Christian churches vernacular translation lower than their own has not only seemed burdensome but also divisively harmful. A Burmese Christian leader complained, for example, that the missionary emphasis on translation into the many vernaculars of Burma had contributed to the current strife and division within the country, and there is an important sense in which such translations did reinforce the divisive effects of colonial language policy there.[12]

This vision of the significance of universality meets up, however, with the reality of particularity, of "distinct worlds." To restrict translation and the expression of the gospel to the more universal languages is elitist, meeting the needs only of people who can handle those languages. Ever since the Ref-

---

[11]Sanneh, *Translating.*

[12]Smalley, "Hierarchy," 256.

ormation itself the central Protestant vision has been that all people should hear, and read. Many missionaries of the Orthodox church have subscribed to that vision as well,[13] and more recently the Roman Catholic church has come to the same position.

The reality of particularity, however, also meets up against the overwhelming number of vernaculars as well as enormously complex sociolinguistic complications. How can you run a Bible school or seminary program, or a hospital in all of twenty-five small vernaculars? or of five? How can one small mission or one small church translate the Bible into all of them?

Whatever their motives, some missionaries and churches have tried in various ways to establish quasi-universal language between a Latin, which everybody who used it would have to learn exclusively as a church language, and the existing multitude of vernaculars. During much of the modern missionary movement colonial languages like English, Spanish and French were the top languages in the hierarchies of areas like South Asia, Latin America and Indochina, for example, and were advocated by some missionaries for roles as more nearly universal church language than the vernaculars.

In the long run vernacular languages generally won out over colonial languages for church use in most parts of the world, but there has nevertheless been lasting value from the use of some former colonial languages now turned into international languages, for some purposes. Today, for example, there are important English-speaking churches in countries like Kenya, India, the Philippines and Papua New Guinea, and French-speaking ones in countries like Cameroon, Zaire, and Haiti. These are not primarily churches for expatriates, which also exist in many large cities, but are made up of citizens of the country. They fill necessary functions in cities where many of the professional and business inhabitants speak numerous different local languages, or have had much of their education in the international language. The use of the international language has also been important for contact between local or national churches and the larger fellowship of Christians, other branches of the church in the same country or in other countries, speaking other vernaculars.

For most individuals and congregations in most situations, however, colonial or international languages have not been enough. In most areas it

---

[13]Stamoolis, *Eastern Orthodox.*

became obvious that not enough local people would learn enough of the international language or learn it well enough to support Christian life. Most missionaries in time therefore rejected using such a language as the only church language.

As a step down from a more universal international language in the direction of more particular vernaculars, most missionaries and churches sought to use one or a limited number of the larger local vernaculars as church languages in areas of linguistic diversity. Then as the church pushed on into smaller language groups it often did so through the medium of these larger languages. The missionaries would thus learn one such major language of the area, preach and teach in it, and perhaps translate into it, and have their message interpreted into lower-level vernaculars from it.

Often many of the people in the smaller language groups were already bilingual, to some degree, in the more widespread language, sometimes knowing it well. These larger languages selected for mission and church use were also easier for local people who did not speak them to learn than were the international languages, because they had more characteristics in common with their own language. In the case of the widely used KiKongo in Zaire, local vernaculars were so similar that thousands of people were able to make the adjustments.[14] Sometimes the larger language and the local dialect shared considerable common vocabulary, and frequently were closely related. Some of the languages chosen as church languages were so important in the areas where they were spoken that they ultimately became national or regional languages in emerging independent countries.[15]

KiKongo in Zaire, Hausa in Nigeria, Urdu in Pakistan and Thai in Thailand are examples of such languages. Of some of the peoples mentioned in this book, the first Hmong Christians were converted through Lao, the Cil and Srê through Vietnamese, and Blaan through Cebuano, for example.

But many missionaries realized that there were limitations in that approach also. It was useful, even essential, but usually was not enough when there were vernaculars below such major languages. Churches speaking lower-level languages needed the higher language for many purposes, but it could not adequately sustain spiritual life for most native speakers of most lower-level vernaculars.

---

[14]Harold W. Fehderau, personal communication.

[15]Sanneh, *Translating*, points out that translation did much to create the climate for independence from colonial rule in many countries. See also chap. 11, below.

Some missionaries therefore sought means of communication close to the vernacular, but more generalized than using all of the particular local form of speech. For a while some Bible translators in Africa tried to produce what were called union versions, often written in artificial dialects which their translator-designers hoped would become common literary levels for groups of fairly different dialects, even different languages. They were supposed to be compromises between various actual vernaculars.

The principles for the formation of OluLuyia, one such artificially produced language in Kenya, for example, were stated as:

> Grammatically the usage of the central dialects (Wanga, Marana, and Shisa).
>
> Written according to the pronunciation of the majority of the AbaLuyia.
>
> Composed of vocabulary in actual use by a majority of the tribes, and, where several phonetic variants were in use, be standard throughout.[16]

At their worst, union versions were unrealistically engineered by translation committees, and the artificiality of the language potentially introduced translational distortion as well. They were often not widely accepted by readers, furthermore, because of the bizarre mixture of dialects. Imagine a translation in English following the grammatical usage of upper-class British English, spelled according to the pronunciation of Scottish English with vocabulary taken from the majority of these forms of English plus Australian English, Indian English, and American English.

However, sometimes the union version was based on more realistic policies and achieved a workable standard for some aspects of the written language. Such was the Igbo Union Version, Bible published in 1913, in which Thomas J. Dennis was the guiding figure. He and his Igbo associates established what became the nearest thing there is to a standardized Igbo writing.[17]

More commonly than trying an artificial dialect, translators did what was earlier described for Srê.[18] They chose one of the dialects in a network. The result was recognizable to speakers of related dialects as the way some people talked. If the dialect carried prestige, as in the case of the Srê,

---

[16]Nida, ed., *Thousand Tongues*, 175.

[17]Ekechi, *Missionary Enterprise*, 231-35.

[18]Chap. 8.

and if other attitudes were positive, it was frequently acceptable to speakers of the other dialects. If not, sometimes nearly duplicate translations had to be made, as in the case of the Mong Leng and Hmong Daw.

Sometimes when one particular dialect has been generally acceptable translators have nevertheless adapted smaller portions of Scripture directly to other dialects as well, so that people could learn the skill of reading the Scriptures in their own dialect, which was easier for them. As they gained experience they could then transfer to reading in the dialect in which the main translation was available. Sometimes notes or glossaries in the major translation gave alternate expressions as found in other dialects.

This survey of approaches to the language of the church should not be taken as chronological, however. Different missions and missionaries began at different points along the scale, and did not necessarily move toward greater use of the vernacular. The Church Missionary Society, for example, had a strong policy favoring use of the vernacular and made an important beginning in the ChiKaguru language of Tanzania, translating three gospels and other works into it by 1894. However, they later abandoned that effort in favor of Swahili, which was higher in the local hierarchy of languages, because they felt that the number of Kaguru people did not justify the effort, and missionaries who knew Swahili could be transferred between ChiKaguru and other languages, but those who knew only ChiKaguru could not.[19]

Probably no translator has ever wanted to translate into every dialect of a language, dialects sometimes differing only in small details from village to village. Everyone sets a limit somewhere, a boundary beyond which translation seems impractical or pointless. As we have seen, however, different translation strategies place the boundaries at very different places, all the way from nearly universal church language down to major dialects of the lowest-level vernaculars.

Translation within Hierarchy. In spite of the universality of the faith, congregations sometimes live side-by-side, unable to talk with each other, unable to worship together. On the other hand, in spite of the particularity of the vernaculars, elsewhere people whose native languages are very different sometimes join together using a common language for worship and for Scripture. Unfortunately church leaders and translators, like society at

---

[19]Beidelman, *Colonial Evangelism,* 113.

large, often see such manifestations of particularity and universality in terms of either-or rather than both-and.

Instead of rejecting the idea of translation into a lower vernacular where need for it has been established by careful evaluation, speakers of upper-level languages who sense the importance of universality would help by learning to understand the language hierarchy at work where they are. Parties at all levels need to realize that translation into a language lower in the hierarchy, although often essential, never stands alone, for example, is never enough. When a church began to grow among one of the Tzeltal groups of Mexico in part through the presence and influence of Marianna C. Slocum, who was translating the New Testament, the Tzeltal Indians were a despised minority. The first time some of the Tzeltal Christians visited a Spanish-speaking church

> . . . none of them understood a word of it [but] sat very still for the entire two hours. . . . Ordinarily, mestizos refused to mingle with Indians, calling them "dogs." But here, among the evangelicals, the mestizos called the Tzeltals "brethren."
> . . . One of the elders . . . welcomed the Tzeltals to the service in their own language. . . . It was the first time they had realized that all over Mexico were "brothers" who were one with them in Christ Jesus.[20]

Later in the development of the Tzeltal church a Spanish-speaking pastor, using an interpreter, helped with marriages and other functions the Tzeltal Christians could not perform for themselves.

Like similar situations elsewhere, Indian churches in Latin America need the Spanish-speaking churches around them, with their much greater resources. As Indian individuals are educated to the point where they can do so, potential pastors will study in Spanish language seminaries and read Christian books in Spanish, for example. Not all individuals will necessarily be able to tap into upper languages of the hierarchy, but without some being able to do so the community may not be able to survive where it is.

When communities which speak languages below the top level in a hierarchy depend in some ways on languages above, that dependency is usually translational as well. This means, for example, that translators into a lower-level language of Indonesia must consider the Indonesian translations seriously because the churches which speak languages lower in the hierarchy will develop in the direction of Indonesian. Some readers of the

---

[20]Slocum and Watkins, *Good Seed*, 88, 103-104.

lower-level Scriptures will eventually also read the Indonesian Bible and may be troubled by differences. They may assume the Indonesian to be correct and the translation in their less-prestigious language to be wrong. This need to emulate in certain ways the translation in the more widespread language creates serious complications, of course, when the higher language translation is not as good as it should be, perhaps not as good as the lower-level one.

Another kind of problem in the relationship between more generalized and more particularized languages was dramatically demonstrated at one training program where translators were using the Thai Bible as a major resource because it was the higher language for them. One day one of them broke into laughter when she realized that other people were retranslating the Bible into Thai at the other end of the same long table at which she and her colleague were working. Part of the foundation of their translation was shifting under them even as they worked.

We have seen that the church needs its more universal languages as well as its more restricted ones. Translations into the vernacular which particularize and localize the gospel, making it clear and relevant, can be in tension with the use of translations in higher-level languages which enlarge and universalize. The tension can be creative, however, if rigid boundaries and ethnocentrism do not stand in the way, if the different languages which are needed by a church are seen as complementary. Without such a pluralistic perspective the effect may be spiritual colonialism imposed by the higher group or spiritual isolationism within the lower.

Spiritual colonialism was not only manifest in the promotion of colonial languages, but was also to be seen, for example, in the type of missionary who restricted translation and education to the vernacular on the grounds that basic reading and writing was enough for religious purposes, and that Christians should be protected from evil influences which would come through a more widely-used language. Such missionaries feared that educated converts would slip out of their control.[21]

A pluralistic view of languages as complementary requires that they be centered categories with open boundaries. The world and the church need open linguistic boundaries rather than fixed ones if the language hierarchy is not unduly to reinforce inequity.[22]

---

[21]Beidelman, *Colonial Evangelism,* 113.

[22]Wolfson and Manes, eds., *Inequality.*

Translation of the Bible into a localized language and use of a Bible translated into a more generalized one have complementary theological significance as well. Translation into the lowest levels of the hierarchy reflects the fact that the Christian gospel is for all people everywhere, no matter what their culture. It is modeled after Christ's own incarnation. It is a particularly Christian phenomenon by comparison with other religions which spread by transmitting intact rituals expressed in an unintelligible language.[23] It not only allows for but also insures at least some degree of the contextualization of Christianity, the development of local Christian forms and indigenous theology.[24]

The use of translations in less restricted languages, on the other hand, reflects the interdependence of the ethnic groups within the church. It is the linguistic expression of the overlapping and intersecting circles of ethnicity in the larger body of Christ, of the cultural transcendence of the faith.

Unity and Division through Translation

The causes of unity and disunity in this body of Christ are many. Among them, the particularity of the lower-level languages leads to some kinds of division, and the greater universality of higher-level languages leads to some kinds of unity. Translation into many vernaculars does not necessarily create disunity, however, as may be seen in Northeast India, where thousands of people speaking many different languages and reading translations of the Bible in many of those languages gather for several days at a time on the occasion of major Christian festivals. They enjoy interethnic solidarity which they had never enjoyed before the time of their common allegiance to Christ. Their loyalty to their respective vernaculars and vernacular translations is meshed in a larger loyalty to Christ and the larger church. English is their strongest unifying language, although only a minority of them know it.[25]

On the other hand, there are churches which speak the same language and have the same translation of the Bible but do not speak to each other because of theological boundaries and the boundaries of different denominational traditions. In the Solomon Islands, as often elsewhere, such differences extend

---

[23]Sanneh, *Translating*, 29.

[24]Chap. 10.

[25]K. Imotemjen Aier, personal communication.

to the place accorded the Bible, and the use which the Christians make of it. Members of Roman and Anglican churches, where church hierarchies mediate the faith, often show little interest in the use of the Bible. The Seventh Day Adventists and the South Sea Evangelical Church, which do not have much hierarchical structure, do make great use of it, treating it as their authority. Attitude toward the very same translation thus contributes to the division, or is at least symptomatic of the division.[26]

The Translation Institutions. The United Bible Societies and the Summer Institute of Linguistics, the two major translating institutions, have both contributed to unity in the body of Christ in spite of and by means of their promotion of translation into the vernacular. Both have also contributed to disunity at times.

The Bible societies were a movement for Christian cooperation long before there were any other forms of interconfessional effort,[27] united around the common task of translating and distributing the Scriptures. Beginning with Protestant churches primarily, that united effort has over time been extended to include the Eastern churches, the Roman church in many areas, and recently the isolated Chinese church. To be able to unite Christians in this common work the Bible societies often had severe self-imposed restraints against sectarianism or the appearance of sectarianism. In the early days even the staff had to be carefully balanced in church background.

After Vatican II and the beginning of the surge of Catholic involvement in Bible translation around the world, many Protestants were suspicious and fearful, resisting cooperation with Catholics whom they remembered for persecuting Protestants wherever possible. The United Bible Societies, however, played an important part in bringing reconciliation within the field of translation and in coordinating the translation efforts of the different traditions. Bible societies have often been able to model what it is like when Christian groups see each other as centered categories rather than bounded ones, and sometimes have been able to enlist others to that perspective.

When Catholics were invited to one Bible society training program for translators, for example, a Protestant mission executive decided that members of his mission would therefore not be allowed to attend. A Bible society translation consultant urged him to reconsider, however, mentioning

---

[26]Ross, "Competition," 170-74.

[27]Chap. 2.

that it was not appropriate for Protestants to take on the role Catholic leaders had abandoned and withhold the Bible from Catholic laity. The mission executive then agreed to the translators attending, but stipulated that they were not to have fellowship with Catholics. Some weeks later, however, one of the Catholic participants spoke enthusiastically about the program, and especially about the fellowship he had experienced with Protestants, among whom he named several from the mission which had forbidden such fellowship.

However, the unifying influence of the national Bible societies which form the United Bible Societies is in itself a cause of disunity. The nonsectarian position of the national Bible societies is proof of their weak Christian faith to some groups who see them as "liberal" and "compromising." A few other Bible societies and similar organizations therefore exist outside of the United Bible Societies in part as alternatives to widespread cooperation, serving missions and churches which are more comfortable with theological and cultural boundaries akin to their own.

The Summer Institute of Linguistics also considers itself nonsectarian, but in a very different sense from the Bible societies. Unlike them, it has rather strict theological restrictions on its members, for example. They are drawn from a particular segment in the Christian cultural spectrum, and must agree to a creed shaped by "evangelical" theology and terminology.

In this way the Summer Institute is typical of many other missionary sending agencies. On the other hand, its services, including its linguistic training programs, are available to all. At one stage long before Vatican II, the fact that the Summer Institute of Linguistics provided services to Roman Catholics brought vigorous criticism from other evangelicals in the United States.

With increasing frequency the Summer Institute is involved in, sometimes invited into, languages where a Protestant church is already present, often leading to increasing cooperation with churches and missions at the grass-roots level, and to serving them ever more extensively. More than that, some individual members of the Summer Institute of Linguistics have found a common bond with Roman Catholic missionaries who have been turned from enemies into fellow servants of Christ as perceptions of bounded denominational categories have changed to centered ones on both sides. For twenty years Mildred L. Larson translated into the Aguaruna language in Peru with the feeling that Catholic priests and nuns working among the same people were her enemies, and the enemies of her work.

They had opposed bilingual schools, insisting on schools only in Spanish; they had opposed the writing system had developed for the Aguaruna language, insisting instead on one which did not adequately record the sounds of the language.

But then the barriers began to crumble because of services provided by the Summer Institute, primarily training programs and conferences. Finally a priest and some nuns asked for a course in Aguaruna grammar.

> . . . I shared a house with the nuns. Each morning and evening we all read Scripture and prayed together. All day, every day, I taught them Aguaruna. Through classes and our daily sharing we came to know and love one another. Trust between us grew. We realized that Christ was central to each of our lives. As members of His body, we learned to be members of one another. God continued to break down the walls I had built. To my own surprise I found that I loved my Catholic sisters.[28]

Wounds in the body of Christ are thus sometimes healed through the services and mediating position of the translating institutions and their agents.

The Translated Book. The book which is printed after translation is finished and the way translation problems were treated in it may also be a source of unity or dissension. New translations into languages which have not had the Scriptures before, but where a church already exists, are generally warmly received and treasured by the Christian people, unless they have a very negative linguistic self-image. This reception is extended sometimes even by people who cannot read. On the other hand, almost every new translation or revision in a language which already has the Scriptures in some form is likely to be welcomed by some people and opposed by others, a fate shared by such great translations as the Latin Vulgate and the English King James version.

Translations of the Bible can also be weapons in the struggle between antagonistic groups of Christians. Although burning translators of the Bible has stopped since the sixteenth century, rivalry between translators and antagonism toward translations recurs periodically. The New International Version of 1978 was produced in English as a countertranslation to the Revised Standard Version of 1952, which had been attacked by many American evangelicals in good part because they were not represented on the translation committee.

---

[28]Larson and Dodds, *Treasure*, 263.

Theological and denominational struggles were apparent, also, when the controversy over the translation of Greek baptizo "baptize" exploded in response to the work of Carey and his colleagues in India. When the Bible society insisted that the term be transliterated rather than translated it was trying to maintain a sound principle, wanting to make Scriptures acceptable to all groups, no matter what their baptismal custom. The solution required of translators, however was unfortunate. At present translators in pioneer situations are often advised to translate *baptizo* rather than borrow it, but to translate in a way which does not highlight a controversial form of baptism, using an expression meaning "water ceremony," for example. But even that might not have satisfied heated tempers in Carey's time.

There are only a few primary issues which generally cause people to attack translations with any vehemence.

1. Sometimes the critics do not like the selection of translators, usually on denominational or other categorical grounds. The translators may be considered too liberal or too conservative, too much influenced by modern biblical scholarship or not influenced by it enough, too much inclined to dynamic equivalence translation or not inclined that way enough. In the case of the baptism controversy part of the problem was that Carey was too much Baptist and not enough Anglican.

2. Unsophisticated critics are often upset by the fact that in some passages the translation does not follow an older translation which they consider standard. More sophisticated people may see the fallacy of judging a translation by comparing it with another translation, but may still be opposed to it on some more fundamental grounds such as disagreement with the Greek text used, or with the principles of translation, or with the exegesis. This is essentially the problem, for example, when translations are attacked for some equivalent of "young woman" rather than "virgin" in Isaiah 7:14.[29]

3. Often there are debates around what receptor-language words should be used for theological concepts and religious behavior. We shall see this in the debate over terms for God in China.[30]

4. Sometimes disagreement is aroused because the translation seems to exclude some interpretation or theological position espoused by the one who is attacking. That was part of the problem in the baptism controversy.

---

[29]Chap. 5.

[30]Chap. 10.

5. Frequently people disagree with the level of language used, or the style. It is too literary or not literary enough, too learned or not learned enough, too colloquial or not colloquial enough, too churchly or not churchly enough, too much like another dialect or not enough like their own.

Whether or not there is any translation at all may be a cause for unity or disunity. Great resentment has sometimes been created when missionaries have not wanted to translate the Scriptures into some languages, and independent churches have even split off as a result. But it is also true that the gaining of Scriptures in the vernacular has resulted in division, especially in Africa.

> Up to this point the missions had had the same absolute control over the Scriptures as they had exercised over the Church. They alone had access to the Hebrew and Greek sources; their interpretation was final. But with the publication of African translations, a momentous change took place: it now became possible to differentiate between missions and scriptures. . . . The vernacular scriptures therefore provided an independent standard of reference that African Christians were quick to seize upon.
>
> . . . In the scriptures, therefore, African Christians gradually began to detect a basic discrepancy between missions and scriptures on what were to them the major points of conflict, namely the traditional customs being attacked by the missions. The slender biblical basis for monogamy was at once noted.[31]
>
> Unrestricted access to the Bible in the vernaculars, with its notions of equality, justice and nonracialism, provided the early converts with a valid weapon which they were not reluctant to employ against the missionaries who brushed these ideals aside in Church administration and in their relations with the converts.[32]

Access to the Bible was therefore one of the significant factors in bringing about the enormous African independent church movement. By 1964 eighty-one percent of all African tribes which had the complete Bible also had independent breakaways from the mission churches. Correspondingly, sixty-seven percent of those with New Testaments and fifty-six percent of those with portions had experienced secessions. Such breakaways had occurred, however, in only ten percent of the groups without a Bible,

---

[31]Barrett, *Schism,* 127-28.

[32]Ayandele, *Impact,* 176.

some of them Christians for more than a hundred years. Some separatist leaders say that reading the Scriptures started their thinking.[33]

Some of the churches which split off from the mission church in part because of what they found in the Bible nevertheless had a unifying effect in other ways. They united Christians across mission denominational boundaries, and even tribal boundaries, for many of the independent churches were not restricted to one language or one country. And then when a few of the new African churches have sought greater fellowship with the larger Christian community in the world, it has been the common understanding of the authority of the Bible which has helped to reestablish the relationship, as we shall see in the case of the Kimbanguists.[34] Fellowship has also increased between some of the ancient churches and more modern ones in different parts of the world, as when the Scriptures were translated into Malayalam.

When we look at the church microscopically we see cracks, divisions, diversity everywhere, symbolized almost always by some language difference: different vernacular, different church variety within the same vernacular, different church language. When we stand back and look at the big picture, however, we see the common faith in Christ which unites this fractured scene, and the astounding fact that the myriad separate parts in this diversity are held together by the translation of the faith, including in a very important way the translation of at least part of the Bible into nearly two thousand languages. It is translation in conjunction with the hierarchy of language use that makes the worldwide Christian community humanly possible.[35]

---

[33]Barrett, *Schism,* 130-32; "Church Growth," 276.

[34]Chap. 10.

[35]Sanneh, *Translating.*

CHAPTER 10

Translation and Indigenous Theology

One of the most intense and bizarre yet serious controversies of the modern missionary movement was over what term should be used for God in the Chinese Bible, and consequently in Chinese liturgy, prayer, devotion, and conversation. The controversy was caused by missionary fear that the term chosen would distort Chinese understanding of God, a concern, in effect, about future Chinese theology.

The problem was difficult, and important. In the seventeenth and eighteenth centuries, long before this particular dispute began, Roman Catholic missionaries to China had also been racked with dissension over such a term. The Pope had finally ruled that they should use *Tianzhu* "heavenly lord," which few Chinese people knew, and which had therefore seemed safe to its advocates because it had few associations with Confucian philosophy, Daoism or Buddhism.[1]

Catholic missionaries with an opposing view had advocated the terms *Tian* "heaven" or *Shangdi* "supreme ruler" as terms for God, both taken from Confucian classical writing. *Shangdi* emerged again in the Protestant controversy, but Protestants started with still a different term, one used by Robert Morrison in translating the Bible into Chinese. It was *Shen* "god, gods, spirit," a popular generic term for the deities of Chinese religion.

The Protestant controversy flared up in the middle of the nineteenth century as Morrison's translation was being revised. Shen was considered by some translators and their supporters to be too generic for the one God, so generic that it included spirits and ghosts. *Shangdi* "supreme ruler" was proposed in its place, but was considered by many others to be too specific for the "gods" of the Bible and even to be the term for a specific god from

---

[1]Covell, *Confucius*, 61-62; Broomhall, *China*, 36-39.

Chinese religion, which they considered made it unsuitable for God. A third group advocated borrowing a term from another language, something without meaning in Chinese.[2]

The missionaries wanted a Chinese term which could be used both as a specific term for "God" the Supreme Being, and also as a general term for other "gods," just as the church had earlier taken Greek *Theos,* Latin *Deus,* and English God, all of which had started as generic terms. Such a solution we now know is possible in some languages, but not in all.

The issue also had roots in diverse missionary backgrounds. British and other European missionaries, for example, generally preferred *Shangdi,* while American missionaries tended to prefer *Shen.* The British and Foreign Bible Society correspondingly published its editions with *Shangdi* and the American Bible Society its otherwise identical editions eventually with *Shen.* However, for some years the ABS even published Scriptures with blank spaces at the point where the term for God should appear, to be filled in at will by different readers![3]

Different assumptions about the levels of language and culture from which Christian terms should be taken also entered in. *Shangdi* came from intellectual Chinese culture, *Shen* from more popular Chinese culture, and was a much more familiar word to ordinary people. All of these are typical issues in translation terminology disputes.

The debate raged for decades. Meetings were held, books and articles written, but the bulk of the written argument was in the form of letters as long as seventy or eighty handwritten pages addressed to mission directors and others back home. In some cases the protagonists wrote first horizontally and then vertically on the same sheet of onionskin paper to save postage.

To this day there are *Shen* Christians and *Shangdi* Christians as well as Catholic *Tianzhu* Christians, each with their Bibles. When Chinese Protestants read an edition of the Bible printed with the other term for God from what they themselves use, they substitute their own word. For Christians, time has apparently leveled the differences between the terms into alternative representations for much the same understanding. Unfortunately the confusion created by three different terms for God has probably been more significant than any theological pitfalls there may have been in using any one of the terms.

---

[2]Covell, *Confucius,* 86-90; Broomhall, *China,* 60-70.

[3]Gibson, *Soldiers,* 128; Dwight, *Centennial History,* 423-24.

Thus, although literal translations and poor selections of theological terms can be theologically misleading and sometimes obscure the faith, as we shall see, biblical terms do come in a biblical context, and are used in other forms of Christian communication as well. Carried by such contexts Christian meanings may develop around many weak and imperfect terms so that they become more adequate, gaining a more biblical meaning as they are used in a Christian way. Meanings of words like terms for God have shifted in languages all over the world and have often been enriched within the Christian faith. Such is one of the forces in the creation of indigenous theology.

Translation Difficulties and Theological Development

Although the controversy over the Chinese term for God may have been unnecessarily severe, a significantly inappropriate term can block understanding or create misunderstanding, sending indigenous theology on a nonbiblical tangent. "Kingdom of God" or "kingdom of heaven," as the terms are often translated literally, is one of the most important concepts in the gospels. They refer to what Christ said he came to do in this world, to establish God's rule among people. The expressions are seriously misleading in English, however, and still misunderstood after centuries of use. In surveys of an adult church school class among people who had been going to church all of their lives, and in college classes of church-raised young people, more than ninety percent believed that the phrases meant "where people go when they die."[4] Similar misconception occurs in many other languages where the expressions are likewise translated literally.

The German common language translation, on the other hand, has not followed such tradition-hallowed phrasing. There these phrases were translated in several different ways according to their implications in different contexts. For example, "preaching the gospel of the kingdom"[5] was rendered "proclaimed the Good News that God would now complete his work." Likewise, "unless your righteousness exceeds that of the scribes and the Pharisees, you will never enter the kingdom of heaven"[6] was rendered "you will only enter God's new world if you fulfill his will better than the teachers of the law and the Pharisees."

---

[4]Surveys conducted at Bethel College, Minnesota.

[5]Matthew 4:23, Revised Standard Version. Kassühlke, "Attempt."

[6]Matthew 5:20.

Of all the translation decisions which impinge on theology, ones like these which involve vocabulary are often the most obvious. Sometimes the options available in the receptor language seem paltry compared to the rich theological meaning of a term in the original. The Hebrew word *Torah* was translated into the Greek Septuagint and then carried over into the New Testament as "law," a weak equivalent without the theological overtones of forming the Jewish people into God's covenant nation.[7] And correspondingly weak it remains when it is translated by similar terms in other languages of the world where laws are made by quarreling legislatures or petty tyrants. Capitalizing the word to indicate that it has significance does not do much for it, either. But there is often no better alternative than a weak word for "law," so in this instance as in many others translation means unavoidable loss, distortion, the price of making the Scriptures accessible in another language.

But then again, sometimes the language into which the translation is being made has richer terminology than does English or some other intermediary language. Instead of a term referring to laws made by rulers, there may be one for the inherited body of social custom descended from the ancestors and sanctioned by the gods. "The custom descended from Moses" or "the tradition God gave to the Jews" may make sense and carry weight and authority in some languages far beyond that conveyed by a word referring to government orders and regulations. The content of the local body of custom will be considerably different from the Torah, but the fact of such differences between peoples is not hard for readers to grasp.

"Messiah", with its promise of the coming national leader sent by God to rescue the Jewish people from their enemies, was feebly translated into Greek as *kristos* "one chosen by anointing," then transliterated into English and other languages as "Christ." This, in turn, has become simply a surname in the combination "Jesus Christ," again with significant loss.

And how do you translate "grace" so that it does not sound like a little inconsequential "kindness"? And how do you translate "glory" so that God does not seem to look like a television screen image or a neon light?

Translators frequently attempt to manufacture high-sounding theological vocabulary. In the traditional Korean translation "faith" was rendered with an artificially constructed noun rather than by a natural verb, "believe," That made it seem like an object, "impersonal, magical quasi-

---

[7]Some of these examples are adapted from Metzger, "Language."

matter," a perception strengthened by literal translation of expressions like "great faith," and "faith as a grain of mustard seed." For other reasons this unnatural term in its verbal form was also taken by some Korean Christians to mean reciting Jesus' name in the repetitive manner in which Korean Buddhists recite the name of the Buddha.[8]

But although vocabulary may be the most salient translational element in the development of theology, more subtle forms of distortion are sometimes even harder for the translator to deal with. Differences of custom between biblical and modern times sometimes create serious misunderstanding of parts of the Bible. In India even some Bible translators understood part of the book of Ruth to mean that

> a young lady, urged on by her mother-in-law, dresses herself up as attractively as possible, and goes sneaking off at night to climb into bed with a man who is her relative. After she seduces him, he agrees to marry her, and he begins to scheme out a way to manage events so as to make their marriage possible.[9]

To avoid such erroneous interpretation of the story, the reader needs to know quite a bit about Hebrew custom at the time, and other information implicit in the telling. A combination of cultural explanation in notes and careful wording to make explicit the implications of the original situation is required in the translation. Otherwise people simply avoid using the story, as they do other parts of the Bible which embarrass them, screening them off from any contribution to indigenous theology.

Part of the problem of indigenous theology, whether in the older churches or the younger ones, is that sometimes multiple views on an issue are to be found in the Bible itself, and people often use the Bible to reinforce their presuppositions rather than to read it self-critically. The Bible has been mustered on both sides of disputes over such issues as slavery, the Sabbath, war and women.[10] But part of the eternal value of the Bible, nevertheless, is that it is self-corrective.

The Bible, for example condones and regulates slavery, but the Bible taken as a whole, in its broader implications, helps make slavery unthink-

---

[8]Kwak, "Korean," 304.

[9]Mundhenk and De Waard, "Missing." Similar problems for Africans understanding Ruth are discussed in Wendland, *Cultural Factor,* 166-88.

[10]Swartley, *Slavery.*

able for the modern Christian. Much of the Bible is also strongly ethno-
centric, the Old Testament rooted in the narrow self-view of a small ethnic
group. There is occasional theological dissent from this view in the Old
Testament itself, as in the books of Jonah and Ruth, and disagreement with
it ultimately became one of the major issues reflected in the New Testament. Because of the struggle against Jewish ethnocentrism in the early
church the Christian faith was universalized.[11] Thus in the broader picture,
the Bible expands such narrow ethnic limitations on the gospel as lie within
it. "There is no difference between Jews and Gentiles, between slaves and
free people, between men and women; you are all one in union with Christ
Jesus."[12]

Responsible translators do not fudge the parts of the Bible which are
embarrassing from their point of view. Translators who believe in nonvi-
olence do not leave out the violence of the Old Testament, and people who
believe that war is justifiable do not leave out "love your enemies." They
translate as much of the Bible as they can so that people can read about all
of the diverse acts of God and of God's people recorded there, and can see
them in relation to each other, providing the biblical raw material for indigenous theology.

Dynamics of Indigenous Theology

Even with a clear translation marred by relatively little distortion, indigenous theology does not necessarily develop in the direction desired by
missionary translators. In fact, the concept of "indigenous theology" is
still incomprehensible to many Western Christians, including some
professional theologians, who see theology as developed and transmitted
only in the framework and logic of Western philosophy and Western presuppositions.

For centuries Catholics sought to control the development of varieties
of theological understanding in part by denying the Bible to people not
trained in official dogma. Many Protestant groups have sought to accom-
plish the same result by insisting that people interpret the Bible only as they
say it should be interpreted. The idea that people from different backgrounds inevitably read the Bible in partially different ways and that they

[11]Sanneh, *Translating*, 9-49.

[12]Galatians 3:28.

inevitably reach partially different understandings does not come easily to many Westerners. Nor does the idea that differences or emphases seen by Asian, African or Latin Christians may not only be better for them but sometimes also enrich people in European and American churches, and sometimes be closer to the meaning of the biblical writers.

Part of the problem comes from the term *theology,* which to many people implies esoteric academic activity carried on only in seminaries and encoded in formulae for inferior beings to memorize, or in abstruse tomes no normal person could possibly read. More significantly used, the term refers to the understanding which any people have of God and of their relation to God, together with the answers which they find as they ask questions of the Bible and of their faith.

Kosuke Koyama has written of Thai theology as carried on at two different levels which he calls the living room and the kitchen of Thai Christian homes.[13] The living room is where theology is discussed. In this Thai case, although not necessarily in other countries or churches, such theology is conventional by missionary standards, theology as learned from missionaries or from Thai pastors and teachers who learned it from missionaries.

The kitchen, on the other hand, is where theology is seasoned to Thai taste, where ''Buddhist salt'' (cultural perspectives arising out of Thai Buddhist world views) is mixed with ''Aristotelian pepper'' (cultural perspectives arising out of Western philosophical theology). The outsider cannot see into the kitchen, but can smell the aroma, and taste the ''ambiguous taste'' of the theology cooked there. Kitchen theology is sensed rather than discussed. It is where emotional involvement in the faith is rooted.

Koyama points out that the Bible says ''God is love,'' but that to the Buddhist ''love'' attaches, engages a person, and attachment brings sorrow and trouble, whereas detachment means release from sorrow and trouble. For the Christian God to be attached, involved, is therefore a very strange message for the person of Buddhist background. For God really to become a human being and live as Jesus did is not seemly, not holy. The Thai convert makes an adjustment by mixing spices. This is not a reasoned reaction, discussed in the living room, but an accommodation in the psycho-cultural kitchen.

---

[13]Koyama, ''Pepper.''

The "living room," of course, stands for many kinds of places. Theology is discussed and formulated in Bible studies, in sermons, and in classes. It is also sung, acted out, or danced. It is pictured, sculpted and expressed in architecture. Typically in the modern world it is also written in books on many levels of abstraction and application. Different kinds of theological communication take place, furthermore, ranging from brain washing and rote indoctrination to people groping for understanding or for a sense of the presence of God. The translated Bible may be used significantly anywhere that communication about theology occurs, and may figure in any type of communication, or it may simply be assumed as background, or sometimes may not even be much of a factor at all.

With all of this uncertainty and indeterminacy, with lack of any control over theological discussion, what many Christian leaders in Western traditions of theology fear the most is "syncretism," the mixture of beliefs from more than one system,[14] the combining of Aristotelian pepper and some other salt. Western Christians forget that the Aristotelian pepper they carry with them is itself a blend of spices from many backgrounds. In addition to Hebrew and Greek biblical elements it includes large measures of Greek philosophy and Western rationalism. There may also be portions of a theology of nationalism, of national security, of capitalism and anticommunism, as preached by Christian religious leaders of the political right. Or there may be elements of a theology of individualism, not to mention scientism or secularism, as fostered by our urban and mechanistic age. Or there may be generous scoops of a theology of prosperity as preached and practiced by some television evangelists. Or, especially for Americans, there may be overtones of the theology of manifest destiny, the perception of America's religious duty to save the world by transforming everyone into its political, economic and cultural image, perceiving the United States to be the modern Israel, the unique people of God.

Many missionaries have assumed that their task was to transplant their unwittingly syncretized theology unmodified from their minds to other minds in the world, a process as undesirable as it is impossible. All people filter the Christian message, notice what is in the Bible, interpret the gospel, through their needs, their preconceptions, their existing beliefs, their

---

[14]For a variety of views by four missiologists, see Yamamori and Taber, eds., *Christopaganism*.

understanding of how things are. They hear the message somewhat differently from what the speaker, the writer, the translator intended.[15]

In so doing they may distort the message badly, twisting it into something unrecognizable as the gospel portrayed in the Bible. They may, for example, enlist God in their campaign of hatred against people whom they would oppress. On the other hand they may find in their filtered understanding that God is present in their situation. They may find that the gospel is relevant to them in ways no outsider can fully imagine.

As kitchen and living-room theologies mature the living room takes on more of the flavor of the kitchen, which in turn is often more influenced by the Bible and other currents. The result is that the theology of each culture reflects God a little differently. The hymns of Vidvan Krishnapillar, which are widely used in the Tamil church, sometimes have overtones of the unreality of human experience or of the worthlessness of the body.[16] These are tones with background in Hinduism more than in the Bible, but they reflect the understanding of a mature Christian person. They are certainly no more strange to the theology of the Bible than are the beliefs of many equally mature western Christians.

The responsible translator seeks to represent the "original meaning" of the Bible to the reader in any language, and so provide an accurate and accessible account of God at work, and of God's people. This provides a base line from which theological thinking can grow and against which theology can be evaluated. An accurate and accessible translation can thus help both to limit distortion in indigenous theology and also to provide people with the basis for fresh insight on any level. Translators have no legitimate role as censors of other people's indigenous theology, although they share with all Christians the responsibility to evaluate any theology in light of the Bible, their knowledge and their experience. They are responsible to avoid translating in ways that they realize could possibly be misunderstood. As they do so, however, all such Christians also need to weigh the theologies arising in other cultures in light of the perspectives which those other cultures bring, not only their own perspectives.

In the long run, however, important as any indigenous theology may be, it does not stand alone under God. Indigenous theologies are highly particular, highly contextualized, and God is always much larger than any

---

[15]See chap. 1, above.

[16]Phillips, *Old Testament*, 16.

of them, or than all of them put together. Cross-cultural theological inquiry helps theologians of different backgrounds to expand their perspective, toward a more complete, more genuinely universal understanding of God.[17]

The Bible and Kitchen Theology

As a missionary language student I was reading the Gospel of Mark with my Thai language teacher, a well-educated woman just back from several years in Scotland where her husband had taken his medical training. As a Buddhist she had not previously read this part of the Bible, perhaps not any part.

Like most other Thai Buddhists, the teacher believed that the world is populated by spirits of many kinds, and it so happens that the first chapters of Mark include several stories in which Jesus drives evil spirits out of people suffering from their effects. As we read these stories my teacher became fascinated. She would stop my reading and tell me stories of her own encounters with spirits, and of similar experiences of her friends and relatives. The stories in the Gospel were speaking to her exactly where she lived. That Jesus had power to cure people afflicted by spirits was intriguing to her, the beginning of a potential theology. Our discussion was taking place in the living room, but clearly the impact was being made in her theological kitchen.

I was aware that at that moment the Gospel of Mark was speaking more powerfully to this Buddhist woman than to me. So strong were the spices of modern science and rationalism in my kitchen, and so remote was spirit possession from my own experience that it did not figure significantly in my theology except as a theoretical concept. My Buddhist teacher understood the Bible better than I did in this respect.

William D. Reyburn wondered why churches in some of the Kaka villages of the Cameroun were poorly attended, although people seemed to want to be members. So he moved into one of the villages for a while, and listened.

One night as people were sitting around the campfire the chief asked Reyburn what his name was. When Reyburn replied that it was "Bill" the chief said no, that was his pagan name. What was his mission name? Fortunately his middle name was David.

---

[17]See Walls, "Gospel," on indigenizing and universalizing forces in the gospel.

So Reyburn asked the chief if he had a mission name. No, he did not; he had too many wives. Reyburn turned to another man. "Do you have a mission name?"

"Yes, God knows me."

"Would God know a Kaka name?" Everyone agreed God would not.

So Reyburn asked what difference it made if God knew their mission name. Satan must know it too.

"Who is stronger, God or Satan?" They were greatly relieved when Reyburn said God was stronger. "What do you care about the strength of Satan? Are you children that you should cry because of Satan?"

The chief spoke up to say that they all cried because of the sorcery Satan puts in them, sorcery which made them kill people or perform other harm in spite of themselves. God would read their names in the mission role book and know whose sorcery to keep under control.

But Reyburn objected that most of the men had more than one wife, and that the mission would not write their names. The men laughed and replied that they enrolled their first wives (the only person in a polygamous marriage the mission would admit to the church roles). God would surely take care of them if they gave their first wives.[18]

This particular kitchen theology of which Reyburn was getting a whiff in the living room was obviously not extensively informed by the Bible, but the theology of an individual or of a group often begins as precariously as that. It may then die out, or grow in directions which have nothing to do with the Bible. Or it may become steadily more influenced by the Bible. The Bible may affect it through worship, sermons, the telling of Bible stories, or through direct reading. In such cases the translated Bible is heard in the living room, but if the theology it engenders is emotionally appropriated it is internalized in the kitchen.

On another occasion Reyburn was in another Kaka village where the same kind of marginal Christians were telling stories around the fire at night. When it came his turn he told the story of Abraham, Sarah, Hagar, Ishmael and Njambie. In the Kaka world view Njambie is the great spider who made the universe and holds the stars in place with a web, but who is not directly concerned much with human affairs.

In the story Sarah could not have children, a terrible disgrace in African society, a plight which all the women in the circle could feel deeply.

---

[18]Reyburn, "Motivations."

So she told Abraham to take another wife, just as any of these women would have done in the same predicament. Hagar the second wife then bore a son and Sarah became jealous, so that Hagar and Ishmael were expelled, sent off into the wilderness to die.

Except, perhaps, for the expulsion, the story had thus far been very natural, very predictable, very Kaka. But then it took a strange, unpredictable turn. Njambie the great creator spider who leaves people pretty much alone, spoke to Hagar the outcast, the second wife, and promised to make her the mother of a great nation. Incredible! No African woman could ask for a greater blessing. And in this story from the Bible, and others like it, the seed of a change in the theology of Njambie is planted. If the idea that Njambie cares for people is taken into the kitchen and becomes part of the theology that is felt, tasted, and smelled, the beginning of a transformation of the people's perception of God will have taken place.[19]

When Simon Kimbangu emerged in 1921 as a prophet in what was then Belgian Congo, now Zaïre, most of his Christian teaching was standard fare learned from the Bible and from the Baptist mission with which he worked. He drew a large following very quickly, however, because of success in healing sick people. In so doing he emphasized the salvation of the whole person without dividing soul from body, a bit of African theology more in line with a biblical perspective than the theology of his missionary teachers. Physical healings were accompanied by the destruction of sacred objects from traditional religion, symbolizing the spiritual healing which was taking place as well.

Kimbangu's growing following quickly attracted attention, arousing the antagonism of the Catholic mission and the suspicion of the Belgian government, so that five months later he was arrested, and then spent the next thirty years in jail, until he died. His movement was also driven underground because the Belgian government persecuted his followers severely.[20] Over the following years a wide variety of theological interpretations developed among Kimbangu's followers and others who continued to join the movement, including some with little or no Christian background. Perhaps the most startling to outsiders was a widespread be-

---

[19]Reyburn, "Transformation."

[20]Andersson, *Popular Movements*; Asch, *Kimbangu*; Kuntima, *Kimbanguisme*; Martin, *Kimbangu*; Bertsche, "Kimbanguism."

lief that Kimbangu was an incarnation of the Holy Spirit.[21] Other prophets also emerged in the name of Kimbangu, with similar emphases on healing, but some of them with little or no Christian element in their message. The heart of the movement, however centered around Kimbangu's wife, and maintained what the core followers felt was Kimbangu's own teaching.

Some time before Zaïre gained its independence in 1960 general leadership of the movement was taken over by the youngest son of Kimbangu, aided by his two older brothers. All of them had some education and some experience in the government bureaucracy. Under them the Church of Jesus Christ on Earth through the Prophet Simon Kimbangu, now grown to several million members, was admitted into the World Council of Churches in 1969 and was constituted the third official church body in Zaïre (along with the Catholic church and the association of Protestant churches) in 1971.

The point of mentioning the Kimbanguists here is that in the process of consolidation the leadership has promoted the study of the Bible and biblical preaching, and established the theological training of ministers in the Kimbanguist Theological Seminary. There is doubtless a considerable gap between the kitchen theology of many village Kimbanguists and that of the more educated, and some (perhaps all?) doubtless still believe that Kimbangu was the Holy Spirit, but the leadership has been pressing the movement towards a more orthodox Christianity through several means, including greater knowledge of the Bible.[22]

As kitchen theology grows and matures in this and other groups it is integrated into the culture of the group and of the individuals in the group who hold to it. If it becomes biblically well informed the theology becomes part of the great network of such theologies spanning the centuries, and the globe. This network is incredibly diverse, but through almost all of it run the themes of God creating people and healing their alienation from their creator, of God freeing people and ruling over them, of obedience to Christ, and of hope because of God's presence and work in the world, and a vision of eternal life.

As for the validity of these various mixtures which are made in the kitchen, God seems more accepting of them than God's followers are of

---

[21]Asch, *Kimbangu*, 139-79.

[22]For official statements of Kimbangu theology see Kimbanguist Church and Manicom, *Kimbanguism*; Kuntima, *Kimbanguisme*, 254-307. See also Fehderau, "Kimbanguism."

each other. But for those Christians who are concerned that their theology be faithful to God, many have the translated Bible in which to examine their theology. The Bible is the common touchstone in all the diversity.

The Bible and Living-Room Theology

One of the outstanding movements in which the Bible is currently central in people's living-room theology is the "base community" movement of parts of Latin America. The conditions under which the community members live hardly seem conducive to discussing theology unless we remember the catacombs, the slaves in the United States, the church under the cultural revolution in China, and many other instances of faith deepening under extraordinary hardship.

Participants in the theological discussions of many of the base communities often have barely enough to stay alive. In some of them hunger is always present, illness a disaster.[23] Descriptions of living conditions contain phrases such as "everything is lacking: employment, housing, food, health and schools." " . . . not enough to live, but only to vegetate." "They live by moral force; they live because they withstand it somehow." " . . . almost no sanitation." "All the children have swollen bellies, and are vomiting with dysentery, which is endless." " . . . deprived of all resources: cultural, social, economic, and political." " . . . established on exhausted land, and also surrounded by large landowners whose infernal circle is increasingly closing in on them." " . . . no medical care or schools in the region." " . . . very listless and prone to alcoholism."[24]

Especially in some Central American countries, participants are also in danger for their lives, many killed because their governments consider their reading of the Bible and their group meetings subversive. In some places people bury their Bibles and hymnals to protect them, taking them out of hiding secretly to use them, because villages are searched for Bibles, which are ripped apart, stamped on, and burned.[25] Sometimes the same treatment is extended to the people who read them:

---

[23]For excerpts from the diary of one of the inhabitants of a Brazilian slum see, de Jesus, *Child.*

[24]Barreiro, *Communities,* 9-13.

[25]Bermúdez, *Death,* 31.

Narcisa and Lorenza died in the fire, along with 225 other people. They were all burned alive. . . . Lorenza was a long time dying. The soldiers shouted in at them, "Well, get up! Get up if you believe in God."[26]

Many of the people in these communities are Indians or African Americans, often displaced from their homes when their land is confiscated or other economic disaster overtakes them. The people and their ancestors have been nominal Christians for generations, but the biblical elements in their kitchen theology have been very superficial until recently. The Catholic church previously had relatively little ministry directly among them as it was generally more concerned with the upper classes.

This base community movement, with its extensive use of the Bible, is relevant to our discussion because it would not have been possible in its present form without simple translations in modern language. The translation used most often in the Spanish-speaking countries is the *Versión Popular,* a dynamic-equivalence common-language translation.[27] The corresponding Portuguese translation is widely used in Brazil. Their low price, down-to-earth language, and faithfulness to the meaning of the Scriptures make them ideal for the base communities.

Although many members of the base communities cannot read, others can, some having learned in the community. Either way, as a part of their worship the Scriptures are read aloud a verse or two at a time, and the people discuss the passage. During one discussion of the meeting between Jesus and Nicodemus in John 3: 1-21, for example, the leader first mentioned that in Greek the same word was used for both "wind" and "spirit" when Jesus said, "The wind blows where it wishes. . . . So also are those who are born of the Spirit." Then:

OSCAR: "The way I see it, the Spirit is like that, like the wind, we just hear it. We don't know where the Spirit's born, where it comes from, or where it's going to wind up from now on. It's invisible, but we are feeling it like we feel the wind. In every answer we give when we're discussing the Bible we're feeling it. We speak through the Spirit, not through the flesh, for we're not educated or important people. This wind is love, too, the spirit is love, and that's what makes us speak here, and we don't know where it comes from. It's speaking through us. I don't know how to explain it."

---

[26]Ibid,, 71.

[27]See above, chap. 6.

* * *

OLIVIA: "I think it's also compared with the wind because the wind goes far, far away, so swift, for it goes thousands of miles, and it's like the spirit carrying the Word of God, it goes invisible like the wind that goes wherever it wants, to the desert, to the mountain, wherever they want to listen to it and understand it. It goes traveling like the wind, like the wind that goes without stopping."

* * *

WILLIAM: "It keeps going in history changing humanity and we don't know how far that change is going to get to in the future.[28]

The deprivation and oppression in which these people live is always at the surface of their thinking, of course. The following excerpts are from a discussion on Luke 18:18-30, the story of the "Rich Young Ruler":

MANUEL: "I think probably that rich man wasn't stealing. If he had been, Jesus Christ would have reproached him for it, because he was no fool. He would have said to him: You did too steal. But let's suppose the man was honest; he is telling him he must get rid of selfishness, that he had respected all the commandments but he still had all that wealth and even though he'd got it honestly, he must give it up."

ALEJANDRO: "There's no wealth honestly acquired."

MANUEL: "But just suppose the man has acquired his wealth honestly."

ALEJANDRO: "No, it's only by stealing that you acquire wealth. They always steal."

MANUEL: "Or inherited."

ALEJANDRO: "Then they've inherited from somebody who stole."

OLIVIA: "God gave the earth to everybody equally; if anybody has anything that others do not have, they must have stolen it in some way."

* * *

ALEJANDRO: "We see that the poor also have things that they can abandon: home, parents, brothers, wife, children, those are riches that the poor can give up."

* * *

OLIVIA: "Yes, we poor can also be selfish and just hang on to the four hens we have."[29]

---

[28]Cardenal, *Solentiname*, 3:19-20.

[29]Ibid., 4:61-69.

The living-room theology revealed in these discussion naturally tends to emphasize those parts of the Bible which focus on deliverance and on God's concern for the poor. These include Exodus with the liberation of the Hebrew slaves to become God's people, the prophets for their denunciation of injustice, the gospels telling of Jesus and his announcement of God's order and rule, his care for the poor, his death and resurrection, the Acts of the Apostles picturing the development of a free and liberating Christian community, and Revelation recounting the struggles of the people of God against oppression.[30]

The theology of the base communities is obviously not restricted to the living room. Enriched, developed and purified there, it has also penetrated deeply into the life and emotions of the individuals and of the groups, into the kitchen. It could not otherwise be as powerful a support in face of persecution as it is.

The significance of what has happened goes beyond the kind of enrichment which many people in more comfortable circumstances have found in Bible study groups. In these communities of the poor and oppressed gathered around the study of the Bible, the first result is for individuals to sense the meaning of God's words:

> I will show love to those who were called "Unloved," and to those who were called "Not-My-People" I will say, "You are my people," and they will answer, "You are our God."[31]

This new identity, this new theology of the self coming in good part from the translated Bible, brings hope, heightened awareness, and stiffened resolve against their conditions, including the oppression. That leads to government fear of subversion. Harsh repression, in turn, leads some individuals to join the resistance against the government.

The Catholic church hierarchy is also threatened. Whereas Archbishop Oscar Romero of San Salvador spoke with prophetic voice for the poor, and was martyred for it by the government, most of the upper leadership of the church is still allied to power and wealth, and would protect its position and power. The ground swell of the base communities, however, supported by many parish priests and nuns, is exerting a strong democra-

---

[30]Boff and Boff, *Introducing Liberation Theology*, 35.

[31]Hosea 2:23, *Good News Bible*.

tizing force within the church, creating the indigenous theology that ''today the church belongs to everybody; all are owners of the church.''[32]

The Bible and Written Indigenous Theology

The living-room theology of the base communities is also both child of and parent of more academic discussion within and outside of the Roman Catholic church, called liberation theology. The seeds of liberation theology led the priests and nuns to find new ways of ministering to the poor and oppressed. Living-room theology in the base communities in turn helped to formulate and develop liberation theology, and the life of the base communities has given it expression. Then dressed up in the language of scholarship, it has been written in books and debated in academic and ecclesiastical meetings, becoming one of the important academic theological inquiries of our time. The perspective, however, remains the perspective of the poor, stated by people who have lived with the poor, ministered to the poor, suffered with the poor, written by people who have seen fellow priests and nuns martyred for the sake of the poor and of the Christ who also died for the poor.[33]

In many other languages in which Bible translations have been made there are other people also writing in their own languages, writing for Christian leaders and lay Christians, providing commentary and exegesis on the Bible as translated into their language, or using the translated Bible as a basis for writing about issues of theology and of Christian life. Some of their writing is imitative, simply taking ideas from western theology and expressing them in the local language. Some of it is indigenous theology, discussing the issues in local perspective. In either case it can be an extremely important extension of Bible translation, interpreting the Bible in relation to the local culture in ways that the translation cannot do. It can be an extension and solidification of much living-room theology.

On another level a few people in the younger churches write indigenous theology primarily to be read by other professional theologians or other kinds of scholars, both in their own countries and outside them.[34] They deal

---

[32]Cook, *Expectation*, 98.

[33]Berryman, *Liberation Theology*; Boff and Boff, *Introducing Liberation Theology*; Boff and Boff, *Liberation Theology*; Cook, *Expectation*.

[34]Muzorewa, *African Theology*.

with biblical issues and themes from their perspectives, thus making contributions to a more global, more universal understanding.[35] In some of this work local Bible translations may not play as significant a part, however, both because much such writing is done in English or some other international language where it gets a wider audience and because writers on this level are able to use the Bible in many languages, often including Greek and Hebrew.

But increasingly the southern continents are becoming the centers of Christian population, and their theology will be the theology of the future, much of it influenced by translations into their languages. Liberation theologians have been showing us how the poor read the Bible. The world church, especially its Western manifestation, also needs to learn more about how people read it when spirits are a prevailing part of everyday life, and how people read it who feel strongly the ties of extended family, including their ancestors. We need to know how the Bible sounds to Christians whose perceptions are still molded in part by Buddhist or Hindu world view as well. We need to know how it sounds to Christians who live under communist and oppressive regimes, both when they are in sympathy with those regimes and when they are not. Translation of the Bible into the vernacular is a crucial step in awakening such voices among the people of God.

---

[35]E.g., Song, *Theology.*

CHAPTER 11

Translation and Modernization

Modernization is an inexorable process which is altering the lives of almost everyone in the world. It is a direction of change in societies and cultures which has very long historical roots, but which has accelerated to overwhelming force in modern times because of such mutually reinforcing developments as the industrial revolution, colonial empires, the rise of science, the proliferation of science-based technology, a worldwide integrated economy, and the population explosion. It is spread by diverse agents like business, government, mass media, education and church, each prompted by a multitude of motives.

And some features of modernization are also spread by translation, translation of James Bond, of Karl Marx, of computer manuals, of science textbooks, and paradoxically of the ancient Bible.

In its various manifestations modernization may cause people to become more individualistic, to depend more on a cash economy, to use mechanical and electronic technology, to be industrialized, to be relieved of heavy manual labor, to be more efficient in a material or economic sense, to rely on a medical technology based on experimental science, to exploit natural resources on a massive scale, to adopt fads emanating from the most modernized societies, and much more. Some elements of modernization have enormous appeal around the world. Sometimes it seems glamorous. It may reduce backwoods stigma by bringing some of the characteristics of the city into the country.

Modernization often makes life physically easier. A Hmong refugee woman in the United States, missing her familiar life in Laos, was reminded by her husband that in Laos she carried all of the water the family used, bringing it up the mountainside to their home from the stream below the village. For many people modernization makes upward mobility possible. Young men and boys in the Cameroun said they went to school because they wanted to "become somebody."[1]

But other people fear modernization, or some manifestations of it, and some resist it selectively. It may introduce forces with which people do not know how to cope, destroying valued perspectives and familiar ways. People whose values center around kin and community, for example, find that their industrialized job has its own requirements, and woe to the factory worker if kin and community interfere with them. More subtly, and less likely to cause fear, the comfort and leisure sometimes associated with modernization can reduce moral and physical resiliency in a people, becoming the new "opiate of the people" and producing "couch potatoes" or "paper tigers," depending on the observer. Modernization also destroys many valuable manifestations of ethnic diversity.

Modernizing Influences on Language

Some of the most direct modernizing influences from Bible translation affect language and the use of language. Languages constantly change, whether because of modernization or not, but modernizing changes tend to make languages seem more like the international languages. We previously saw that the work of the Serampore missionaries stimulated the development of prose writing in Bengali, a more modernized literary form than poetry.[2]

In a language with established writing traditions a Bible may be only one translation among many. Some Asian-language bookstores, for example, carry translations of works on subjects ranging from medicine to political science to fiction. In such languages Bible translation plays only a modest part in language modernization. In a language without prior writing traditions, on the other hand, a Bible translation may be one of the most important forces in the early stages of linguistic modernization.

Translatability. One of the most direct modernizing effects of translation on language is greater translatability. That means that when a text is translated from English or any other source of modernization into a somewhat modernized language like Malay, for example, the translation will typically be easier to understand than such a translation would have been

---

[1]William D. Reyburn, personal communication.

[2]See chap. 3, above.

if made before the modernization took place. It also means that dynamic equivalent translation is easier to achieve in a modernized language.

This increased translatability is not entirely a linguistic phenomenon, however, because through modernization people learn more about the world outside local experience and about subjects which highly modernized people write about. They are thus able to interpret a translation better than premodernized people can, partly because of more generalized knowledge.

Greater translatability can sometimes be demonstrated from the different types of problems characteristic of successive Bible translations into the same language. Many times, for example, an initial translator struggled with how to translate terms for many animals, physical objects and cultural concepts of the Bible because local people knew nothing about them. "Camel" may have been rendered as "large animal called camel," "synagogue" as "building where Jewish people worship God," and "circumcision" as "cutting the flesh." But then after people had become more educated, or had heard considerable Christian preaching, teaching and explanation, and after they had used the Bible regularly, they came to picture what a camel was like, could imagine more clearly what a synagogue was for, and understood what circumcision involves.

But along with that generalized knowledge came linguistic change as well, as standard terms for such strange creatures and customs also became established. Translators who followed later, therefore, did not have to invent new terms for the same meanings.

In addition to new terminology, increased translatability may take the form of new grammatical constructions, or of existing grammatical constructions used in new ways. Passives of any kind were uncommon in premodern Thai writing, which does not mean that premodernized Thai was impoverished, but simply that people expressed themselves effectively without passives. Various Thai expressions used to translate the English passive construction have become more common over much of the past two hundred years, however, occurring more commonly in translations from English than in original Thai writings, and more frequently in original Thai writing about modern subjects than in those about traditional subjects.[3]

Such an effect of translation on the use of passive constructions has occurred in other languages as well. Other grammatical features which sometimes emerge partly because of translation include relative clauses,

---

[3]Prasithrathsint, "Passive Constructions."

grammatical tenses, and a more frequent than normal use of plurals in languages where a distinction between singular and plural is not required by
the grammar, unlike English.

Increased translatability does not make literal translation of the Bible desirable, however. It is never a legitimate excuse for anything less than the best
dynamic equivalence translation possible. In fact, many modernized linguistic elements remain translationisms, sounding strange or foreign because they
originated in literal translation. Translatability may thus result in a stilted
translation-based level of the language, restricted in use primarily to translated documents and ones in which modernized people write about modern
topics such as economics or international politics. Translationisms may also
be significant elements in a church variety of the language,[4] although some
of them may be assimilated eventually into the mainstream of the language
and become very natural. Indeed, some new vocabulary needed as modernization takes place may be assimilated quickly.

Elaboration of Language Roles. Where no previous writing tradition
exists Bible translation may also help establish a written level within a language or dialect. This, too, is now a modernizing process, although some
written languages long antedated current modernization, and so did the effect of translation on their development. A modern case we have already
discussed is Haitian, where a written level with a role beyond informal
speech is being developed, and where translation of the Bible is playing an
important part.[5]

Establishing a written role where none existed before means elaborat-
ing the hierarchy of levels within the language. Along with the new written
level, in some cases the spoken dialect on which writing is based may also
take on new prestige and become normative for speakers of other dialects.
It does not usually replace those other dialects, but their speakers may begin to use it, or elements from it, in formal situations or in church, reserv-
ing their home dialect for informal use. This produces at least three levels
within the language: written, formal spoken and informal spoken.

Srê, as we have seen, was one among a number of dialects, but translation also made it the basis of the writing which speakers of the other dialects read.[6] The selection of Srê for translation not only influenced the

---

[4]Chap. 9.

[5]Chap. 8.

[6]Chap. 8.

incipient written level, but also helped to give the various related dialects a new common identity which was eventually given the name, Ko'ho. Speakers of these mutually intelligible dialects all read the Scriptures in their common written language, increasingly called Ko'ho, and also came to perceive themselves as speaking different forms of Ko'ho, a perceptual realignment which made their dialect hierarchy more elaborate.

The push of modernization is generally toward greater universality in language. When leaders of nationalistic movements sometimes selected a local language to be the official language of a country rather than choosing an international language, they may seem to have been moving toward the particular rather than toward the universal, and on one level they were. But that national language was usually selected from among several vernaculars, and became more universally used in the country. And at still another level the national language was always established with the assumption that government, business, education, and other elements in national life would also use one or more international languages where needed. Sometimes an international language was made official along with the national language in the country, and in any case the teaching of international languages remained high in government educational priorities.

Occasionally a language which emerged as a national language or was selected to be an official language for an emerging independent country had been partially "prepared" for that role by the development of its written level in Bible translation and other church and mission literature. That was clearly the case in Haitian, and Bible translation also played a part, for example, in the development of such diverse languages as modern written Swahili, an official language of Kenya and Tanzania, Tok Pisin of Papua New Guinea,[7] and of Samoan.

Literacy. The assumption that every normal person should be able to read is modern. So are the stigma attached to being "illiterate" and the idea that someone is handicapped or deprived if not able to read and write. In many parts of the world, even in Europe until the eighteenth century and after, many high-status, cultured people could not read and write, and felt no need to do so.[8] To this day in some parts of the world like India, scribes will read aloud whatever limited documents villagers need to have read, or will write letters for a small fee. In such cases the ability to read and

---

[7]Norm Mundhenk, personal communication.

[8]Klem, *Oral Communication,* 9-10.

write is a specialized skill which people pay to have performed for them when necessary, like some Americans pay to have their income tax forms filled out.

And many people in some societies are not interested in learning to read and write. On the one hand they may see no need for literacy, especially if some other member of the family can already read or there is a professional scribe in the neighborhood or village. Or they may be amused or puzzled by the missionary emphasis on reading and writing when the only value they can see in books is as a source of cigarette paper.[9] On the other hand they may also resist literacy because to them it symbolizes something they are not or do not want to be.[10] It may be identified with a hated dominant culture, or represent being coopted by an oppressive system, or symbolize the destruction of old values such as are embodied in oral culture, to be discussed below.

And in some societies people have no motivation to read and write their vernacular at its low level in the hierarchy even if they would like to be literate in the national or international language. Reading and writing is not one of the traditional functions of that level in the hierarchy of languages.

In other societies, on the other hand, desire for literacy in the vernacular may be intense, reflecting a desire for some of the trappings of modernization. In many societies where no interest in literacy previously existed, furthermore, translation of the Scriptures has stimulated desire for the ability to read. Here was an important book which many Christians wanted, the very word of God in their very own language.

However motivated, some people found other uses for the new skill after they started to read and write. One of the signs that literacy has begun to catch on in a society is the flow of letters for the first time from village to village, or between people away at work in the city and their families at home. Many Hmong in Laos, for example, learned to read and write so that soldiers could keep in touch with their families. They used a system of writing which had been introduced to make Bible translation possible, but Hmong who were not Christians began to learn it rapidly when such other uses were discovered. From then on one person taught another.[11]

---

[9]Lawless, "Ethnohistory," 14.

[10]Ogbu, "Opportunity."

[11]Smalley, Vang, and Yang, *Mother*, 153.

Sometimes literacy is taken on as a package with other institutions. After a literacy teacher had been struggling for several years to teach a few children to read,

> one day the four or five senior elders of the village informed him that they wanted to learn to read, and would begin the next day. And indeed, the next day they all appeared, carrying small slates and chalk. Before the teacher could begin, the oldest man said they must pray first, and he promptly folded his hands and bowed his head in an imitation of what he had seen the teacher do (the elders were not Christians). As the elder began "praying," his words quickly showed the teacher that the men had not simply decided they wanted to learn to read, but had taken the decision to improve the lot of their people, and were at one time taking on modernization, Christianity and education (including literacy) as a package deal.[12]

In many societies some people also found that it was easier to learn to read the national or international language after they could read their own. They sometimes became skillful in reading two languages almost for the effort of learning one. The ability to read the national language as well as the vernacular was important because literacy in the mother tongue led only to a restricted range of uses. People needed literacy in the language above it in the hierarchy as well in order to read documents they had to sign, or to gain economic advantage, or to deal with the government, or to get some education or modern vocational training, or to follow road signs, or to read newspapers and magazines.

Primarily in the vernaculars low in the hierarchy of languages, but also sometimes in higher ones, missionaries, especially missionary translators and their associates, pioneered in promoting adult literacy and in developing ways to help adults learn to read.[13] Some members of the Summer Institute of Linguistics have also led in developing and applying sophisticated linguistically based systems of literacy training.[14]

Writing Systems. A script, an alphabet, some kind of writing system is obviously a prerequisite to Bible translation, and also a significant element in modernization. Missionary contribution in this area started at least as early as when the missionary (but also native speaker) Ulfilas developed a writing system for Gothic in the fourth century, followed by Mesrop for

---

[12]Stine, "Read," 6.

[13]Laubach, *Silent Billion*; Watkins, *Literacy*. See also Freire and Macedo, *Literacy*.

[14]Gudschinsky, *Literacy*, and *Manual*.

Georgian and perhaps Armenian in the fifth century, and Cyril for Slavonic in the ninth. Then John Eliot, missionary but not a native speaker, developed one for Massachuset in the seventeenth century.[15] During that long period most of the native speakers who produced writing systems were priests or rulers.

But with the modern missionary movement beginning in the nineteenth century came a flood of missionary writing systems in previously unwritten languages, some of them matching the spoken languages badly, others brilliantly. During these past two hundred years missionaries have developed more writing systems for use by native speakers of more previously unwritten languages than any other class of people or institutions in all of history, by far.

Besides making writing and literacy possible in a language, and affecting the place of that language in the language hierarchy, a writing system has sometimes become a crucial symbol of a society's modern identity. Would the writing be based on French or English in Africa? Would it be Romanized or based on Thai in Thailand? What kinds of cultural alignments would such decisions symbolize? The Tartar case in the Soviet Union in the last half of the nineteenth century dramatizes some of the implications of such questions:

> The services were in Slavonic and there were no native Tartar clergy.
> . . . The problem was compounded by the translation committee's use of
> . . . the Arabic script, since the Tartars possessed no script of their own.
> Thereby the Tartar's link with Islam, instead of being severed by the work
> of the translation committee, was actually being strengthened.
>   It was [Nicholas] Ilminsky who proposed breaking this link by . . .
> substituting Russian characters for the Arabic script.[16]

This development of a Cyrillic alphabet for the Tartar language shifted a major identity symbol for literate Christian Tartars, but does not mean that a non-Arabic script would necessarily be most appropriate in all languages where the people have Muslim background. There are many complicating factors.[17]

We have seen that most Inuit (Eskimo) people in the Hudson Bay area of Canada are bilingual in Inuit and English, and that their culture has been

---

[15]Chap. 2.

[16]Stamoolis, *Eastern Orthodox*, 34.

[17]Smalley, "Non-Roman Script."

heavily modified by influence of the dominant Canadian culture.[18] But the widely used syllabic script adapted to Inuit by missionaries as a medium for Bible translation and other Christian literature has become a strong symbol both of ancient Inuit identity and of modernity, going beyond Christianity. In this case the fact that the script is not Roman strengthens ethnic pride and self-confidence, as most of these Inuit assume that their ancestors themselves invented the script.

Roman letters and modifications thereof have been much more widely used for new writing systems in the past two hundred years than has any other script, however. The Roman alphabet was the system most missionaries knew, and use of it meant that people who were literate in the vernacular could more easily learn to read the colonial language in earlier times, later the international and national languages. In spite of these alien associations, Roman systems have also frequently become strong symbols of modern identity for some peoples, in part because they look like the writing of the most modernized peoples. In other cases people have wanted their writing to be in the non-Roman script of the national language, or to be unique.[19]

Some writing systems are easy to learn, so that bright native speakers get the idea within a short time, and can read and write pretty well within a few weeks. That is possible when the sound systems are relatively uncomplicated and the writing represents them well.

In other languages sound systems and other complicating factors are very complex, or the writing system poorly designed, so that learning to read and write is difficult. In some African languages, for example, there is no consistent tradition for writing tones, which sometimes seriously hinders literacy.

The difficulty in the Nigerian language of Yoruba is so great, for example, that pastors who can read English often check the English Bible to figure out what some of the words in the Yoruba translation are supposed to mean so they can know with what tone they should be pronounced. Without preparing in this way the pastors can only guess at these words as they read a passage aloud in church.[20] This inadequate writing tradition was

---

[18]Chap. 8.

[19]Smalley, Vang, and Yang, *Mother*, 160.

[20]Klem, *Oral Communication*, 22.

started before anyone preparing writing systems in Africa knew how to handle tones in writing, but attempts to improve it have not been successful because of the complicated ways in which tones change in context.

But the majority of writing systems which accompanied Bible translation have been very useful. Many of them represent the language better than some European writing systems do their respective languages, much more consistently than English writing represents English. More recently with the rise of greater linguistic knowledge among translators, the effort has also been put on a more professional footing.

These few points barely introduce the modernizing effect of Bible translation on languages and linguistic culture in many societies. There is no room here to deal with its contribution in such other important areas as language standardization, literature production, and new skills learned in the process of translation. Nor can we discuss its relation to the vast undertaking of missionary education both in vernaculars and international languages, as well as in bilingual education.[21] Although modernization would have eventually taken place without Bible translation, Bible translation and associated activities have in fact very often been a powerful part of the process, starting it earlier than it would otherwise have started, and channeling its direction to a significant degree.

Nonlinguistic Modernization

Print Culture. One of the most powerful manifestations of modernization is print culture, which differs profoundly from oral culture in ways far beyond language. Print culture has changed people's perceptions, the way they organize data and thought. In print culture chronology has become more fixed, myth giving way to history. Accuracy of detail has sometimes taken over from more holistic perception of truth. Private individual study has become pervasive, diminishing the place of interactional learning in socially structured apprenticeship. Reasoning has become more abstract as written statements can be taken out of context, preserved and repeatedly reexamined. Intellect has been elevated and emotion made suspect in religion, academic discussion and many other parts of life. Worship involves less participation and more intellectualized spectatorship. And

---

[21]Larson and Davis, *Bilingual Education.*

all of this and much more has been caused by the way people use the communication tools, ancient and modern, which they have available.[22]

But writing or printing alone does not produce print culture. Instead, script culture first emerged around oral culture after writing was invented in ancient times. This was oral culture with a writing component added to it. Thus, for several thousand years writing existed as a projection of speech, a way of preserving speech over time and of transmitting it over distances, without producing some of the radical changes in culture and cognition to be found in print culture. In some Asian countries to this day young students in school recite loudly in unison, almost in a chant, as script culture communal learning has not yet been obliterated by print culture focus on the isolated individual. But even those government schools where such recitation takes place are more oriented toward print culture than are some of the Buddhist monasteries or Islamic schools in the same country.

Print culture was made possible by the invention of printing in the West, but did not actually come into being in Europe or America until the mass literacy of the last three centuries, when the enlightenment, rationalism, modern education and modern scholarship also brought profound changes in communication and thought. These all came to deal with written texts as physical objects abstracted from the settings in which they were composed, to be read silently by individuals rather than to be shared by reading aloud or recited in interpersonal communication.[23]

The various parts of the Bible were composed by people in oral and script cultures and were then transmitted for centuries by script culture people, but modern Protestant missionaries almost always translated the Bible and presented the translation in print culture terms. Few taught people to sing the new Bible translations (or made them singable in local music patterns). Not many dramatized them. Missionaries did not model reading them aloud at great length, with group interaction. They did not encourage people to memorize whole books of the Bible and recite them all at one sitting, taking pride in the quality of the recitation, as when people recite the Qur'an. So extreme was the print culture fixation of some missionaries in Africa that they even required converts to be able to read

---

[22]Graham, *Beyond*, 11-17; Ong, *Orality*; Goody, *Interface*; Scribner and Cole, *Literacy*.

[23]Graham, *Beyond*, 30-44.

before admitting them to church membership, so that they would be able to read the Bible.

The oral use of language has not stopped with increase in print culture, of course, but much of value in oral culture has often disappeared. The recitation of proverbs which call up the moral foundations of a people's culture has frequently been replaced, for example, by legal arguments and judicial precedents. Colonial powers and missionaries could not understand the proverbs or the view of reality on which they were based, so they substituted their own "logical" and "efficient" judicial system.

Not only were local Christians thus deprived of the richness which they might have gained from the Bible shared in script culture ways more suited to their traditional cultures, but much that was rich in traditional culture was stifled in the church. Myths and legends were relegated to ignorance and superstition. Dance was evil. Proverbs were patronized as quaint. A sense of nature as alive, and of cooperation and communication with nature was simply beyond the understanding of most print culture missionaries. The people selected for leadership in the church were also the educated and modernized young men, those learning print culture, not the wise and the mature, among whom wisdom was couched in oral culture terms, and in those few places where church leadership was given only to nonliterate traditional leaders, the rush of modernization in other areas of life soon forced the church to change.

Certainly widespread literacy is of utmost importance to many people today, creating high motivation also for some aspects of print culture. Certainly the educated elite in most societies have profited by learning major aspects of print culture, and any society is at a great disadvantage if none of its members who deal with the outside world can understand print culture behavior. Certainly the church has been enriched in many ways by print culture and its products. John S. Mbiti, the African theologian, who is obviously a child of print culture, expressed that perspective as follows:

> The Church has revolutionized Africa through introducing literacy. . . .
> The power of one written page in Africa is greater than a hundred sermons from the pulpit.[24]

But the cry of pain at loss of oral culture is to be heard in different terms:

---

[24]Mbiti, *Crisis*, 6.

My husband has read much
He has read extensively and deeply
He has read among whiteman
And he is clever like whiteman
And the reading has killed my man
In the ways of his people
He has become a stump . . .

For all our young men
Were finished in the forest
Their manhood was finished
In the classrooms
Their testicles were smashed with large books.[25]

Sadly, writing is not typically synthesized with orality in the mission-ary-founded churches which have the translated Bible; a script culture expression of faith has not normally also been developed in those churches as an option for Christians, alongside print culture.

That this is no small matter may be seen especially in the several thousand independent church movements in Africa[26] and in many independent Pentecostal movements elsewhere. Movements like Kimbanguism flourished as oral or script cultures when they broke off from the mission-founded churches, removing themselves from the influence of the missionaries and from that of the print culture local leadership. Catholic churches around the world also showed traditionally more script culture characteristics than do the typical Protestant churches descended directly from mission activity.

Print culture has not completely won out in all Protestant churches, however. Missionaries in the Pacific islands at first prohibited dancing, which had been a major form of communication by the islanders, but later some missions and churches relented, and in some places dances with Christian themes emerged.

Perhaps the fullest development of dancing to biblical themes took place in the Ellice Islands. There in marvelously graceful and intricate group dances the young people performed the stories of the Hebrew patriarchs or of the birth in Bethlehem or of later church experiences in their own era. This was carried on week by week under the critical eyes of the village

---

[25]Okot p'Bitek, ''Song of Lawino,'' quoted in Klem, *Oral Communication,* 160, after Rubadiri, ''Writing,'' 153-54.

[26]Chap. 10.

elders who commended and commented on each performance in order to
improve the quality of the art.[27]

Concerned with the implications of the suppression of oral culture,
Herbert V. Klem conducted an experiment in musical communication of
the Bible. A Yoruba translation of the book of Hebrews was adapted and
set to music by Yoruba composers. Several different Bible classes studied
the book, some only in its original translated form, some only as set to music, and some in both written and musical forms together. Learning took
place equally well with either medium alone, but was superior when the
two types of study were combined. More than that, however, people enjoyed either of the types of session in which the music was used much more
than they did the sessions with book alone, and sessions with music also
attracted more visitors. As people left those sessions, furthermore, they
continued to sing the Scripture, and found themselves doing so through the
week while they performed their daily tasks.[28]

But print culture dominates Bible translation, and dominates the use of
translations in the missionary movement and in most of the churches which
resulted directly from that movement. Because of this manifestation of
modernization potentially powerful culturally appropriate ways of communicating the Bible and expressing the faith have been lost.

Print culture has never been uniform through any modernized society,
of course, as it is most characteristic of the educated elite and their imi-
tators. But now in the modernized countries many such people are also repudiating elements of monolithic print culture. The world is moving on,
and it is not yet clear what is replacing, or will in time replace, the narrow
extremes of print culture. Certainly the church should not repudiate print
culture, for in some degree and some forms it is likely to be needed in the
modern world of the future. Certainly developing peoples cannot compete
in today's world without it. Perhaps, however, multiple ways of communication will emerge, so that oral and script cultures are not wholly swal-
lowed up by print culture.

Revitalization. The Bible is in good measure a book about God revitalizing societies which were suffering or perplexed under stress. Deliverance from slavery in Egypt was the mighty act of God to which Old

---

[27]Forman, *Island Churches,* 108.

[28]Klem, *Oral Communication,* xv, 167-78.

Testament writers never stopped looking back. The trying experience in the wilderness was the crucible in which Yahweh was revealed as the God of the Hebrews and gave the Law. Stress in the midst of hostile surrounding peoples in Canaan brought nationhood, new self-understanding and new understanding of God, as described in the historical books of the Old Testament. Later conquests by kingdoms to the east reshaped the Israelites again through insights voiced by the prophets, and so did the captivity which followed.

The followers of Jesus were floundering after he died, but were galvanized by his resurrection and by Pentecost. The Roman occupation of Palestine, which is backdrop to the gospels, and the later sporadic persecution of Christians living in the Roman empire helped to form the Christian community. Even more importantly, so did the conflict between those who would require Gentiles to follow the Jewish law in order to be Christian and those who would not, as reflected in some of the epistles. Because that controversy was resolved in favor of ethnic inclusiveness, Christians gained a more generalized, transethnic identity.

In this respect the ancient Bible is very timely, a very modern book. Translation has made this book about revitalization, about the repeated reformation of a people, accessible to contemporary peoples in analogous distress. In society after society more powerful ethnic or other social groups are forcing themselves upon a people, or overwhelming economic forces are destroying them, or a government is grinding them down, or a majority of the population is persecuting them or the demands of the spirits have become too oppressive, or land is too scarce because it has been expropriated, or population is too large, or crops are too small, or moneylenders are extorting too much, or modernization is too bewildering, or change is too rapid, or traditional values are being lost. Forces, alien or local, have made requirements of people which they do not want to meet, or cannot meet. They cannot cope, their self-understanding based on their previous pattern of life is being undermined, and sometimes they are being physically destroyed as well.

There are numerous different reactions to unbearable stress, such as flight, resistance, or defeatism. Or as in the events mentioned above from the Bible, sometimes cultural revitalization takes place. This involves a shift in world view and in values on the part of the people undergoing stress, a reinterpretation of reality which enables them to cope with their new situation, to understand it in new terms, to establish an identity within it, to rise above it emotionally, and to form a new cultural strategy for life, replacing the one which has become ineffectual. Such a change sometimes brings people to Christ in large numbers, producing a "people movement."[29] Or it may lead them to some other religion such as Islam, or to spirit cults.

People subject to the forces of modernization may have no alternatives but either revitalization or disintegration, and in modern times revitalization usually involves modernization. Sometimes a revitalizing shift in world view results in adopting much from the impinging culture, or some other accessible neighboring culture. People decide to take on new ways as far as they can, or to do so selectively. They learn new farming technology or look for new medical treatment or adopt a new religion. They often look to modernized countries as models.

In other cases the revitalization centers around some form of revolution, as people look for ways of overturning the oppresors. Sometimes such a reaction is to be found in the church base communities of Latin America.[30]

Then again, the new attitude is often nativistic as people look to local cultural processes and to a reinterpreted past for their solutions, believing that by relying on tradition and on what they think the past was like they will resolve their present crisis.[31] Nativistic movements would thus seem to be the opposite of modernization, reactions against modernization; and emotionally they are, but the vision of the past to which people turn is in many ways reinterpreted through modernization lenses, and the movement often uses modern tools.

When nativism is primarily political we call it nationalism, rejection of foreign dominance through local resources rooted in tradition. When it is religious it is known by a number of terms: messianism, prophetism, millennialism and revivalism, among others. Both political and religious nativism may enable people to rise above the crisis, to have hope and to proclaim hope, although at other times attempted revitalization is ineffectual, even self-defeating, and leads to deeper disappointment and frustration.

---

[29]Pickett, *Mass Movements*; Reed, "Modernization."

[30]Chap. 10.

[31]This revitalization typology has been adapted from Linton, "Nativistic Movements," and Wallace, "Revitalization Movements." See also Lanternari, *Religions*. Kamma, *Korreri,* 231-319, and O'Connor, *Moro Movement,* 306-531, are surveys of the extensive literature. For a non-Christian nativistic movement in which writing played an important part, see Smalley, Vang, and Yang, *Mother.*

Lamin Sanneh makes the point that nationalism was awakened, aroused, in part "with mission deliberately fashioning the vernacular instrument that Africans . . . came to wield against their colonial overlords."[32] Translation of the Bible gave the languages importance, contributed to writing them, accentuated the boundaries between them, gave the people a sense of self-worth. It also provided the account of God at work freeing the Jews from their oppressors, declaring the importance of justice, of fairness, of righteousness, themes with which these Africans in distress identified very well.

Religious nativism, likewise, is often stimulated by the Bible, whether the resulting movement is Christian or not. The movements like Kimbanguism[33] which broke off from the mission churches to live out their faith in oral culture terms often found nativistic revitalization also in the integration of their reinterpreted past with their understanding of the Bible.

Secularization. People tend to become more secular as one of the overall results of modernization. In the premodern world a sense of spiritual or cosmic power is far more pervasive than it is in the modern world, because one of the characteristics of modernity is to seek explanations in natural laws rather than in supernatural intervention. Modern world views often substitute inanimate natural forces like evolution or chemistry and electricity for spirits and for God. The modern Christian prays for the sick, but in the case of serious illness, if it comes to a choice between praying and taking the baby to the doctor, the doctor will usually get the business. As one Nigerian member of an independent church remarked, Westerners go to the doctor first, and if that doesn't work they pray, whereas Africans pray first, and if that doesn't work they go to the doctor.[34]

Mechanistic and secular modernizing ideas may come to people through the literacy which Bible translation stimulated, through the reading which that literacy made possible, and through the education created to support a reading church. They come also through missionary teaching and the example of the missionary.[35] The missionary doctor is one of the most effective Christian agents because of the importance of healing to vulnerable

---

[32]Sanneh, *Translating*, 5, 88-125.

[33]Chap. 10.

[34]Philip C. Stine, personal communication.

[35]Miller, "Missionary."

people, but the doctor also promotes secularism because the causes of illness as the doctor understands them, and against which the doctor works
so effectively through modern medicine, are more fully natural causes than
the causes of illness in the world views of people who have undergone less
modernization. The missionary doctor may stress verbally the spiritual side
of healing, and believe in it, but pills, shots and surgery are still the powerful immediate causes of healing.

The different world views held respectively by the Christian community undergoing modernization, the modernized missionary community and
the Bible writers unaffected by modernization never fully match. Missionaries, no matter how literally they think they believe the Bible, have selected certain elements from the world views of the biblical writers, and
have passed over others. They normally believe, for example, in one God
who is creator and sustainer of the universe and of the people in it, and in
Jesus Christ as God in human form, who came to earth to save people. But
on the other hand, even if they argue for Genesis 1 as a literal account of
creation few believe in an earth covered by a dome with windows in it to
let the rain through, as is implied there.

With respect to local cultures, furthermore, many missionaries have not
been able to understand how dead ancestors could be important for Christians, and have often considered any reverence given ancestors to be idolatry. But in many parts of the world ancestors continue to be integrated
into the extended families of their descendants, who believe deeply that
ancestors should be respected, symbolically fed, consulted, honored, and
sometimes worshiped. Just as some missionaries required men to divorce
all their wives except the first one in order to be admitted to the church, so
they also forced Christians in effect to expel their dead parents and grand-
parents from the family, to repudiate their ancestry and deny their heritage. They believed that ancestor worship was idolatry. But people to whom
ancestors were important sometimes found support in the biblical geneal-
ogies and in the commandment to love father and mother, just as men with
more than one wife found support in the many wives of the Hebrew patriarchs and of Solomon.

In parts of the Old Testament Yahweh, the God of the Israelites is the
greatest among all of the gods,[36] while in other parts God is universalized

---

[36]E.g., Exodus 20:1-2.

as the true God of all peoples.[37] That universal position is also a major theme in the New Testament,[38] and is strongly held by missionaries, sometimes with qualifications. However, whereas some missionaries believe the local supreme deity is that same God, others do not, so that today some African Christian theologians are reconstructing what their ancestors knew about God in order to reattach the African roots of their Christian faith which they feel were ignorantly pruned away by missionaries.

Paul G. Hiebert has described the predicament of the missionary who stands between the Bible and people of a culture that has not been extensively modernized, as in Table 5. He pointed out that there are two basic worldview metaphors in the world, one organic, the other mechanical. Both are ancient metaphors, with some religious systems like Christianity rooted predominantly in the organic metaphor, some like Buddhism rooted primarily in the mechanical, but most mixed in various proportions, partly depending on the sophistication and orthodoxy of the believer.

Within each of these metaphors there is a gradation between high religion at the top and folk science at the bottom. Between these two ex-

Worldview Metaphors	TABLE 5
ORGANIC METAPHOR	MECHANICAL METAPHOR
Based on the concept of living beings relating to other living beings. Stresses life, personality, relationship, function, health, disease, choice, etc. Relationships are essentially moral in character.	Based on concept of impersonal objects controlled by forces. Stresses impersonal, mechanistic and deterministic nature of events. Forces are essentially amoral in character.
HIGH RELIGION BASED ON COSMIC BEINGS	HIGH RELIGION BASED ON COSMIC FORCES
Cosmic gods, angels, demons, spirits of other worlds.	Kismet, fate, Brahman and karma, impersonal cosmic forces.
FOLK OR LOW RELIGION	MAGIC AND ASTROLOGY
Local deities, ancestors and ghosts, spirits, demons and evil spirits, dead saints.	Mana, astrological forces, charms, amulets and magical rites, evil eye, evil tongue.
FOLK SOCIAL SCIENCE	FOLK NATURAL SCIENCE
Interaction of living beings such as humans, possibly animals and plants.	Interaction of natural objects based on natural forces.

Sources: Adapted from Hiebert, "Excluded Middle," 40. See also Nida, *Religion*, 20-47.

---

[37]E.g., Amos 9:7.

[38]Galatians 3:28; Colossians 3:11.

tremes the organic metaphor has local gods, spirits, ghosts and dead saints, whereas the mechanical metaphor has astrological forces, charms, amulets, magic and the evil eye. It is on this middle level that religion operates most significantly for most people in the world, and this level simply does not exist or is not very real for many modern Christians, including many missionaries. Hiebert calls it the "excluded middle."[39]

Many people with a modern world view tend to reject the organic metaphor and adopt the mechanical one as manifested in science or astrology. Secularism in the extreme is a world view focused narrowly on the observable world, particularly in the mechanical metaphor, ignoring everything else or subsuming it within the material world.

The missionary has always accepted the organic metaphor for God as alive, working, loving, speaking. But for the observable world the modern missionary also typically accepts the mechanical metaphor to some degree. The missionary believes most scientific explanations and in the working of natural forces. Much of the missionary's understanding of causality is pushed into science. Such a missionary is thus partially secular by comparison with many converts.

The missionary world view, then, is often organic in categories at the top of the diagram, partly organic and partly mechanical at the bottom, and empty in the middle, unlike the bulk of religious life to be found among most people in the world. Some Catholic missionaries populate the middle with dead saints, and that is where much traditional Latin American Christianity centers. The charismatic movement now sweeping the world places the Holy Spirit in the middle. How secular the missionary is depends on the interplay between the top and bottom, and the presence or absence of a significantly functioning middle. Ignoring the middle has a strongly secularizing effect on people whose religious life lies there. For many Christians the top and the bottom seem effectively compartmentalized, with only vague interconnections.

The Bible writers themselves normally reflect the organic metaphor on all levels, but when the translated Bible is presented by missionaries more secular than their converts, and accompanied by other secularizing forces, the mechanical metaphor in its modern scientific manifestation sometimes overshadows the organic one. A scientific perspective certainly has its le-

---

[39]Hiebert, "Excluded Middle."

gitimate place in the world view of modern Christians, but it needs to be theologically integrated with the organic on all levels.

And without an adequate understanding of differences in world view between missionaries, Bible writers and local church members, a secularism which leaves only marginal room for God may win out by default. The missionary may have come to terms with a degree of secularism, but to assume that degree of secularism is the best way for Christians in another culture to understand God and God's works may be fallacy and folly.

The modernization which comes with or without the translated Bible can be dynamite. It's power may build or destroy a people. Some of the instances of destruction are plain to be seen around us, as in some Native American and some other minority populations in the United States, in the Black majority of South Africa and in the slums of the world. But in other cases, the translated Bible frequently stimulates revitalization along with modernization, guides people to what they perceive as greater wholeness through the thickets of conflicting perceptions, and leads to participation in the church under God's authority in the face of spreading secularism.

CHAPTER 12

The Translated Book

One time when I was in a border area of northern Thailand we heard that a new group of refugees had just crossed over from Burma. This was not an unusual occurrence as the areas of Burma to the north and west of Thailand have for many years been racked by armed conflict between various ethnic groups, opium warlords and the Burmese government, all struggling for control.

We went out and found the refugees walking along the trail. They were Lahu people, part of a large minority group living in Burma and China, with smaller numbers in Thailand. They had been sent on by the Thai border authorities to a place where they could camp while awaiting resettlement. Adults and young people were carrying heavy loads on their backs, some with live chickens tied at the top. Many were also carrying infants. A few men were leading pigs on leashes.

We could not talk with the people because we did not share any language, but the next day we took an interpreter with us and found their camp, where they had built small banana-leaf shelters, and were now busy cooking, washing clothes, and resting. We learned that more than one hundred of them had come, having left home twenty days before, usually walking through the jungle at night and sleeping in the daytime to avoid military patrols and bands of marauders. Sometimes they had camped in one spot for two days or so if they needed to rest, as they did when a baby was born on the way. They had brought with them everything they could carry or lead, mainly rice, blankets and a few utensils. They had abandoned what other belongings they could not sell.

As I was looking around the camp I suddenly noticed a pile of four black books in one of the shelters, recognizing them immediately to be two New Testaments and two hymn books. I asked to whom they belonged, and told the owners I knew the missionaries who had worked with the Lahu people in translating that New Testament and in compiling the hymn book. The pastor of the group identified himself, and said he had been a student of those missionaries. I asked if I could take some pictures.

Then as I was adjusting the camera I realized that other people had gone to their shelters for their New Testaments and hymn books as well. Almost every adult had a pair; they had carried two large books for all those days, along with the rice, chickens and babies! They had not brought just one pair of books per couple or one to serve the whole village, but all had carried the weight of the Scriptures as translated into their language, and of the hymn book of their people.

Bible society annals are full of such accounts showing how some people value the translated book. Not so frequently recounted, of course, are the times when Scripture portions are torn up after a distribution campaign, to be used as cheap cigarette paper or to wrap small packets in the market. We need to look at the range of what happens to the translated and published Scriptures if we are to understand more fully the role of Bible translation in the modern missionary movement.

Christians without the Translated Book

The transition from being people without the translated book to ones who have it can be very dramatic.

The incomparable, living word from Nazareth arrived in Nazaret [an interior village in Peru] in written form, in words every Aguaruna could savor and hold, on October 14, 1975. The message, almost two thousand years in transit, arrived clothed in the plastic wrappings of the twentieth century. . . .

The village was full of Aguaruna, eager to buy copies of their book—the first big book [the New Testament] in their language! They crowded into the school building, impatient for the selling of the Scriptures to begin. Handsome young Rudolfo was there. A naked little boy when I first knew him in 1954, he had helped with the final proofreading of the New Testament in 1972.

"Are you ready to buy your own copy?" someone asked him.

"Yes!" he beamed. "I have saved up enough money to buy ninety New Testaments. I will leave by trail tomorrow morning to take books to those who could not come out here to the main river."

. . . Tomas was so enthusiastic that he was soon surrounded by a group of noisy young people asking questions about the New Testament. He began teaching them right on the spot. They had never seen the Gospel of

Matthew; he opened it up to chapter five and began reading to them. Immediately they fished ballpoint pens out of their shoulder bags and began underlining the verses he was sharing.

As people bought books, they sat down and eagerly pored through them. Some sat outside under the trees to read, away from the loud hum of excited voices. The buying didn't slow down until about 700 copies of the New Testament had been sold. Then Alias led everyone in songs of praise and in prayer. Tomas read Scripture. A special dinner for everyone, with wild meat, fish, manioc and bananas followed. . . .[1]

A new era in the life of the church in another language had begun.

On the other hand, there are occasionally situations where the translated books arrive among people indifferent to them. Or the people may be mildly curious at first, or even temporarily enthusiastic, but for some reason they turn out not to want this Bible in their own language, or not many of them want it. Perhaps it is not an idiomatic translation, or is difficult to understand or unpleasant to read, or perhaps people believe that the Bible in a foreign language is superior, or that a different dialect would be more suitable, or perhaps they do not see any value to the Bible at all. In any case the translators either did not adequately assess people's attitudes or else did not adequately prepare people for Scriptures in their own language, or they took a calculated risk that the work would be accepted, and lost.

But even in the first joyful instance, what about the church before the books came? And what about people who cannot read? And in the second case, does rejection mean the church is without the Bible? And what about the church in languages where the books have not come, will not come?

We saw earlier that the church existed before the New Testament or any part of it was written, and that there were believers among the Hebrew peoples before the Old Testament existed. We have also seen that some churches lasted a long time without the Bible in their own language, or without widespread ability to read the Bible. There were also Christians who could not own their own Bible for various reasons even if it had been translated into their language and they could read. In most churches today people at least say that it is very important for Christians to have and be able to read the Bible, but from a historical and theological standpoint we realize that the Holy Spirit is not limited to situations where everyone has their own copy of the translated book.

---

[1]Larson and Dodds, *Treasure,* 270-73.

Furthermore, when the first shipment of the New Testament arrived at Nazaret and places like it, many people previously had part of the Bible. In many translation situations, for example, as the draft of a gospel is completed it is mimeographed or even printed in a trial edition to get it into people's hands, to test how well people understand it, and to find out what mistakes may be found in it. Various other books of the Bible often follow in similar fashion, so that some people own a stack of dog-eared, torn, well-thumbed booklets of various sizes and quality of translation. Some people carry all of them to church every Sunday, and use them in Bible classes and in their own study of the Bible. Part of the delight of getting the full New Testament or Bible under such circumstances is the fact that they now have a nice, bright, new, complete and well-printed volume, all in one piece.

But in other cases people without any translated book have sometimes known the contents of the Bible even better than some who do possess it. They may have heard it repeatedly read and preached in another language they know. Or the preaching may have been in their own language even though there was no Bible, and the preachers not only told the Bible stories but also translated portions of the Bible aloud in a rough way in the worship service as they read the passage from a Bible in another language. When the Bible is deeply a part of people's lives, furthermore, they discuss what they have heard of it and retell the easily remembered parts to each other. They use the stories in bringing up their children, who hear them many times. Illiterate people may have memorized great parts of the Bible if it has been translated into their language.

Even in Roman Catholic churches before Vatican II, when there were few translated Bibles published, parts of the Bible were nevertheless usually present in some form such as catechism and teaching. Unpublished translations of the Sunday readings were also read aloud in some churches.[2]

It is very hard to pin down objectively what spiritual difference it does make for people to own and use the book translated into their own language. Certainly there are many clear cases where the translation had an important effect on people's lives. A few of them are mentioned in this chapter by way of illustration, but such descriptions do not show whether or not the same effect might have been reached in some other way.

----

[2]Adrian Hastings, personal communication.

There seem to be few if any studies with careful anthropological, sociological or theological comparison of a church or of a society or even of individuals "before" and "after" Bible translation. Nor do there seem to be such comparisons between two separate but similar societies, one of which gets a translation in its own language and the other does not.[3] Nor is it easy to sort out the effect of the translated book from other influences in the society. People do not usually bother to record and analyze the failures, either, the cases where the translation did not make much impact, although why the failures occurred would be important to know.

The Latin American poor people discussing the Bible and gaining hope in their base communities[4] contrast radically with some of their fellow citizens without the Bible. But their renewal is not due to the use of the Bible alone, as the incarnational ministry of some deeply dedicated priests, sisters and lay leaders among them has had its impact also. We have also seen that the leadership in the Kimbanguist church in Zaïre used Bible teaching, among other things, to help move the church more in the direction of other Christians elsewhere in the world. We do not know, however, how much of the change in theology is due to the Bible and how much to other influences at work.

Some observers have also pointed out that the great North African church of the early centuries after Christ crumbled and disappeared under the Muslim advance across North Africa, but that the Egyptian and Ethiopian churches did not, although they were greatly weakened. Nor did the Armenian church to the north disappear, or the Nestorian church in Syria, Mesopotamia and Iran.[5] The North African church which was completely

---

[3]Dye, *Strategy* seems to be the nearest. It is based on a survey of some of the churches which have been started or influenced through translation work done by the Summer Institute of Linguistics, trying to determine what effect translation has actually had as a mission strategy, and what other activity needs to accompany and support translation activity itself. Tippett, *Solomon Island* also has an excellent chapter describing the village use of the Bible in various Solomon Islands churches.

There are some descriptions of churches established through the influence of Bible translation activity, especially that of the Summer Institute of Linguistics. These are missionary genre success stories, but some of the people who have written them are careful observers with many years of experience among the people about whom they write, and the events they record are remarkable. Some examples are Larson and Dodds, *Treasure*; Steven, *Different*; Slocum and Watkins, *Good Seed*; and Rossi, *City*.

[4]See chap. 10, above.

[5]Westermann, *Africa*, 107; Oosthuizen, *Post-Christianity in Africa*, 1-2; Cooksey, *Vanished Church*, 21-22.

eliminated outside of Egypt was a Latin church, without Scriptures or significant biblical teaching in any of the North African vernaculars. The Latin
church survived elsewhere, of course. The Egyptian and Ethiopian churches
which did survive had vernacular Scriptures, although by the time of the
Muslim sweep the languages had sometimes become archaic and the rise
of Arabic as the dominant language eventually prompted the churches from
Egypt to Mesopotamia to prepare literature and Scripture translation in Arabic, adapting to the new vernacular.[6]

But on the other hand, the Christians existed in South India for centuries without written Scriptures in any language.[7] They did not suffer a
Muslim conquest, to be sure, and perhaps were not severely persecuted in
the Indian cultural system which permits diversity, although it segregates
diverse groups sharply through the caste system. Then again, the Chinese
Nestorian church, with no Bible and no Muslim invasion either, did not
survive. Obviously many forces were involved in all these cases, and the
presence or absence of the Bible in the vernacular may have played a significant part, but it is hard to be sure.

But even if the translated Scriptures have not always been essential to
Christian life, their value is overwhelmingly demonstrated. Oral communication of the Bible is present to some degree in any church even if the
written Bible is not, but oral communication needs some kind of standard
to keep it from becoming corrupt. Some people need to be able to verify
the stories, the teachings, the prophetic utterances, the praise of God; they
need to renew them, to see them in context, in order to keep them from
becoming increasingly fanciful and to distinguish them from nonbiblical
material which grows up around them.

In this modern age, furthermore, where there is not just one church
which represents ''authority'' and speaks monolithically for God unchal-
lenged, the translated Bible provides an authority universally accepted as
such among Christians, but independent of individual churches and individual missionaries. The translated book sometimes helps to separate God
and the Christian faith from the missionary.[8]

With widespread education and literacy, with widespread publication
of all kinds, the printed page has also become a major source of informa-

---

[6]Latourette, *History*, 2:303.

[7]Chap. 2.

[8]Barrett, *Schism*, 127-28.

tion and inspiration throughout the world for people except for those on the lowest social and economic levels, and even for some of them. True, there are vast numbers of people on those lowest levels, people to whom the printed page is not relevant. And not everybody on other levels profits by this printed resource, even though capable of doing so, but many do. We will glimpse examples of their experience as we go along.

Distribution of the Translated Book

In 1988 member societies of the United Bible Societies distributed Scriptures all over the world in the enormous numbers shown in table 6. To these figures should be added the sales by all commercial publishers of Scriptures plus distribution by numerous other publishers like the International Bible Society, Living Bibles International, World Home Bible League, the Gideons, some churches, and some missions. The sheer quantity of Scripture distributed each year is staggering, and increases regularly.

In much of the world, however, the only bookstores which carry Scriptures are those run by the local Bible society or other Christian agencies, to be found only in the largest cities, often only in one city per country. Churches, mission stations or individual Christian homes therefore frequently stock Scriptures for local sale. All Bible society publications are inexpensive, the price usually subsidized below full cost, calculated according to what people living in the local economy should be able to pay, and people who want copies are normally expected to pay that small amount as they will value the book more if they buy it.

Scripture distribution also extends far beyond existing churches and missions, however. Vast numbers of selections and portions are sold or

United Bible Societies Scripture Distribution, 1988	TABLE 6
Bibles...14,091,439	
Testaments.....................................12,909,437	
Portions*..37,524,751	
New-Reader Portions*.........................15,547,771	
Selections†.................................... 569,785,689	
New-Reader Selections†.......................42,895,838	
TOTAL................................. **692,754,925**	

*Portion = a complete book of the Bible, less than a testament.
†Selection = less than a complete book of the Bible.

Source: United Bible Societies, *Annual Report*, 24.

given for evangelistic purposes to people who are not Christians, some of whom never knew about the Bible before. In recent years such distribution is most typically carried out by teams of trained volunteers from local churches, who may canvass an area or work in a market place, testifying to what the Bible has meant to them, and urging people to buy a portion or selection.[9]

But other, less conventional ways of getting Scriptures to people have also been used. During the Chinese cultural revolution Bibles were widely destroyed, and Christians could not get replacements. Radio programs were therefore beamed into China with passages of the Chinese Bible read at dictation speed, so that people could write down what they heard. There was widespread response to such broadcasts, received in secret. Some people also copied whole books of the Bible for themselves by hand from copies which did survive.[10]

An important older method of distribution, not as often followed these days when Christian churches are more widespread in most countries, is the work of the individual colporteur employed by a Bible society or some other Christian agency. Such people sell inexpensive Scriptures, often to people who would otherwise have no contact with the Bible. In earlier years the Bible society colporteur sometimes worked in a country or a region even before there was any church or missionary there, at least any Protestant who would promote the use of the Bible.

Sometimes colporteurs travelled from town to town on foot with their load of books. They would display their books in the town square or in the marketplace, perhaps drawing a group by talking about Christ and the Bible. Later when mass transportation became more common they sometimes worked in railroad stations or bus depots, urging the passengers to buy. Sometimes they would buy a ticket to board a train and would walk through the cars, selling their portions to the passengers.

In early days colporteurs were often not able to sell many Scriptures because of low literacy and/or low interest on the part of the population. In the late 1800s for example, one colporteur in Brazil sold forty-two Bibles and seven hundred and thirty-four New Testaments in one year as he walked

---

[9]One such type of program, with the training which prepares for it, is described in Wolfensberger, *Multiplying*, 29-45.

[10]Brown, *China*, 173.

long distances over the roads and trails of the country.[11] This averaged just over two books per day. That meant that distribution was expensive for the Bible society, but often the colporteurs paved the way for missionaries to enter later and work with believers and even with congregations already in place.

Some colporteurs have showed marvelous ingenuity. One man in the Philippines could not himself read, but used his lack of literacy to advance his colportage work. He would approach someone by asking if that person could read. If the person could, he would say that he had a wonderful book, but he could not read it himself, and ask the stranger to read some passages he had previously selected. He would thus gain the interest and curiosity of the reader, who might not only buy a book, but also go to church with him the next Sunday.[12]

There are cases where colporteurs showed heroic faithfulness under persecution and hardship. In various parts of the world they have been expelled from towns, beaten, imprisoned and even killed. But along with such dedicated heroism there have also been a few cases of fraud. One of the most notorious was perpetrated on Charles (Karl) Gutzlaff in Hong Kong. Gutzlaff was a bold, imaginative, and controversial missionary who, among other things, translated parts of the New Testament into Thai and Japanese as well as Chinese. He formed a Chinese Christian Union of his converts, through which they served as witnesses, preachers and colporteurs. By 1848 there were eighty colporteurs in the union, some of whom went out in pairs for journeys lasting weeks or months. Several hundred people were converted through their work, and joined together in small congregations.

But without Gutzlaff realizing it, among the colporteurs were some Hong Kong confidence men. After they took the colporteur training, Gutzlaff gave all of the colporteurs Scriptures, other books and travel money, but the confidence men then sold the books back to the printer who had printed them. He, in turn, resold them to Gutzlaff whenever Gutzlaff ordered more. In the meantime the confidence men pocketed the travel money and concocted elaborate fake diaries of the trips they were supposed to have taken, complete with sermon outlines and lists of converts.[13]

---

[11]Morris, *Brazil*, 25.

[12]Laubach, *Philippines*, 175-76.

[13]Broomhall, *Hudson Taylor*, 340-61.

In spite of such occasional abuses, for many years the colportage system has had a very important place in the distribution of the translated book, and is still used in some places. And whether it be the colporteur or the volunteer, when an individual Christian testifies to the value of the book and tells about Christ, the potential reader is more likely to take the book seriously, buy and read.[14]

Use of the Translated Book

There are many ways in which the translated book is used by the people who ultimately get them. These are not usually mutually exclusive, but may overlap and intermingle in different proportions with different individuals and churches. Some uses are more significant than others, more in keeping with what the church in other places has found to be true of the Bible. All have pitfalls, and can be subject to abuse. We can mention only a few of them here.

When people buy Scriptures from a colporteur or volunteer they may do so out of curiosity, looking at these translated books as *cultural artifacts* of a strange foreign religion. Many people have heard of Christianity or of Jesus or at least of Christian churches, and the opportunity to buy an inexpensive booklet is an unexpected chance to read about the exotic subject, to browse like a tourist in a strange domain. Occasionally the experience may unexpectedly turn out to be a very powerful one for such people even if they do not commit themselves to Christ. Passages such as the Sermon on the Mount have influenced some readers profoundly.

Then again, in Haiti there are people who sometimes rip out of a Bible a page on which is printed one of the psalms which contain curses pronounced on the psalmist's (or God's) enemies.[15] They boil the page in water and make the water into tea for someone against whom they have a grudge. They expect that the curses will be carried out on the person who drinks the tea. The Bible from which they take the pages is usually a French Bible, not one in Haitian, partly because whole Bibles were not available in Haitian until 1985, but perhaps also because Scriptures in an international language like French are considered more powerful.

---

[14]Colportage stories are to be found frequently in publications about Bible distribution or the Bible societies. See Chirgwin, *Bible*, 93-110, and Wolfensberger, *Multiplying*, 70, 75-79.

[15]E.g., Psalm 83:9-18 or Psalm 109:6-20.

Magical use of the Bible is not always antisocial, however. Soldiers of many countries sometimes carried New Testaments in their pockets during World War II to protect them from danger, and healing prophets in some African independent churches hold Bibles over people's heads as part of their healing ceremony. In all such cases, whether the effects desired are positive or not, the Bible is a *fetish*. The sacred book is used as a magically powerful object. It does not matter whether the user can read or not, understand it or not, follow it or not. The physical book itself performs its work by its presence.

Many people who use the Bible as fetish use it in other ways as well, however. They may also read it, preach from it, guide their lives by it. One significant movement in which the Bible was fetish but more than fetish was the Prophet Harris movement of West Africa, beginning about 1914.[16] William Wadé Harris was a Liberian Episcopalian of deep conviction and charismatic influence who walked through the cities, towns and villages of the Ivory Coast for a few months. The result was one of the most remarkable movements in the history of Christianity.

Harris carried an English King James Bible, the prevalent version of the Bible in his home country of Liberia. He preached simply of God, telling people to destroy the fetishes of their traditional religion, to rest on Sunday, and not to commit adultery. He told the thousands who came to him, heard his message, and were converted, to wait for people who would come to teach them the Bible. Some of the converts went to the Catholic churches in the area but found no evidence of the Bible, and so built their own churches and waited. Whether they could read or not, many of the groups bought a Bible for their church (sometimes the King James version, like Harris's own Bible, although they were in a French colony). Most of the ''Harris Christians,'' in fact, were not literate.

Some years later Methodist missionaries heard of these Harris people and started working among them. Here, at last, were people who taught the Bible, and many of Harris's followers became members of Methodist churches. Others did not, for various reasons remaining independent Harris Christians.

For many people the Bible is partly, or mainly, a *law book*. In Africa there are, for example, religious movements sometimes called Judaistic:

---

[16]S. Walker, ''Message''; Groves, *Africa*, 4:124.

There may be . . . emphasis on laws, rituals, and taboos, upon baptisms,
and purifications and festivals; a sense of exclusiveness may appear in
hostility to the white race and in messianic expectations focused on a "Black
Messiah" who will see justice done at last to the suffering African people
of God; . . .[17]

Many of the laws and prescriptions of the Judaistic groups are derived from
the Old Testament, which is more important to them than the New. Christ
is not central in these movements, so they are not fully Christian although
they may have the New Testament as well as the Old in their languages.

The Bible is often a law book among Christians as well. In many parts
of the world missionaries treated it as such, especially in the earlier years.
They emphasized the ten commandments, but more salient yet were laws
about tithing, Sunday, wearing clothes; dancing and drums were usually
forbidden, as were polygamy, veneration of ancestors, and many other activities, the details depending on the mission. These rules were all justified
by the Bible, although in some cases the biblical support for them was very
slight. Parts of the Bible, furthermore, proscribed much more strongly activities which the missionary thought nothing about. Missionaries, for example, ate pork, which is prohibited in the Old Testament, with only
indirect, slight possible hints of modification in the New,[18] but they prohibited multiple wives although that practice was followed by some of the
major characters of the Old Testament and there is no unequivocal prohi-
bition of it anywhere in the Bible. For these missionaries the Bible was a
law book reinterpreted through Western culture.

And the Bible is to some degree a law book for most of the churches in
the world, although the laws enforced often vary considerably from church to
church as they are likewise reinterpreted. Sometimes the laws are perpetua-
tions of the missionary selection of laws, but elsewhere they may differ sharply
from them. Some African independent churches were founded partly in revolt
against missionary laws, in some cases including those prohibiting multiple
wives, for example. When those churches read the translated Bible they found
no justification for laws enforcing monogamy.[19] The same applied to mis-

---

[17]Turner, "Typology," 85.

[18]As in the vision where Peter was told to eat the "unclean" animals. In the meaning
of the vision, however, the animals represented the gentile peoples. Acts 10:9-43.

[19]Some other African independent churches prohibit multiple marriages as strongly as
the missionary-founded churches they have rejected.

sionary laws against drumming and dancing. On the other hand, the same churches often have laws against fetishes from the traditional religion, and other proscriptions. In some cases the African reading of the Bible as a law book is more true to the ancient Israelite cultural scene portrayed in the Bible than was the missionary reading.

A reverse twist on the Bible as law book occurred in Zaïre when some prophets interpreted "Now concerning virgins I have no commandment of the Lord: yet I give my judgment . . . to be faithful."[20] They declared that since there was "no commandment" (no law) concerning unmarried women the women were free to do as they desired sexually. That they should be "faithful," furthermore, meant that they should give themselves to anyone who asked![21]

Another use for the translated Bible is *textbook,* a use most noticeable where school education is unavailable for any reason. In some societies, particularly in earlier times when mass communication was less extensive than it is now, people pored over the Bible so diligently that it became their main source of information on things outside their own experience, providing an expanded worldview and glimpses of other cultures, times and places. Ancient history beyond their own legends of the past were formed out of the accounts of the Hebrew people and of the first Christians. If the Bible was reasonably well translated the Old Testament stories and those of the Gospels and Acts were easy to understand, reflecting experience with which people in many parts of the world could identify. The Bible even became a source of the personal names many people gave their children.[22]

In the first half of the present century, for example, there was wide biblical knowledge in some of those South Pacific islands where Scriptures had been translated for some time.

> Every tortuous detail and obscure point in the entire book seemed to be common knowledge. . . . Even where translations had not been made or where church tradition placed little emphasis on Bible study, there was a surprising degree of familiarity with the main outlines of the Bible story. . . . In Tahiti and the Cook Islands [Bible studies] were the most popular of all church functions, when a passage would be raised for comment or a clever question raised for discussion by the pastor, and the people would

---

[20] 2 Corinthians 7:25, King James version.

[21] Andersson, *Grass Roots,* 145.

[22] Ibid., 88.

vie with each other for hours on end, sometimes the whole night long, in providing commentary or suggestions.[23]

Today when other sources of information about the world are more common, many people nevertheless use the Bible as a textbook on theology, if nothing more. For most Christians it is the primary and authoritative source of knowledge about God and God's work in the world, the only such source of information about Jesus, his life, ministry, death and resurrection. It is also the most important source of information about how people have responded to God as God has dealt with them.

Another use of the Bible is as a *reference book,* usually in conjunction with one or more of the other uses. People need to be reminded of the details of a story or teaching in the Bible, or they want to tell somebody about it, so they look it up. One of the major values of chapter and verse markings is to make the reference function easier. Many people use the Bible very legitimately as a reference book, but probably many other people never read the Bible or any portion of the Bible as they would any other book, but only look things up, as when a Bible study passage or a sermon text is announced. Many individual passages are familiar, but a book like Mark as a total book is not; much less Amos.

Using the Bible only as a reference book can also be a means of control over what people hear from it. Silas Eto, a ''post-Christian'' prophetic leader in the Solomon Islands used the Bible as a reference book to testify to himself, but kept it from his followers.

> [Eto] knew he was no match for [missionaries] in exposition, and he knew the Bible was their norm and authority. He declared that the Bible was like a dictionary or an A B C, to be used only for reference. It should never be read as a book, for this would lead only to confusion.[24]

Another use of the translated Bible is as a *behavioral manual,* a model for morals, individual life, the church community, and worship of God. As such it may be used in a legalistic way (the Bible as law book), or more sensitively and contextually, trying to understand from the Bible what present life and worship should be like in present-day circumstance. From the Bible people may see their need for ''covenant,'' some kind of relationship with God, some kind of corporate life that reflects that relation-

---

[23]Forman, *South Pacific,* 95.

[24]Tippett, *Solomon Islands,* 263.

ship, some kind of worship that expresses it more directly. Out of such needs met in different ways come different life styles, different church organizations, different liturgies. Often what people read about in the Bible is not actually the same in form as the behavior they find satisfying for themselves and their church, but the way in which they construct their Christian life style nevertheless resonates for them in some way with the biblical message.

One of the scandals of the modern missionary movement has been how some missionaries sought to reproduce their own life styles, corporate structures and worship patterns in their converts. This creating of God and the Bible in the missionary's image was not done maliciously, but out of ignorance and ethnocentrism. One of the great evidences of the Holy Spirit at work in many of the younger churches has been the way in which some of them have found more suitable forms of life and expression in the interaction between the Bible and their own traditions.

Nowhere is such reinterpretation more dramatically demonstrated than in the African independent churches where missionary patterns of organization and behavior which are perceived to be unsuitable have been rejected and others more African adopted.[25] Often the innovations are justified by reference to the Bible. Sometimes outsiders find the biblical evidence for some practice slim or stretched, but usually no more so than the biblical support adduced for some missionary requirements like monogamy.

The Church of the Lord (Aladura) in Nigeria and some other countries of West Africa constitutes a famous example.[26] *Aladura* means prayer, which reflects part of their emphasis. The church is of the prophet-healing type,[27] which refers to their strong belief in revelation from the Holy Spirit through prophets, and in healing as an integral part of salvation. These are African themes, but are also to be found in the Bible.

African drums dominate the music in an Aladura worship service, which lasts several hours, whereas they were banned from most mission churches, at least in colonial days. The service is animated and participatory, with everyone "making a joyful noise unto the Lord." At times there is dancing in the aisles and Spirit possession of a few individual worshipers. All of

---

[25]Chap. 10.

[26]The classic study is Turner, *History of an African Independent Church* and *African Independent Church*, a two-volume set.

[27]Turner, "Typology," 97-101.

this is in direct contrast to the solemn and intellectualized service in many of the mission-founded churches.

In the Church of the Lord (Aladura) hymns are lined out by the leader before each musical phrase. He thus provides the words of the next line for the largely illiterate congregation to sing. The singing therefore does not depend on people's ability to read the hymn book, whereas many mission churches in Africa had a literacy requirement for membership.

In the service of dedication for newborn infants sheep are killed as an offering of thanksgiving, then later cooked and eaten in a thanksgiving dinner. The offering of the sheep is accompanied by reading from Leviticus and the eighth Psalm. This ceremony is held after the mother has been purified from the defilement of childbirth, an African custom with parallels in Old Testament culture.

One of the most important ritual acts which people perform in the Church of the Lord (Aladura) is to roll, often naked, on the "Mercy Ground" for up to an hour, praying fervently for spiritual power. This is one of the cases where biblical precedent cited for a custom seems somewhat strained: "David fasted, and went in and lay all night upon the ground"[28] and "Ezra prayed and made confession, weeping and casting himself down before the house of God. . . ."[29]

The Bible, of course, is also used very often as a *devotional book,* a worship book. It is read and sung in ritual and individual devotional life. People meditate on what they find in it, and use it as a stimulus to prayer, and to thank God. We saw such use of the Bible in the base communities of Latin America. It is strong in the Kimbanguist church and the Church of the Lord (Aladura).

A Chinese man bought some gospels from a colporteur and then put them on a shelf and forgot them until some months later when he was opening a school. He got them down to take a closer look and became so engrossed with them that he spent much of his spare time reading them. As a result of his reading he wanted to worship God although he did not know what to do. He did know God was in heaven, however, so he regularly went outside before breakfast and knelt to pray. He did not know

[28]2 Samuel 12:16.

[29]Ezra 10:1. This and other examples from the Church of the Lord used here are from Brown, "Worshiping with the Church of the Lord." He observed a church in Monrovia, Liberia.

what else to say, so he would repeat, "God, I truly worship you! I truly worship you!" He did this for several months until Christians heard about it and got in touch with him, and a Christian community was established.[30]

Many Christian families and individuals in some parts of the world have their own simple worship service every day, in which reading of the Bible, often a chapter, is an integral part. In one survey in Zaïre forty-one percent of the families reported doing so.[31]

> . . . we sometimes sang hymns from the church hymnal in our mother tongue, Kikamba; sometimes we read passages out of the New Testament; . . . And before eating together, or going to bed at night, we prayed, not only in our home but also when we were guests in the homes of other people, regardless of whether they were or were not Christian.[32]

In some new churches before there are educated ministers Sunday worship services consist largely of reading the Bible and of the worshipers discussing it. Elsewhere, and more commonly, a service includes preaching based on a Bible text. One survey of 8,000 texts used in churches of The Church of the Lord (Aladura) compared with 1,300 in the Anglican churches in the same area, showed a similar range of Bible texts in both. In the Church of the Lord the Old Testament was used proportionately slightly more than in the Anglican church, but in both cases they used the New Testament far more than the Old, contrary to stereotypes of African independent churches being oriented to the Old Testament. In the Church of the Lord, in fact, half of the New Testament books (the most frequent being James, Matthew and Ephesians) were used more often than the most greatly used book of the Old Testament (Ecclesiastes, followed by Genesis 1-11 and Proverbs).[33]

Underlying almost all of these other uses of the translated Bible is the Bible as *oracle*, people hearing God speak in and through it. Some people who use the Bible in this way take the translated book to be the actual eternal words of God; God is literally speaking KiBamba or Srê or Sema Naga, as the case may be. Others hear in it the word of God for them in their particular situation. There are many other variations in what people believe

---

[30]Marshall Broomhall, *China*, 161-62.

[31]Andersson, *Grass Roots*, 79n29.

[32]Mbiti, *Bible and Theology*, 9.

[33]Turner, *Profile*.

as well. In any case, people look to the translated book for guidance, support, conviction and hope.

Often what seekers hear in the Bible is commonplace and predictable, but it gives them the strength and assurance to carry on. Occasionally what seekers hear is life-shattering and world-shaking for them. Such are some of the radical conversions with which the history of Christianity is studded, and the calls to change from a stable life to unpredictable service.

One way people use the translated book as oracle is by finding it to be a mirror in which they see themselves as they read. Much written African theology seems to start this way. African culture and African religion were so strongly repudiated by some missionaries and the churches they established that as Africans are reading the Bible for themselves they are constantly finding in it their repudiated selves, some of their traditions, some of their traditional understanding of God, some of their religious culture. Sometimes this traditional African perspective enriches their Christian understanding of God.[34]

Sometimes the use of the Bible as oracle is reflected in prophetic criticism. One young African man spoke up to a high-ranking minister in the church after the minister had announced that God had revealed certain things to him:

> . . . you said that God told you that he did not understand why the members have cut their assessments down, and many have failed to pay anything. . . . I, a staunch believer in prophecy, dream, and vision, find it very difficult to treat that . . . with respect . . . that construes God as not understanding the actions of men! . . . According to you, God asked you to tax the Church members. . . . to build the Church . . . There is no parallel to this order in the Bible. . . . To me God is love. He will not put more weight on us than we can bear . . . you construe God different from being merciful and loving. . . .[35]

Some people use the Bible as oracle only by finding texts which seem superficially to speak to their situation. Others do so by studying it carefully in its full scope, examining and weighing everything they find in it. It is clear that all people read the Bible through the eyes of their experience and their presuppositions, but growth in hearing the Bible as oracle comes

---

[34]One summary of the issues in African theology is Tutu, ''African Theology.'' Some other articles in the same volume are also useful.

[35]Turner, *African Independent Church*, 2:136.

when experience is tested against the Bible, and the resulting understanding is tested against experience in the world in which the believer lives, and that new outlook in turn is tested again against the Bible, and so on.[36]

If the book is only fetish and is available in languages considered more powerful than the local language it does not need to be translated. For each of these other uses, however, translation is critical to the degree that people do not understand any other language in which the Bible is available. But more than that, for devotional use and for hearing God speak, the most important language is almost always the person's primary language, even though the Bible in their primary language is not always acceptable to some people because of feelings of language inferiority or unsuitability. The primary language is the language which best touches people's thinking and emotions, in which their understanding and feeling is the most creative.

And if the historical meaning of the Bible, what it meant in its original situation, is to have any bearing on the use of the Bible, the translation must be clear. People will always interpret the Bible through their own presuppositions, their own experience, even their own preference, because the message of the Bible, or anything else, never passes from the mind of the writer into the mind of the reader unchanged.[37] This filtering of the message has both its good and its bad aspects, and the history of interpretation illustrates the great range of differences in interpretation which result.[38] Clarity of translation will not eliminate divergence, nor should it, because multiple reader perspectives are very important. But clarity of translation will help to provide an accurate base for whatever varieties of interpretation there may be.

---

[36]Cook, *Expectation,* 104-105.

[37]Chap. 1.

[38]See Childs, *Exodus,* for a commentary which gives the history of interpretation of a book of the Bible, with its amazing variety in both Jewish and Western Christian faith.

CHAPTER 13

Translation, Mission Past and Mission Future

When the "modern missionary movement" started at the beginning of the nineteenth century, and when the Moravians (United Brethren) were pioneering mission work in the century before that, Europeans and Americans were extremely ignorant of peoples and cultures outside their own historical tradition. Carey performed impressive research for his brief *An Enquiry into the Obligations of Christians to Use Means for the Conversion of the Heathens,* published in 1792, but even this pamphlet demonstrates how sketchy and spotty such knowledge was. In those earliest days, furthermore, most missionaries shared with other people of the North Atlantic a belief in their own superiority, and part of the missionary vision was often to spread the blessings of European civilization.

Unfortunately, such ideas are not dead yet among some missionaries, but even from early on, other sensitive and thoughtful ones rejected assumptions of superiority, in part or in whole. And even when they did maintain such attitudes, many missionaries nevertheless learned that they could not effectively communicate with other peoples without at least modifying some assumptions. Many developed new perspectives as they were forced into them by the realities of their work, including, for some of them, the process of translating the Bible.

In the middle of the eighteenth century, for example, Moravian missionaries working in Greenland lived under bitterly harsh circumstances. They received supplies only sporadically, so had to fish in the open ocean to survive, even without the skills to do so effectively. They lived underground in the bitter cold, suffered severe illnesses, and nearly died.

In spite of their conspicuous inferiority to the Greenlanders (Eskimo) in coping with that environment, the missionaries considered the local people to be rude savages. When the language had no terms to translate biblical ideas literally missionaries saw this lack as depravity.[1] The Green-landers, in turn, were contemptuous of the bumbling ineptitude and pov-erty of the Moravians who posed as teachers but scarcely knew how to keep themselves alive.

The Moravians tried to preach by telling of "the existence of God, the creation of the world, the fall of man; a mode of instruction which appears a priori, not merely the most rational, but the only plan that could be adopted with any prospect of success."[2] The Greenlanders, however, responded with indifference and even hostility.

Then one day in 1738, after having been in Greenland for five years, the missionaries were recopying a corrected draft of a translation of part of the Gospels when some Greenlanders dropped by and asked what they were doing. The missionaries read aloud stories of Jesus Christ and described his life, suf-fering and death, and spoke of salvation. This produced a much more positive response, and before long one of the people was converted.

The missionaries therefore began in time to build a new strategy, re-flecting a revised understanding of their task:

> They . . . directed the attention of the savages . . . to Christ Jesus, to his incarnation, his life, and especially to his sufferings and death. . . . The subject so warmed and animated their own hearts that the words flowed from their lips with wonderful fervor and affection; they were astonished at each other's powers of utterance. Happily, this was attended with cor-responding effects on the Greenlanders. Their darkened understandings were enlightened, their stubborn hearts melted, and in their cold icy breasts was kindled the flame of spiritual life.[3]

Ethnocentrism and misunderstanding on both sides remained strong, and expressions like "savage" and "darkened understanding" would not go out of missionary vocabulary for a long time, but Greenlanders and Mo-ravians moved toward each other as they both moved in different ways to-ward Christ. The stories of the translated Bible had proved more effective than rationalistic exposition. The Holy Spirit was at work. And mission-aries learned more of their task, more about people.

As time went on other translators all over the world also learned in many different ways from people into whose language they were translating.

---

[1]Brown, *History* , 212-18, 208.

[2]Ibid., 215.

[3]Ibid., 213-15.

Some of the new lessons were individual ones; others became part of the missionary culture in a particular mission or mission area. Today, in the new era of nonmissionary Bible translation,[4] the continuing process of translation has lessons of a different kind as well for local churches which are translating into their own languages.

Translation and Missionary Self-Understanding

Gospel and Culture. Missionaries share with Christians everywhere a tendency to see their own culture as to some degree an absolute embodiment of the gospel. No matter how much sin they may recognize in their own culture they tend to identify the gospel with what they do approve of in it, or take to be "normal," and at some points to measure other cultures and the behavior of other people by it.

For example, in some highland areas of Irian Jaya, the Indonesian part of New Guinea, standard traditional dress for a man consists exclusively of a thin gourd some fifteen inches long, worn as a penis sheath. The lower end, into which the penis is inserted, is tied to the exposed scrotum, while the upper end comes to a point about eight inches in front of the chest, held in place by a cord.

Missionaries who began working among various groups in interior Irian Jaya after World War II sensibly made no issue of clothing, having learned from mission experience elsewhere, interpreted through missiology. Scripture translation was undertaken and sizable churches grew to the point where one of the churches decided to send its own missionaries to people in the lowlands. So the missionary party, consisting entirely of Irian Jayans, travelled across the mountains, eventually reaching a group of people whose men wore nothing but rattan cords around the waist. Faced with this unimaginable depravity, after they cleared an airstrip the missionary party arranged for inbound planes to come loaded with penis sheaths.[5]

But in spite of this recurring tendency to see missionary culture as the norm which others should be taught to follow, through the history of Christianity the missionary frontier has also been the area where the validity of other cultures to be vehicles of Christian life and faith has repeatedly

---

[4]Chap. 2.

[5]John D. Ellenberger, personal communication.

been rediscovered. It was discovered first by Paul himself, of course, the missionary who insisted that what mattered was faith in Christ Jesus, not the observance of irrelevant requirements of the missionary sending culture.[6] Of course faith in Christ itself entails major changes in world view, in the very heart of culture, but ramifications which follow are not always predictable or controllable by missionaries.

Many missions had both their Pauls and the Judaizers (the group which wanted to force religious behavior of the missionary culture on Paul's new converts). Often the Judaizers won the battle within the missions. The Pauls, however, won the war, because once local people accepted the faith they often ran away with it,[7] and the church as it spread around the world has become a kaleidoscope of cultural diversity, particularly in its independent indigenous manifestations.[8]

And yet, when some later missionaries less clear-sighted than Paul did not recognize validity in diversity, when they imposed requirements from their own cultures on their converts, they nevertheless often unwittingly undermined some of their own ethnocentrism by the use of the local vernacular and by translating the Scriptures into it. For example, even at the very heart of the Christian faith, the term for God,

> presented an unprecedented difficulty, for the multiplicity of languages in Africa meant a corresponding multiplicity in the terms by which God is addressed. And since each term carried widely differing connotations in the concept of God, missionaries could not be sure what precise implications might come to attach to usage. It thus came about that in the religious and theological sphere, missionaries became ultimately helpless in the face of the overwhelming contextual repercussions of translation.[9]

Missionaries in general, but especially Bible translators, had to learn from the people they had come to evangelize the basic vernacular information they needed: the language, the vocabulary, the meanings of terms,

---

[6]For example, Galatians 2:15-21.

[7]One intriguing missiological question is why Africans seem to have assimilated the gospel into their own cultural framework more radically, or at least more overtly radically, than Asians. Nothing in Asia matches the size, volatility, and diversity of the African independent church movements.

[8]Chap. 10.

[9]Sanneh, *Translating*, 158.

the religious system, the meaning of behavior.[10] To be sure, some of them papered over what they learned, equating many local terms with what they considered to be corresponding terms in their own languages, unconscious of the differences of implication, or sometimes ignoring those differences if they did suspect them.

Other missionaries, among whom Maurice Leenhardt was notable,[11] saw far beneath such superficial equivalences and struggled with the implications of difference. In Leenhardt's terms, culture-bound missionaries themselves had to be converted. That is, they had to recognize how essential cultural pluralism is within Christianity, how fundamental some cultural relativism is in the outworking of the gospel.

In the gospel Christ is Lord of all, but the cultural manifestations of loyalty to Christ, including those of the missionary, are all tainted by sin, and Christians at different times and places have found myriad ways of expressing their relationship to God. In the gospel, also, there is only one undivided humanity, neither Jew nor Greek, slave nor free, male nor female,[12] but that humanity has myriad expressions in different languages and cultures. Right from the first, Paul insisted that Christian behavior in other cultures could not be judged on the basis of the missionary culture, but that what mattered was obedience to Christ.

This fact, which the church regularly forgets and has to relearn, is the basis for the translatability of the gospel, and the Bible.

> It was Paul's achievement that while he disentangled the gospel from any exclusive cultural definition, he retained the particularity of culture as the necessary saddle for launching Christianity in the world. For instance, he faced the combined demands of Jewish particularity in seeking messianic consolation and the Greek expectation of philosophical emancipation by affirming the cross as the promise and the gift. He writes to the church at Corinth: "For the Jews demand sign and the Greeks seek wisdom, but we preach Christ crucified, a stumbling block to Jews and folly to Gentiles, but to those who are called, both Jews and Greeks, Christ the power of God and wisdom of God" (1 Corinthians 1:22-24). The gospel is thus recognized by both "Jew" and "Greek" as a confirmation of their respective particularity. In Paul's mind Christ came into the world, risky as it was,

---

[10]Ibid., 158-64.

[11]Chap. 3.

[12]Galatians 3:28.

not to make a composite montage of our differences but to bring our true stature into God's own picture.[13]

Paul's lesson kept being relearned in many ways and to varying degrees. The Leenhardts who learned to see it clearly were in the minority, but many missionaries were drawn into living and working as though the cultural manifestations of the gospel were multiple and relative even though they would have been uncomfortable saying so.

Some missionary translators tried to maintain both positions, translating the Scriptures in the vernacular but trying not to yield to cultural diversity in many other ways. Sometimes they translated the Bible in as shallow a way as possible, so that the words and spellings were from the local language but the translation was as much in the syntax of the missionary language (or the original) as they could possibly make it. Other missionaries decided that the Scriptures should be allowed to speak for themselves in the local idiom.

Many translators never thought about it, but when they did turn to native speakers for information, when they really sought to communicate[14] and asked native speakers if a translated passage was clear, and when they changed wording because they discovered that it was not clear or was misunderstood, they were actually turning a measure of translational adequacy over to local people. They saw this technique as a practical tool for insuring the usefulness of the translation, but what it implicitly did was to put local language and the relevant parts of local culture in some ways on a par with the missionary language and culture and the languages and cultures of the Bible.[15]

Missionaries were against sin, of course, and to speak in these terms of the diversity of Christianity is not to imply that all of the diverse behavior of Christian churches is equally valuable, equally just, equally in obedience to Christ. The diversity of Christianity creates a diversity of sinning as well as a diversity of manifestations of God's grace. Translation into the vernacular, however, helped force many missionaries to give up regulating the sins of other peoples as well as regulating God's grace, yielding to God and to the local church the responsibility for judging and

---

[13]Sanneh, *Translating*, 34.

[14]Chap. 1.

[15]Sanneh, *Translating*, 3.

to the Holy Spirit the responsibility for the direction of the church's development. This did not mean giving up nurturing the church supporting it, and serving as a catalyst as it made its decisions, but it did mean a step toward giving up paternalism and superiority.

Translation and Missiology. The struggle to accept peoples of other cultures and to understand the missionary task within cultural diversity was not long confined to individual missionaries or within individual missions. Mission theorists began to develop by the middle of the nineteenth century, building both on theology and on the rapidly growing experience of missionaries from all over the world. Discussion of cultural differences and of the nature and practice of mission was broadened in various ways over time, coming to a head periodically in international mission conferences. The International Missionary Council was formed in 1921. Books were written, and journals such as *International Review of Missions* were established.

However, Bible translation as such apparently did not contribute much directly to the development of missiological discussion in the nineteenth century. Missionaries assumed translation to be important, even essential, but without thorough missiological reflection, and without explaining its theological and cultural implications. The major problem they discussed with respect to translation was the limitation they saw as inherent in the languages and cultures into which the translation was being made, a belief exhibiting missionary ethnocentrism once again.

But the Bible societies, on the other hand, with their long record of interconfessional cooperation, and the experience of translators with different backgrounds working together in translation committees were very important in the development of other cooperative institutions and of missiological thought. The motives for translator cooperation had usually been pragmatic, or at least had started that way with individual translators. Some people cooperated in translation, for example, because they could not afford to translate and publish another Bible by themselves. But whatever the motives, the effect was often greater mutual understanding.

The embryonic social sciences, furthermore, had little to contribute in the early years of the development of missiology. In fact, some missionaries were themselves accumulating data which would later be used in the development of modern linguistics and anthropology. By the end of the nineteenth and the early twentieth centuries, however, Bible translators like Robert H. Codrington[16] and Maurice Leenhardt in Melanesia, and Edwin

---

[16]Codrington, *Melanesians.*

W. Smith[17] in South Africa had made major anthropological contributions. Catholic missionary anthropologist led by Wilhelm Schmidt,[18] although not Bible translators, were also producing the major anthropological journal *Anthropos*. Such people helped to establish a foundation for what followed.

Then, beginning in the middle of this century the professionalization of translation[19] brought linguistics, then anthropology, then sociolinguistics and sociology solidly into missiological discussion. At least it did so in some circles, although in many major seminaries mission is still seen more exclusively in theological and historical perspective, and in relation to the philosophical study of world religions. Dynamic equivalence translation[20] articulated the rationale for letting the Bible speak in all vernaculars on its terms and theirs, emphasizing the validity of all vernaculars as vehicles for translation which is as free as possible of literalism. It was and is an explicitly missiological theory of translation, conceiving translation as having a missiological purpose and being conducted in a missiological context.

At the same time, the principles of culture and communication[21] opened new perspectives in other aspects of missiology as well. During that period Eugene A. Nida wrote several popular books about issues broader than translation alone, about mission as seen from an anthropological and communication perspective.[22] For nearly twenty years he and several other Bible society translation consultants also sponsored, edited, and contributed heavily to a journal, *Practical Anthropology,* in which social science insights, particularly ones from cultural anthropology, were explored for the light they could throw on the missionary task, and on development of the church in diverse cultures.[23] Partly independently, some of this same perspective was being explored at the Kennedy School of Missions of the

---

[17]Chap. 4.

[18]Schmidt, *Religion.*

[19]Chap. 2.

[20]Chap. 6.

[21]Chap. 1.

[22]Nida, *Customs, Animism, Message, Religion,* and *Communication.*

[23]Some of the articles from *Practical Anthropology* were reprinted in Smalley, ed., *Readings,* and Loewen, *Culture.*

Hartford Seminary Foundation, by some members of the Summer Institute of Linguistics, later at the School of World Mission of Fuller Theological Seminary,[24] and more recently at Asbury Theological Seminary.[25] Roman Catholic missionaries contributed to *The Anthropological Quarterly,* and among them Louis J. Luzbetak wrote a major textbook.[26]

These social science contributions to missiology, often byproducts of translation, or influenced by developing dynamic equivalence translation theory, were helpful to many missionaries in making the transition from colonialism to nationalism, from paternalism to partnership, from mission churches to independent churches. They have also continued to influence the thinking of some missionaries entering societies with no previous expression of the gospel, and to missionaries translating into new languages.

In spite of contributions from translation to missiology, however, and in spite of the crucial place translation occupies in the spread and development of the church, it still gets very little attention by most missiologists except those who are translation specialists. In a survey of articles in *The International Review of Missions* and *Evangelical Missions Quarterly,* 1965-1986, less than .5% of the articles dealt with Bible translation and distribution. In a similar survey of book reviews appearing in *Missiology,* 1973-1986, only 1.4% of the books reviewed were described as including themes of Bible translation and distribution.[27] Correspondingly among translators, *The Bible Translator* deals very little with broader missiological questions raised by translation.

More recently, however, Lamin Sanneh's *Translating the Message: The Missionary Impact on Culture* has placed translation, including Bible translation, squarely where it belongs in the heart of missiology. It has also moved the missiological discussion of translation into a historical and theological mode of discourse with less of the social science emphasis of modern translation theory. Some of Sanneh's points, including the theme that translation is essential to the very nature of historic Christianity, are not entirely new,[28] of course, but Sanneh's book-length treatment gives

---

[24]See esp. Kraft, *Christianity.*

[25]Whiteman, *Melanesians* and *Missionaries.*

[26]Luzbetak, *Church.*

[27]Hesselgrave, *Choices,* 244, 249.

[28]E.g., Walls, ''Culture.''

them much greater prominence, and enlarges the scope of missiological discussion dramatically.

Perhaps most missiologists do not write about translation because it is a highly specialized activity with which they do not feel at home. Perhaps they overlook it because in modern times the task itself has been largely relegated to special agencies like the United Bible Societies and the Summer Institute of Linguistics. Perhaps translation is too fundamental, too much a part of the water of Christianity for the fish swimming in it to notice, too much below the level of consciousness except when a particular translation becomes controversial, too much taken for granted.

The Changing Missionary Role in Bible Translation. In the last decade of the twentieth century we are now well into the era of nonmissionary translation.[29] But before discussing the developing modern role of native speakers as translators, we need first to look at what is happening to missionary translators amid the changes.

Traditionally, missionary translators were very powerful people, even though they worked for many years on a task which often attracted little attention until it was done. They were powerful because they decided what the Bible meant, and watched to see that the meaning they understood was the one conveyed to a whole church. They were the gatekeepers of truth. If anyone on the translation team knew the original languages, they did, or at least they were the ones who had access to the commentaries and to other translations to help them. They could stop any argument, quell any uneasiness about awkward or misleading wording in the translation by insisting that "That is what the Greek says!" More than one native speaker helping in a Bible translation has pointed to the array of books the missionary was using for reference and has asked when all of them would be translated as well!

Ultimate decision making about the translation lay in the hands of those missionary translators, although they usually collaborated with highly capable native speakers, who sometimes even made the initial drafts. Missionaries controlled the procedures, the process, organization of translation, and held the purse strings. They were also the people with whom the Bible Societies dealt.

Through the years, as native speakers of local languages gained more education, as local leaders emerged, as nationalism increased, as mission-

---

[29]Chap. 2.

ary sensitivity to the unequal relationship was sharpened, as Bible societies exerted pressure, as church leaders spoke up, and as missiology
matured, that traditional missionary translator role has increasingly diminished. Control is now frequently in the hands of the local church and/or the
national Bible society of the country, and in those cases if any missionaries
have any role at all in the translations or revisions they are invited to participate by those in charge because they have some needed skill not available in the church. Missionaries who insist on dominating or on keeping
power are not often invited.

There still remain many situations, however, where native speakers do
not have extensive education, or where missionaries want to promote
translation into a language where there are no Christians, or where the
church is unable to exert leadership in the translation for some other reason, such as not knowing what to do. Under such circumstances some missionaries still assume that the traditional role of missionary-in-control is
the only way to go.

The traditional translator role, furthermore, is itself still very attractive
to some missionary translators and would-be translators. In Scripture
translation they have a long-term chance to exercise complex, unusual and
impressive skills, sometimes to prepare a writing system for an unwritten
language, sometimes to analyze the grammar of a language previously unknown to outsiders, to explore its meaning system, to study the Bible at
whatever level they are capable, to elicit the closest natural equivalent from
native speakers serving as their translation helpers. All this, although it may
call for self-denial and self-sacrifice, can be extremely rewarding, satisfying desires to engage in pioneering activity, to work at the fringes of
knowledge, to be responsible almost single-handedly for bringing the Bible
to a people in the tradition of the legendary missionary translators of history, and to be the boss in an important job, too.

In taking that traditional role, however, translators may not be facing up
to a very important part of missionary responsibility. In wanting to bring the
Scriptures to the people they may overlook the opportunity for enabling a
church to get the Scriptures for itself. Enabling someone else may be a harder
task in some ways than doing it yourself, but it has greater ultimate significance. To participate as a missionary in that task involves most of the skills
required for doing the translation, plus some rare personal ones. It requires
the ability to encourage people to come to wise decisions on the basis of judiciously derived knowledge without telling them what to decide, to support

without dominating, to suggest alternatives without forcing the way, to serve faithfully without resentment, in short to be a catalyst who makes possible an effective, skillful translation team of native speakers.

In fact, as traditional translation projects have moved along in recent years, some missionary translators have increasingly realized the importance of native speakers doing the translating, while missionaries take a consulting or serving role, if that is needed. Sometimes they have been influenced by the example of other translators or by the Bible societies. At other times a natural growth has occurred in which missionaries stepped back from power as native speakers gained skill. Sometimes, for example, an Old Testament project was established with much more responsibility in the hands of native speakers than had been true in the earlier New Testament project.

One of the temptations in the increasing missionary role of consultant or exegete or partner, instead of primary translator, however, is the temptation to reduced commitment to the greatest possible missionary competence in the language and culture of the translation. If native speakers are responsible for the wording of the translation missionaries may feel less necessity to know the language as well as though the wording were their own responsibility. For English-speaking missionaries, reduction of commitment toward learning the language is reinforced by the general negative attitude toward learning other languages which some may feel from their position at the top of the world hierarchy of languages.[30] For a generation imbued with the concept of narrow specialization, reduced commitment to competence in the local language and culture seems consistent with a logical division of labor.

The measure of the depth of the missionary contribution, however, continues to be the degree of its insight into local language and culture as well as into those of the Bible. It is ironic that our perverse human minds can take a move toward greater local control over translation and treat it with missionary ethnocentrism, finding in the increased role of the native speaker a reason for falling back into a less taxing avoidance of submersion in language and culture. To be a true partner in translation, however, requires more of the missionary, not less.

Part of the problem for a missionary taking a helping role in Bible translations, of course, is knowing how to do it. One way is demonstrated

---

[30]Chap. 8.

by Ernst R. Wendland working simultaneously with Bible translation projects in two Central African languages, ChiChewa in Malawi and Chi-Tonga in Zambia. The translators whom he advises, coordinated by Joseph Tenthani for the ChiChewa and by Salimo Hachibamba for the ChiTonga, are educated people but Wendland's role would be appropriate for working with less well-equipped translators as well.

Wendland's own qualifications are obvious from his books[31] and articles. He has a good knowledge of the original biblical languages and of biblical exegesis, as well as of ChiChewa and ChiTonga languages and cultures, including the no small advantage of having spoken ChiChewa from childhood. He also has anthropological skills, and his understanding of linguistic theory and of translation is outstanding. As adviser to the two translation projects he has sought to foster insight and skill in the translators at all levels of the work. At every point he seeks to support the deepening of the translators' activity, discovering with them what the translation should be. He is enabling these ChiChewa and ChiTonga translators to bring a much better Bible to their own people than they would otherwise have been able to do, helping them grow over the years in the process.

The role Wendland plays is truly a postcolonial role, truly a helping one, missiologically much more significant than the traditional missionary translator role, the antithesis of any role which grows out of feelings of superiority.

The Future in Non-Missionary Translation

The growing percentage of non-missionary translators of the Bible in the younger churches forms the ultimate capstone of translation as mission. Historically these translators bring the story of translation full circle, back to the norm before the modern missionary movement began, when translation was almost always into translators' own languages. Missiologically they represent a church growing in a society to the extent that people want the Bible in their own languages and are prepared to translate it for themselves. Theologically they underscore God speaking directly to each people, with less foreign mediation. Socially they embody the maturation of the local church as it accepts and undertakes this major task at whatever level it is able to work effectively. Translationally, they have the potential for doing a far more adequate job than foreigners can ever do.

---

[31]Wendland, *Language* and *Cultural Factor*.

It is hard to exaggerate the built-in advantage of people translating into their own languages. Native speakers normally have a feel for their own language that foreigners cannot fully learn as adults. Among them are gifted people whose language sense is especially keen, the writers or potential writers. The advantages they have are often stifled by misleading folk theories of translation, or even by an education which downgrades their vernacular, but once released they can be harnessed to produce translations which sing in comparison to translations produced by foreigners.

In some major languages, especially of Asia and Latin America, the process of people revising Bible translations or retranslating into their own languages is little different from the process in Europe or North America. Committees are formed from among native speakers who are all biblical scholars: seminary professors, pastors or priests with strong training in biblical languages and talents in exegesis. Bible society translation consultants frequently work with them on the implications of dynamic equivalence translation for their work.

Unfortunately, however, such committees sometimes have not only the same strengths as their North Atlantic counterparts, but also the same weaknesses. Like committees of Western biblical scholars, their perspective on translation is often not a missiological one, is sometimes formed by the literalism inculcated in seminaries and in classical education,[32] or stemming from theological predispositions.[33] Lacking a sense of translation as communication, a missiology of translation, they sometimes see dynamic equivalence translation as beneath their scholarly dignity. In the eternal balance between accessibility and distortion in translation they may want to make accessible the structures of the original text to a degree which too heavily casts the reader as an eavesdropper rather than as one who hears a direct communication.[34]

The fact is that without training in translation theory and practice most native speakers, whatever their level of education, are usually just as inclined to literalism in Bible translation as missionaries are, and for much the same reasons. Reverence for the text, biblical training which treats the Bible as an artifact to be deciphered rather than as a message to be read,

---

[32]Chap. 6

[33]Chap. 5.

[34]Chap. 1.

and other issues which have been discussed in earlier chapters[35] inhibit native speakers as much as they do missionaries. In the era of non-missionary translators, however, the solution is not for missionaries who are convinced of the value of dynamic equivalence to try once again to take charge and produce the ''right kind'' of translation, but to cultivate and encourage native speakers who will themselves eventually be able to make the message of the Bible more accessible.

A committee consisting primarily of biblical scholars is relatively rare in the younger churches around the world, however, because normally there are not enough native speakers of a language with that level of training to make up a translation team. Instead, other educated people in the churches frequently learn to translate into their own languages, and may bring essential writing skills or other contributions to the project, skills which biblical scholars themselves do not necessarily have. Typically translators or potential translators of this kind recognize that they lack the original languages and training in exegesis. Without prior training they are not usually as aware of their need for an adequate understanding of the translation process, but they usually welcome opportunity to grow in this respect, also, if the opportunity becomes available.

In some translation programs like this a missionary serves as the biblical exegete, and consultants from the United Bible Societies help to train everyone in translation theory. A less frequent but major advance beyond that arrangement involves something along the Wendland model, providing long-term in-service training to the members of the translation team, helping them learn to do their own biblical exegesis, to make their own necessary analysis of language and culture, and to apply translation principles as they go along. This requires far more than an occasional visit from a translation consultant, but where possible it could enrich the translation and the church enormously.

Translators handbooks published by the United Bible Societies on different books of the Bible and other helps for translators are also critical in helping native speakers without extensive biblical training to take their places as Bible translators.[36] They summarize exegetical information in simple form, warn of translational pitfalls in the passages, and make suggestions for solutions to translation problems. Translators who would be

---

[35]Chaps. 5 and 6.

[36]Chap. 4.

lost in typical commentaries written for scholars can get much of the essential information they need in the handbooks. Unfortunately, however, only translators with a good command of English can use most of the handbooks. Only a few have been written in French or adapted to French, none to Spanish, two of the other international languages most frequently used in areas where translation is being done.

Also critical for helping people with limited biblical background to translate well are modern translations in which the meaning of Scripture is readily accessible in languages the translators know. In some cases these people translate from both a moderately literal translation such as Revised Standard Version and a dynamic equivalence translation such as the *Good News Bible,* to help them work out the closest natural equivalent in their own language.[37] Under the principles of dynamic equivalence translation they should not translate either of these literally, of course.

Then, on another level, come the languages spoken in churches where nobody has very much education, where skills resembling biblical exegesis do not exist, and where there is little knowledge of biblical cultures. Some knowledge of the national language or of an international language and rudimentary knowledge of the Bible is all that can be expected. Here missionaries often tend to take over once again. Local people are obviously not qualified, from their point of view, and often the local people would agree.

Prospective missionary translators in such situations often do not see as clearly, however, that they, too, are equally unqualified because they do not know the local language and culture. Neither do they tend to see that overcoming the church's lack of qualifications rather than theirs would be of more help to the kingdom of God. Sometimes this can be accomplished by reciprocal learning, in which local people help the missionaries with what they need to learn about local language and culture to serve effectively, while missionaries help the local translators with what they need to learn about the Bible and about translation in order to translate effectively.

Finally, in those situations where no church exists and no local people desire the Scriptures, there may not be any native speakers to take responsibility for the translation at the beginning, if translation is warranted for other reasons. The missionary may have to start the work, hiring the best help posible among native speakers. But as a church begins to grow and

---

[37]Loewen, "Bantu Translators."

as bright prospects emerge among the converts, the process of training them to be the translators could start far sooner than it has usually started in the past.

Mildred L. Larson has described the steps by which a preliterate un-educated person eventually became a skilled and effective Bible translator in such a society. Not to have had a previous chance for an education, or even to become literate, is no sign of lack of ability, of course. Nor is it a sign of lack of knowledge about the person's own culture.

> When we began working with the Aguaruna, in Peru, the level of educa-tion and lack of any biblical background meant that we started with myself as an Acquired Language Translator working with a Language Helper. Then as speakers of the language received more basic education, and be-came bilingual, and received training in translation principles, we moved into truly Co-translator relationship. Later the Co-translator improved his Spanish and received more training in Biblical matters. I became the Ad-viser and he worked as a semi-independent Mother Tongue Translator on a number of books. Finally, after the New Testament was published, this mother-tongue speaker translated Genesis and other Old Testament ma-terial as an Independent Mother Tongue Translator and I only served as a Consultant. It was an excellent translation but years of training in trans-lation principles, Spanish, and Biblical Studies made it possible.[38]

Bible society consultants have also trained many people with relatively little education or background knowledge of the Bible to translate into their own languages.[39] Consultants generally give translation-based training, with native speakers first preparing drafts on their own and then discussing them together with other translators and the consultant, learning to apply the principles of analysis, transfer and restructuring[40] which the consultant introduces and reinforces as appropriate. The consultant also continues to support the translators through repeated contacts over time. Such a pro-gram, however, is limited at best. If a translation is desired in a language in which no one has the basic qualifications to be a translator, then the Lar-son experience just described, or that of Wendland, would be far superior in many situations, both in depth of training and in quality of translation produced. Such expatriates would ideally be ones who are already in the

[38]Larson, "Indigenizing."

[39]Loewen, "Training;" Fry, "Training."

[40]Chap. 6.

area for some other reason, know the people, speak the language, and have the necessary talents and skills.

Westerners with academic perspectives on translation are sometimes horrified that the Bible societies allow, even encourage such ''unqualified'' people to translate if that seems the best alternative available. But when talented native speakers learn to be free from literalism so that they can express the meaning of Scripture creatively, and when they learn to find the meaning of the text in responsible and skillful ways, the chances of having a better translation than one produced under missionary dominance are excellent, and the process of translation itself has been a greater contribution to the church which speaks the language than it would have been if a missionary had done it. Members of the church have gained skills to which the church would not otherwise have had access. The church has also had a better chance of understanding the nature of the Bible and of the translation by which it gained access to the Bible than it would have been if the missionary had ''given'' it the completed translation.

Recognizing their deficiencies in the receptor language, sometimes even after twenty years of speaking it fluently, missionary translators have almost always sought help from native speakers, some deeply, some superficially. Somehow their language deficiency has generally not seemed as serious to them as deficiency in knowledge of the Bible on the part of native speakers. The change in that missiological bias may be what has most drastically altered participation in translation in the past two decades or so, as missionaries became the ''translation helpers.'' In either case, whether the translators are native speakers or missionaries, God's Spirit uses imperfect vessels. Today, however, the imperfections of native speakers are no longer seen as often through the lens of missionary superiority.

Babel and Pentecost

The stories of Babel and Pentecost stand at two critical points in the Bible, two great stories about language, about community, and ultimately about the missiology of translation.

The story of the confusion of languages at Babel (Babylon) is told just before the events which lead to the establishment of the ethnically particular Hebrew nation and its covenant with God; Babel highlights the particularizing character of language,[41] how language is related to individual

---

[41]Chap. 8.

groups of people, how it divides and how its diversity is caused by division, how it interferes with wider communication. Babel is the biblical story of vernaculars.

Babel is also the story of how people can feel too powerful if too many of them can communicate too easily, and of how that power can turn against God. In that sense it is a warning for the speakers of international languages today, especially for speakers of English. It can be a warning also against relying too much on higher-level languages within the church.[42]

The story of Pentecost is told just before the events which lead to bursting the bounds of the Hebrew tradition and the establishment of the church—the ethnically universal people of the new covenant. Pentecost highlights the universalizing character of language,[43] how language can transcend individual groups even while it is so closely tied to them, how it unites through wider communication than the vernaculars. Pentecost is the biblical story of breaking the limits on vernaculars to enable universal communication of the word of God in spite of them, and through them, and of people who speak different vernaculars turning to God as they hear "of the glorious works of God in our native language."[44]

The linguistic miracle of Pentecost has never been repeated. Glossolalia, or speaking in tongues, is not a reenactment of Pentecost, as any reading of Paul on the subject makes clear, because people who hear glossolalia do not hear in their own vernaculars.[45] But although the linguistic miracle was unique, the missiological miracle of communicating "the glorious works of God in our own native language" has been repeated innumerable times through translation; and the miracle of gathering a people of God out of all ethnic groups, which was so dramatically highlighted at Pentecost, has multiplied geometrically, still gaining steam in some parts of the world today.

The modern missionary movement was, for a time, a major part of the modern Pentecost. It audaciously pushed translation of the Scriptures down into ever lower levels of language hierarchies, and in so doing sometimes raised people up in their social position as well as opened up the Kingdom

---

[42]Chap. 9.

[43]Chap. 8.

[44]Acts 2:11, Phillips, *New Testament*.

[45]1 Corinthians 14. See also the analysis by a sympathetic linguist in Samarin, *Tongues*.

of God to them. Increasingly now, however, the modern Pentecost is and will be the movement of those gathered peoples translating for themselves, into their own languages.

But just as different churches at different times and places have seen translation of the Bible in different lights, so will these churches now emerging into the potentiality of translation. In time some of them will move toward rigid and archaic church languages, fossilized in an attempt to encapsule holiness in verbal formulae. Some will sanctify an existing translation, making it "The Holy Bible" and reject all deviation from it, no matter how solidly based such "deviation" may be in the Scriptures themselves. Some will neglect their own vernacular Bible, feeling that translation into a higher language is more fitting for the word of God.

More than that, some churches will twist the Bible, interpreting it in ways which are comfortable to them but muting its prophetic voice among them. Some will limit the right to interpret the Bible to a select class of people, and insist that only authorized dogma, standard ways of reading the Bible are legitimate. Some will seek to protect the Bible by stoutly defending their own presuppositions in its name, setting themselves up as the keepers of God's mind. Some will ignore it.

And none of this will be new. The church in its various manifestations has gone through periods when it has done all of these things, and examples of all of them are to be found in different churches today. But eventually, even in the face of such attempts to bind the Spirit of God, the Spirit will again break out in Pentecost somewhere. The church in any of its various forms cannot for ever silence the prophets in its midst, cannot for ever keep the pens out of the hands of the translators, not even with an Inquisition, not even with tightly guarded separatist boundaries.[46] In time the Spirit frees the Bible to speak for itself once more. Once again fresh translations are made. Once more people hear—people are allowed to hear—in their own native languages, of the glorious works of God.

> . . . at the moment we are living in the middle of another of those decisive shifts in Christian history. By the end of the century a considerable majority of Christians is likely to be living in what we call, loosely, the southern hemisphere (including . . . India, the Philippines, Nigeria, Mexico, all geographically north of the Equator). . . . It will be the fruit . . . of awkwardly obstinate nineteenth-century missionaries, of the power of bib-

---

[46]Chap. 8.

lical translation . . . but—above all and in all—of a sudden sense of recognized identity between the masses of the third world and Jesus, a crucified carpenter, a man who wrote nothing and had nowhere to lay his head: a leap of faith and hope. . . . The impact of the figure of the martyred Archbishop Romero of El Salvador says it all, or of Bishop Tutu, or that strange prophet of Zaïre who spent thirty years in a colonial prison and whose son, whom he never spoke to, leads today a church of more than a million faithful—Simon Kimbangu. One could go on, almost indefinitely, naming teachers, martyrs, prophets, who have been incarnating Christianity anew in lands where until recently it barely existed: creating for it new sources of dynamism, new heartlands.[47]

At the beginning of the modern missionary movement some of those "awkwardly obstinate" missionary translators who worked to make the modern Pentecost possible bore names like William Carey (Bengali, India), Henry Martyn (Persian, Iran), Adoniram Judson (Burmese) and Robert Morrison (Chinese). Now almost two hundred years later their mantle has fallen on people with names like Jared Mwanjalla (Swahili, East Africa), Esther Hutagalung (Minangkabau, Indonesia), Aurelio Flores (Cuzco Quechua, Peru) and Maika Bovoro (Fijian).

The future of Bible translation, and to some degree the future of Pentecost, lies with people like them.

Of such is the Kingdom of God.

---

[47]Hastings, *Hurricane*, 99.

REFERENCES

Abbott, Walter M., ed. *The Documents of Vatican II*. New York: Herder and Herder and Association Press, 1966.

Aland, Kurt. "Der Deutsche Pietismus als Wegbereiter für die Arbeit der Bibelgesellschaften." In *On Language, Culture and Religion*, ed. Black and Smalley, 3-21.

_____. *A History of Christianity*. Vol. 1. *From the Beginnings to the Threshold of the Reformation*. Philadelphia: Fortress Press, 1985.

_____. "The Text of the Church?" *Trinity Journal* n.s. 8 (1987): 131-44.

Aland, Kurt, Matthew Black, Carlo M. Martini, Bruce M. Metzger, Allen Wikgren, et al., eds. *The Greek New Testament*. 3rd ed. corr. Stuttgart: United Bible Societies, 1983; ³1975; ¹1966.

Alter, Robert, and Frank Kermode, eds. *The Literary Guide to the Bible*. Cambridge MA: The Belknap Press, 1987.

American Board of Commissioners for Foreign Missions. *Constitution, Laws, and Regulations of the American Board of Commissioners for Foreign Missions*. Boston: ABCFM, 1839.

American Revision Committee. *The Holy Bible Containing the Old and New Testaments. . . .* Standard Edition. "American Standard Version." New York: Thomas Nelson & Sons, 1901; c1929.

Andersson, Efraim. *Churches of the Grass Roots: A Study in Congo-Brazzaville*. London: Lutterworth Press, 1968.

_____. *Messianic Popular Movements in the Lower Congo*. Studia Ethnographica Upsaliensia XVI. London, 1958.

Ansre, Gilbert. "To Unify or Dialectize? Some Sociolinguistic and Psycholinguistic Factors in Language Development for Bible Translation." In *Issues in Bible Translation*, ed. Philip C. Stine, 187-206.

Arichea, Daniel C., Jr. "The Christian Translator and the Old Testament: Some Translational Issues." Paper presented to the UBS Triennial Workshop, 1984.

_____. "The New Testament for Children." *The Bible Translator* 37/2 (April 1986): 239-48.

_____. "Taking Theology Seriously in the Translation Task," *The Bible Translator* 33/3 (July 1982): 309-16.

_____. "Theology and Translation," *United Bible Societies Bulletin* 140-41 (1985): 7-24.

_____. "Translating the Old Testament for Children: Genesis as a Test Case," *United Bible Societies Bulletin* 148-49 (3rd–4th quarters 1987): 7-17.

_____. "Who Was Phoebe? Translating *Diakonos* in Romans 16.1." *The Bible Translator* 39/4 (October 1988): 401-409.

Arichea, Daniel C., Jr., and Eugene A. Nida, *A Translator's Handbook on Paul's Letter to the Galatians*. Stuttgart: United Bible Societies, 1976.

Arichea, Daniel C., Jr., and M. K. Sembiring. "Promoting a Common Language Translation." *The Bible Distributor* 27 (October-November 1986).

Asch, Susan. *L'église du Prophète Kimbangu: De ses origines à son rôle actuel au Zaïre (1921–1928)*. Paris: Editions Karthala, 1983.

Ayandele, E. A. *The Missionary Impact on Modern Nigeria, 1842–1914: A Political and Social Analysis*. London: Longmans, Green, 1966.

Baëta, C. G., ed. *Christianity in Tropical Africa*. London: International African Institute, 1968.

Banker, John. *Semantic Structure Analysis of Titus*. Dallas: Summer Institute of Linguistics, 1987.

Barr, James. *The Semantics of Biblical Language*. London: Oxford University Press, 1961.

Barreiro, Alvaro. *Basic Ecclesial Communities: The Evangelization of the Poor*. Maryknoll NY: Orbis Books, 1982.

Barrett, David B. "Church Growth and Independency as Organic Phenomena: An Analysis of Two Hundred African Tribes." In *Christianity in Tropical Africa*, ed. C. G. Baëta, 268-86.

_____. *Schism and Renewal in Africa*. Nairobi: Oxford University Press, 1968.

_____, ed. *World Christian Encyclopedia: A Comparative Study of Churches and Religions in the Modern World 1900–2000*. Nairobi: Oxford University Press, 1982.

Bassnett-McGuire, Susan. *Translation Studies*. London: Methuen, 1988.

Beegle, Dewey M. *God's Word into English*. Ann Arbor MI: Pryor Pettengill, 1960.

Beekman, John, and John Callow. *Translating the Word of God*. Grand Rapids: Zondervan Publishing House, 1974.

Beidelman, T. O. *Colonial Evangelism: A Socio-Historical Study of an East African Mission at the Grassroots*. Bloomington: Indiana University Press, 1982.

Belete, Million, and Frank Robbins. "The United Bible Societies in Africa and the Africa Area of the Summer Institute of Linguistics: A Joint Statement." 1988.

Bergsland, Knut. "Eskimo-Aleut Languages." In *The New Encyclopedia Britannica*, macropaedia 6:962-64. Chicago: Encyclopaedia Britannica, 1974.

Berlin, Brent, and Paul Kay. *Basic Color Terms: Their Universality and Evolution*. Berkeley: University of California Press, 1969.

Bermúdez, Fernando. *Death and Resurrection in Guatemala*. Maryknoll NY: Orbis Books, 1986.

Berryman, Philip. *Liberation Theology: Essential Facts about the Revolutionary Movement in Latin America and Beyond*. New York: Pantheon Books, 1987.

Bertsche, James E. "Kimbanguism: A Challenge to Missionary Statesmanship." In *Readings in Missionary Anthropology*, ed. William A. Smalley, 373-93.

Bird, Phyllis. "Translating Sexist Language as a Theological and Cultural Problem." *Union Seminary Quarterly Review* 42/1-2 (1988): 89-95.

Black, Matthew, and William A. Smalley, eds. *On Language, Culture and Religion: In Honor of Eugene A. Nida*. The Hague: Mouton, 1974.

Blair, Frank. "Survey on a Shoestring." Prepublication draft. Dallas: Summer Institute of Linguistics, 1990.

Bloch-Hoell, Nils E., ed. *Misjonskall og Forskerglede: Festkrift til Professor Olav Guttorm Myklebust*. Oslo: Universitestsforlaget, 1975.

Bloomfield, Leonard. *Language*. New York: Holt, 1933.

Boff, Leonardo, and Clodovis Boff. *Introducing Liberation Theology*. Maryknoll NY: Orbis Books, 1986.

_____. *Liberation Theology: From Dialogue to Confrontation*. San Francisco: Harper & Row, 1986.

Bond, George, Walter Johnson, and Sheila S. Walker, eds. *African Christianity: Patterns of Religious Continuity*. New York: Academic Press, 1979.

Boutilier, James A., Daniel T. Hughes, and Sharon W. Tiffany, eds. *Mission, Church, and Sect in Oceania*. ASAO Monograph no. 6. Lanham MD: University Press of America, 1978.

Bratcher, Robert G., John J. Kijne, and William A. Smalley, eds. *Understanding and Translating the Bible: Papers in Honor of Eugene A. Nida*. New York: American Bible Society, 1974.

Brend, R., and K. Pike, eds. *The Summer Institute of Linguistics: Its Work and Contributions*. The Hague: Mouton, 1977.

Broomhall, Marshall. *The Bible in China*. Repr. San Francisco: Chinese Materials Center, Inc., 1977; ¹1934.

Broomhall, A. J., *Hudson Taylor and China's Open Century*. Vol. 1. *Barbarians at the Gate*. Sevenoaks, Kent: Hodder & Stoughton, and The Overseas Missionary Fellowship, 1981.

Brown, G. Thompson. *Christianity in the People's Republic of China*. Atlanta: John Knox, 1983.

Brown, Kenneth I. "Worshiping with the African Church of the Lord (Aladura)." In *Readings in Missionary Anthropology II*, ed. William A. Smalley, 394-419.

Brown, William. *The History of the Christian Missions of the Sixteenth, Seventeenth, Eighteenth, and Nineteenth Centuries. . . .* Vol. 1. 3rd ed. London: Thomas Baker, 1864.

Callow, Kathleen. *Discourse Considerations in Translating the Word of God*. Grand Rapids MI: Zondervan, 1974.

Canfield, R. L. "Accusation as 'Anthropology'." *Reviews in Anthropology* 10 (1983): 55-61.

Canton, W. *A History of the British and Foreign Bible Society*. 5 vols. London: John Murray, 1904.

Cardenal, Ernesto. *The Gospel in Solentiname*. 4 vols. Maryknoll, NY: Orbis Books, 1982.

Carey, Eustace. *Memoir of William Carey, D.D. . . .* Boston: Gould, Kendall and Lincoln, 1836.

Carey, S. Pearce. *William Carey D.D., Fellow of Linnaean Society*. London: Hodder and Stoughton, 1923.

Carey, William. *Dialogues Intended to Facilitate the Acquiring of the Bengalee Language*. 3rd. ed. Serampore, India: Mission Press, 1818.

_____. *A Dictionary of the Bengalee Language in Which the Words Are Traced to Their Origins and Their Various Meanings Given*. 2 vols. (vol. 2 in two parts). Serampore, India: Mission Press, 1818, 1825.

_____. *An Enquiry into the Obligations of Christians to Use Means for the Conversion of the Heathens*. Repr. London: The Carey Kingsgate Press Ltd., 1961; orig. 1792.

_____. *A Grammar of the Bengalee Language*. 2nd ed. with additions. Serampore, India: Mission Press, 1805.

_____. *A Grammar of the Bengalee Language*. 3rd ed. Serampore, India: Mission Press, 1815.

_____. *A Grammar of the Mahratta* [Marathi] *Language, to Which are Added Dialogues on Familiar Subjects*. Serampore, India: Mission Press, 1805.

_____. *A Grammar of the Punjabee Language*. Serampore, India: Mission Press, 1812.

_____. *A Grammar of the Sungskrit Language, Composed from the Works of the Most Esteemed Grammarians, to Which Are Added Examples for the Exercise of the Student and a Complete List of the Dhatoos and Roots*. Serampore, India: Mission Press, 1806.

Carey, William, and Joshua Marshman. *The Ramayana of Valmeeki, with a Prose Translation and Explanatory Notes*. 3 vols. Serampore, India: Mission Press, 1806–1810.

Carson, D. A. "The Limits of Dynamic Equivalence in Bible Translation." *Evangelical Review of Theology* 9/3 (July 1985): 200-213.

Cherry, E. Colin. *On Human Communication*. New York: Wiley, 1957.

Childs, Brevard S. *The Book of Exodus: A Critical Theological Commentary*. Old Testament Library. Philadelphia: Westminster Press, 1974.

Chirgwin, A. M. *The Bible in World Evangelism*. New York: Friendship Press, 1954.

Clark, David J. "Patterns of Inverted Parallelism in Genesis." In *Understanding and Translating the Bible*, ed. Bratcher, Kijne, and Smalley, 44-60.

Clifford, James. *Person and Myth: Maurice Leenhardt in the Melanesian World*. Berkeley: University of California Press, 1982.

_____. "The Translation of Cultures." *Journal of Pacific History* 15/1 (1980): 2-20.

Codrington, Robert H. *The Melanesians: Studies in Their Anthropology and Folklore*. Repr. New Haven CT: Human Relations Area Files, 1957; orig. 1891.

Colwell, Ernest C. "The Greek Language." In *The Interpreter's Dictionary of the Bible*, ed. George A. Buttrick, E-J: 479-87. New York and Nashville: Abingdon Press, 1962.

Cocordant Version of the Sacred Scriptures. . . . Los Angeles: The Concordant Publishing Concern, 1930.

Conus, Georges. "Le créole, une langue pour l'Église en Haïti." *Neue Zeitschrift für Missionswissenschaft* 43/2 (1987): 98-107.

Cook, Guillermo. *The Expectation of the Poor: Latin American Base Ecclesial Communities in Protestant Perspective*. Maryknoll NY: Orbis Books, 1985.

Cooksey, J. J. *The Land of the Vanished Church: A Survey of North Africa.* London: World Dominion Press, n.d.

Correll, Thomas C. "Language, Christianity, and Change in Two Eskimo Communities." In *Rethinking Modernization,* ed. J. Poggie and R. Lynch, 292-331.

Covell, Ralph R. *Confucius, the Buddha and Christ: A History of the Gospel in Chinese.* Maryknoll NY: Orbis Books, 1986.

Cowan, George. *The Word That Kindles.* Chappaqua NY: Christian Herald Books, 1979.

Crapanzano, Vincent. Preface Maurice Leenhardt, *Do Kamo: Person and Myth in the Melanesian World,* vii-xxix.

Crim, Keith R. "Translating the Poetry of the Bible." *The Bible Translator* 23/1 (January 1972): 102-109.

Culshaw, Wesley J. "William Carey—Then and Now." *The Bible Translator* 18/2 (April 1967): 53-60.

Daniels, Boyd, ed. *The UBS at 40.* Special issue of *United Bible Societies Bulletin* 144-145 (3rd-4th quarters, 1986).

Das, Sisirkumar. *Early Bengali Prose from Carey to Vidyasagar.* Calcutta: Bokland Private Ltd., 1966.

de Jesus, Carolina Maria. *Child of the Dark: The Diary of Carolina Maria de Jesus.* New York: New American Library, 1962.

de Waard, Jan, and Eugene A. Nida. *From One Language to Another: Functional Equivalence in Bible Translating.* Nashville: Thomas Nelson, 1986.

de Waard, Jan, and William A. Smalley. *A Translator's Handbook on the Book of Amos.* New York: United Bible Societies, 1979.

Deissmann, Adolf. *Light from the Ancient East: The New Testament Illustrated by Recently Discovered Texts of the Graeco-Roman World.* New and rev. ed. Trans. Lionel R. M. Strachan. New York: Doran, 1927.

Duthie, Alan S. *Bible Translations and How to Choose Between Them.* Exeter UK: The Paternoster Press, 1985.

Dvornik, Francis. *The Slavs: Their History and Civilization.* Boston: American Academy of Arts and Sciences, 1956.

Dwight, Henry Otis. *The Centennial History of the American Bible Society.* New York: The Macmillan Co., 1916.

Dye, T. Wayne. *Bible Translation Strategy: An Analysis of Its Spiritual Impact.* Rev. ed. Dallas: Wycliffe Bible Translators, 1985.

Dye, T. Wayne, and William A. Merrifield. "Anthropology." In *The Summer Institute of Linguistics*, ed. R. Brend and K. Pike, 165-82.

Ekechi, F. K. *Missionary Enterprise and Rivalry in Igboland 1857–1914*. London: Frank Cass, 1972.

Ellingworth, Paul. "Exegetical Presuppositions in Translation." *The Bible Translator* 33/3 (July 1982): 317-23.

_____. "Translation and Exegesis: A Case Study (Rom 9,22ff)." *Biblica* 59/3 (1978): 396-402.

Elson, Benjamin F., ed. *Language in Global Perspective: Papers in Honor of the 50th Anniversary of the Summer Institute of Linguistics, 1935–1985*. Dallas: Summer Institute of Linguistics, 1986.

Fehderau, Harold. "Kimbanguism: Prophetic Christianity in Congo." *Practical Anthropology* 9/4 (1962): 157-78.

Fenn, Eric. "The Bible and the Missionary." In *The Cambridge History of the Bible*, vol. 3, ed. S. L. Greenslade, 383-407.

Forman, Charles W. *The Island Churches of the South Pacific: Emergence in the Twentieth Century*. Maryknoll NY: Orbis Books, 1982.

Freire, Paolo, and Donaldo Macedo. *Literacy: Reading the Word and the World*. South Hadley MA: Bergin and Garvey Publishers, 1989.

Fry, Euan McGregor. "Training Nationals as Bible Translators." *The Bible Translator* 23/4 (October 1972): 430-35.

Gibson, John M. *Soldiers of the Word: The Story of the American Bible Society*. New York: Philosophical Library, 1985.

Goetchius, Eugene van Ness. *The Language of the New Testament*. New York: Charles Scribner's Sons, 1965.

Good News Bible: The Bible in Today's English Version. New York: American Bible Society, 1976.

Good News for Modern Man:The New Testament in Today's English Version. New York: American Bible Society, 1966.

Goody, Jack. *The Interface Between the Written and the Oral*. Cambridge: Cambridge University Press, 1987.

Graham, William A. *Beyond the Written Word: Oral Aspects of Scripture in the History of Religion*. Cambridge: Cambridge University Press, 1987.

Greenslade, S. L., ed. *The Cambridge History of the Bible*. Vol. 3. *The West from the Reformation to the Present Day*. Cambridge: Cambridge University Press, 1963.

Greenstein, Edward L. "Theories of Modern Bible Translation." *Prooftexts* 3 (1983): 9-39.

Grimes, Barbara F., ed. *Ethnologue: Languages of the World.* 11th ed. Dallas: Summer Institute of Linguistics, 1988.

Groves, C. P. *The Planting of Christianity in Africa.* 4 vols. London: Lutterworth Press, 1948–1958.

Gudschinsky, Sarah C. "Literacy." In *The Summer Institute of Linguistics,* ed. R. Brend and K. Pike, 39-56.

_____. *A Manual of Literacy for Preliterate Peoples.* Papua, New Guinea: Summer Institute of Linguistics, 1973.

Guiart, Jean. *Destin d'une église et d'un peuple: Nouvelle-calédonie 1900–1959, étude monographique d'une oeuvre missionnnaire protestante.* Paris: Mouvement du Christianisme Social, 1959.

Guidelines for Interconfessional Cooperation in Translating the Bible. Rome, 1987.

Guiding Principles for Interconfessional Cooperation in Translating the Bible. United Bible Societies and Secretariat for Promoting Christian Unity, 1968.

Hall, Edward T. *The Hidden Dimension.* New York: Doubleday, 1969.

_____. *The Silent Language.* New York: Doubleday, 1973.

Hall, Robert A., Jr. "Le créole haïtien et sa grammaire." *Le Nouvelliste* (9 April 1949).

_____. *Haitian Creole: Grammar, Texts, Vocabulary.* Memoire 74. Menasha WI: American Anthropological Association, 1953.

Halle, Morris, et al., eds. *Semiosis: Semiotics and the History of Culture. In Honorem Georgii Lotman.* Michigan Slavic Contributions. Ann Arbor: University of Michigan, 1984.

Halliday, M. A. K. *Explorations in the Functions of Language.* London: Edward Arnold, 1973.

Hargreaves, John. "The Story of the Yoruba Bible." *The Bible Translator* 16/1 (January 1965): 39-44.

Hastings, Adrian. *In the Hurricane: Essays on Christian Living Today.* London: Collins, 1986.

Hatton, Howard A. "Maha-Katoey and the Popular Thai New Testament." In *Issues in Bible Translation,* ed. Philip C. Stine, 172-86.

_____. "Translation of Pronouns: A Thai Example." *The Bible Translator* 24/2 (April 1973): 222-34.

Haugerud, Joann. *The Word for Us: The Gospels of John and Mark, Epistles to the Romans and Galatians, Restated in Inclusive Language*. Seattle: Coalition on Women and Religion, 1977.

Hefley, James, and Marti Hefley. *Uncle Cam: The Story of William Cameron Townsend, Founder of the Wycliffe Bible Translators and the Summer Institute of Linguistics*. London: Hodder & Stoughton, 1974.

Hesselgrave, David J. *Today's Choices for Tomorrow's Mission: An Evangelical Perspective on Trends and Issues in Missions*. Grand Rapids MI: Zondervan, 1988.

Heywood, Christopher. *Perspectives in African Literature*. New York: African Publishing, 1971.

Hiebert, Paul G. "Conversion, Culture and Cognitive Categories." *Gospel in Context* 1/4 (October): 24-29.

_____. "The Flaw of the Excluded Middle." *Missiology* 10/1 (January 1982): 35-47.

Hooper, J. S. M., and W. J. Culshaw. *Bible Translation in India, Pakistan, and Ceylon*. Bombay: Oxford University Press, 1963.

House, Juliane. *A Model for Translation Quality Assessment*. Tübigen: TBL Verlag Gunter Narr, 1977.

Hvalkof, S., and P. Aaby, eds. *Is God an American?* Copenhagen: International Work Group for Indigenous Affairs, 1981.

Inclusive Language Lectionary, An: Readings for Year A. Atlanta: John Knox Press, 1983.

Information Services Department. "General Statistics." Dallas: Summer Institute of Linguistics, August 1988.

International Information Services. *Bible Translation Needs* 1. Dallas: Wycliffe Bible Translators, 1988.

Jerusalem Bible, The. Garden City NY: Doubleday & Co., 1966.

Johnson, Edna. *Semantic Structure Analysis of 2 Peter*. Dallas: Summer Institute of Linguistics, 1988.

Jordan, Clarence. *The Cotton Patch Version of Luke and Acts: Jesus' Doings and the Happenings*. New York: Association Press/A Koinonia Publication, 1969.

_____. *The Cotton Patch Version of Paul's Epistles*. New York: Association Press/A Koinonia Publication, 1968.

Kamma, Freerk Ch. *Korreri: Messianic Movements in the Biak-Numfor Culture Area*. The Hague: Mouton, 1972.

Kassühlke, Rudolf. "An Attempt at Dynamic Equivalent Translation of *Basileia tou Theou.*" *The Bible Translator* 25/2 (April 1974): 236-38.

Kaufman, Paul L. *An Introductory Grammar of New Testament Greek.* Palm Springs CA: Ronald N. Haynes, 1982.

Khubchandani, Lachman M. *Plural Languages, Plural Cultures: Communication, Identity, and Sociopolitical Change in Contemporary India.* Honolulu: University of Hawaii Press, 1983.

Kietzman, Dale W. "Field training Programs." In *The Summer Institute of Linguistics,* ed. R. Brend and K. Pike, 69-83.

Kimbanguist Church, and Peter Manicom. *Out of Africa: Kimbanguism.* London: Christian Education Movement, 1979.

King James [Authorized] Version. *The Holy Bible, Containing the Old and New Testaments. . . .* Repr. London: Cambridge University Press, 1950; orig. 1611.

Klem, Herbert V. *Oral Communication of the Scripture: Insights from African Oral Art.* Pasadena CA: William Carey Library, 1982.

Kohlenberger, John R. *The NIV Interlinear Hebrew and English Old Testament.* Grand Rapids MI: Zondervan, 1987.

Kooiman, William Jan. *Luther and the Bible.* Philadelphia: Muhlenberg Press, 1961.

Kornfield, W. " 'Fishers of Men or Founders of Empire'?" *Evangelical Missions Quarterly* (October 1983): 308-13.

Koyama, Kosuke. "Aristotelian Pepper and Buddhist Salt." In *Readings in Missionary Anthropology II,* ed. William A. Smalley, 109-14.

Kraft, Charles H. *Christianity in Culture: A Study in Dynamic Biblical Theologizing in Cross-Cultural Perspective.* Maryknoll NY: Orbis Books, 1979.

Kubo, Sakae, and Walter F. Specht. *So Many Versions? Twentieth-century English Versions of the Bible.* Rev. and enl. ed. Grand Rapids MI: Academia Books, 1983.

Kuntima, Diangienda. *Histoire du Kimbanguisme.* Kinshasa: Editions Kimbanguistes, 1984.

Kwak, Nosoon. "The Korean Bible: A Linguistic Diagnosis." *The Bible Translator* 26/3 (July 1975): 301-307.

Langer, Judith A., ed. *Language, Literacy, and Culture: Issues of Society and Schooling.* Norwood NJ: Ablex, 1987.

Lanternari, Vittorio. *The Religions of the Oppressed: A Study of Modern Messianic Cults.* New York: Alfred A. Knopf, 1963.

Larson, David K., and Mary Rhea. "God Brings the Increase for Blaan: A Case Study." *Notes on Scripture in Use* 14 (July 1987): 18-26.

Larson, Mildred L. "Indigenizing of the Translation Process: The SIL Perspective." Paper read to a symposium on "Bible Translation and the Spread of the Church—The last Two Hundred Years," 28-30 October 1988.

_____. *Meaning-Based Translation: A Guide to Cross-Language Equivalence.* Lanham MD: University Press of America, 1984.

_____. "The Summer Institute of Linguistics and Translation." Paper read to a symposium on "Bible Translation and the Spread of the Church—The last Two Hundred Years," 28-30 October 1988.

Larson, Mildred L., and Patricia M. Davis. *Bilingual Education: An Experience in Peruvian Amazonia.* Washington: Center for Applied Linguistics, 1981.

Larson, Mildred L., and Lois Dodds. *Treasure in Clay Pots: An Amazon People on the Wheel of Change.* Palm Desert CA: Person to Person Books, 1985.

Latourette, Kenneth Scott. *A History of the Expansion of Christianity.* 7 vols. Repr. Grand Rapids MI: Zondervan Publishing House, 1970; orig. New York: Harper, 1938–1945.

Laubach, Frank C. *Forty Years with the Silent Billion.* Old Tappan NJ: Fleming H. Revell, 1970.

_____. *The Peoples of the Philippines: Their Religious Progress and Preparation for Leadership in the Far East.* New York: George H. Dorand, 1925.

Lawless, Robert "An Ethnohistory of Missionaries in Kalingaland." In *Missionaries and Anthropologists,* ed. Frank A. Salamone, 1-18.

Leenhardt, Maurice. *L'Art d'Océanie.* Paris: Edition du Chêne, 1947.

_____. "La Bible en mission." *Évangile et liberté* (21 October 1934).

_____. *Do Kamo: Person and Myth in the Melanesian World.* Trans. Basia Miller Gulati. Chicago: University of Chicago Press, 1979.

_____. *Do Kamo: La personne et le mythe dans le monde Mélanésien.* Repr. Paris: Gallimard, 1971; orig. 1947.

_____. *Documents néo-calédoniens.* Travaux et Mémoires de l'Institut d'Ethnologie 9. Paris: Institut d'Ethnologie, 1932.

_____. *Gens de la Grande Terre.* Repr. Paris: Gallimard, 1952; orig. 1937.

_____. *La Grande Terre: Mission de Nouvelle Calédonie.* Paris: Société des Missions Évangéliques, 1922.

_____. *Langues et dialectes de l'Austro-Mélanésie.* Travaux et Mémoires de l'Institut d'Ethnologie 46. Paris: Institut d'Ethnologie, 1946.

_____. *Notes d'ethnologie néo-calédonienne.* Travaux et Mémoires de l'Institut d'Ethnologie 8. Paris: Institut d'Ethnologie, 1930.

_____. "Notes on Translating the New Testament into New Caledonian." *The Bible Translator* 2/3, 2/4 (July, October 1951): 97-105, 145-52.

_____. *La structure de la personne in Mélanésie.* Milan: S.T.O.A. Edizioni, 1970.

_____. *Vocabulaire et grammaire de la langue Houaïlou.* Travaux et Mémoires de l'Institut d'Ethnologie 10. Paris: Institut d'Ethnologie, 1935.

Leenhardt, Raymond-H. *Un sociologue Canaque: Le Pasteur Boesoou Erijisi, 1866-1947, Houailou, Nouvelle-calédonie.* Cahiers d'Histoire du Pacifique 4. Paris, 1976.

Lewis, Jack P. *The English Bible, from King James Version to NIV.* Grand Rapids MI: Baker Book House, 1981.

Linton, Ralph. "Nativistic Movements." *American Anthropologist* 45/2 (June 1943): 230-40.

Living Bible, Paraphrased, The. Wheaton IL: Tyndale House Publishers; London: Coverdale House Publishers, 1971.

Loewen, Jacob A. *Culture and Human Values: Christian Intervention in Anthropological Perspective.* Pasadena CA: William Carey Library, 1975.

_____. "The Inspiration of Translation: A Growing Personal Conviction." In *Understanding and Translating the Bible,* ed. Bratcher, Kijne, and Smalley, 86-99.

_____. "The Training of National Translators." *The Bible Translator* 20/4, 21/1 (October 1969, January 1970): 131-42, 10-20.

_____. "Training Translators to Translate Biblical Poetry." From a paper presented to the American Translators Association, Metroplex Chapter, Arlington TX, 1983.

_____. "Why Bantu Translators Use R.S.V. and T.E.V. as their Textual Base." *The Bible Translator* 25/4 (October 1974): 412-16.

Louw, Johannes P., and Eugene A. Nida, with Rondal B. Smith, and Karen A. Munson, eds. *Greek-English Lexicon of the New Testament Based on Semantic Domains.* 2 vols. New York: United Bible Societies, 1988.

Loving, Richard. "Increasing Vernacular Scripture Use in the Sepik Region of Papua New Guinea." *Notes on Scripture in Use* 16 (April 1988): 11-26.

Luzbetak, Louis J. *The Church and Cultures.* Techny IL: Divine Word Publications, 1963. New ed. *The Church and Cultures: New Perspectives in Missiological Anthropology.* Maryknoll NY: Orbis Books, 1988.

Manley, Timothy M. *Outline of Srê Structure*. Honolulu: University of Hawaii Press, 1972.

Marshall, Alfred. *The Interlinear Greek-English New Testament*. London: Samuel Bagster and Sons, 1960.

Marshman, John Clark. *The Life and Times of Carey, Marshman, and Ward. Embracing the History of the Serampore Missionaries*. 2 vols. London, 1859.

Marshman, Joshua. *Elements of Chinese Grammar. . . .* Serampore, India: Mission Press, 1814.

Martin, Marie-Louise. *Kimbangu: An African Prophet and His Church*. Oxford: Blackwell, 1975.

Matejka, Ladislav. ''Church Slavonic as a National Language.'' In *Semiosis: Semiotics and the History of Culture*, ed. Morris Halle et al., 333-46.

Mbiti, John S. *Bible and Theology in African Christianity*. Nairobi: Oxford University Press, 1986.

_____. *The Crisis of Missions in Africa*. Mukono, Uganda: Uganda Church Press, 1971.

McLoughlin, William G. *Cherokees and Missionaries 1789–1839*. New Haven CT: Yale University Press, 1984.

Metzger, Bruce M. *Introduction to the Apocrypha*. New York: Oxford University Press, 1957.

_____. ''The Language of the New Testament.'' In vol. 7 of *The Interpreter's Bible*, ed. George A. Buttrick, 43-59. New York and Nashville: Abingdon Press, 1951.

_____. ''Versions, Ancient.'' In *The Interpreter's Dictionary of the Bible*, ed. George A. Buttrick, R-Z:749-60. New York and Nashville: Abingdon Press, 1962.

Meyendorff, John. ''Eastern Orthodoxy.'' In *The New Encyclopedia Britannica*, macropaedia 6:152-62. Chicago: Encyclopaedia Britannica, 1974.

Mickelsen, Berkeley, and Alvera Mickelsen. ''Does Male Dominance Tarnish Our Translations?'' *Christianity Today* (5 October 1979): 23-26, 29.

Miller, Elmer S. ''The Christian Missionary: Agent of Secularization.'' *Missiology* 1 (1973): 99-107.

Minkoff, Harvey. ''Problems of Translations—Concern for the Text versus Concern for the Reader.'' *Bible Review* 4/4 (August 1988): 34-40.

Moffatt, James. *A New Translation of the Bible, Containing the Old and New Testaments*. Rev. ed. New York: Harper & Brothers, 1935; orig. 1913–1925.

Moore, Bruce R. "Translation Theory." In *The Summer Institute of Linguistics,* ed. R. Brend and K. Pike, 147-64.

Morris, C. H. *The Bible in Brazil.* London: British and Foreign Bible Society, 1954.

Morrison, Robert. *Grammar of the Chinese Language.* Serampore, India: Mission Press, 1815.

Mounin, Georges. *Les Belles Infidèles.* Paris: Cahiers du Sud, 1955.

Mundhenk, Norm. "The Subjectivity of Anachronism." In *On Language, Culture and Religion,* ed. Matthew Black and William A. Smalley, 259-73.

_____. "Translation and the Form of the Source Language." In *Current Trends in Scripture Translation,* ed. Heber F. Peacock, 33-42.

Mundhenk, Norman, and Jan de Waard. "Missing the Whole Point and What Do about It—With Special Reference to the Book of Ruth." *The Bible Translator* 26/4 (October 1975): 420-33.

Muzorewa, Gwinyai H. *The Origins and Development of African Theology.* Maryknoll NY: Orbis Books, 1985.

Neill, Stephen. *A History of Christian Missions.* Rev. for the 2nd ed. by Owen Chadwick. Harmondsworth UK: Penguin Books, 1986.

_____. *A History of Christianity in India.* Vol. 2. *1707–1858.* Cambridge: Cambridge University Press, 1985.

New American Standard Version. *New American Standard Bible.* Chicago: Moody Press, 1973.

New International Version. *The Holy Bible, New International Version, Containing the Old and the New Testaments.* New Brunswick NJ: New York International Bible Society, 1978.

Newman, Barclay M. "And a Child Shall Lead Them." *United Bible Societies Bulletin* 148-149 (3rd-4th quarters 1987): 18-25.

_____. "Toward a Theology of Translation." In *Current Trends in Translation,* ed. Heber F. Peacock, 10-21.

Newman, Barclay M., and Eugene A. Nida. *A Translator's Handbook on Paul's Letter to the Romans.* London: United Bible Societies, 1972.

Newmeyer, Frederick J. *The Politics of Linguistics.* Chicago: University of Chicago Press, 1986.

Nichols, Anthony. "Dynamic Equivalence Bible Translations." *Colloquium: The Australian and New Zealand Theological Review* 19/1 (October 1986): 43-53.

Nida, Eugene A. *Bible Translating: An Analysis of Principles and Procedures.* Rev. ed. New York: United Bible Societies, 1961; ¹1947.

_____. *Communication of the Gospel in Latin America.* Cuernavaca, Mexico: Centro Intercultural de Documentación, 1969. Repr. as *Understanding Latin Americans, with Special Reference to Religious Values and Movements.* Pasadena CA: William Carey Library, 1974.

_____. *Componential Analysis of Meaning.* The Hague: Mouton: 1975.

_____. *Customs and Cultures.* New York: Harper & Row, 1954.

_____. *God's Word in Man's Language.* New York: Harper & Row, 1952.

_____. *Good News for Everyone. How to Use the Good News Bible (Today's English Version).* Waco TX: Word Books, 1977.

_____. *Learning a Foreign Language.* Rev. ed. New York: Friendship Press, 1957; [1]1950.

_____. *Message and Mission.* New York: Harper & Row, 1960.

_____. *Morphology: the Descriptive Analysis of Words.* Ann Arbor MI: University of Michigan Press, 1949.

_____. ''A New Methodology in Biblical Exegesis.'' *The Bible Translator* 3 (1952): 97-110.

_____. *Religion Across Cultures: A Study in the Communication of the Christian Faith.* Pasadena CA: William Carey Library, 1968.

_____. *Toward a Science of Translating.* Leiden: E. J. Brill, 1964.

_____., ed. *Book of a Thousand Tongues.* Rev. ed. New York: United Bible Societies, 1972.

Nida, Eugene A., and William D. Reyburn. *Meaning Across Cultures.* Maryknoll NY: Orbis Books, 1981.

Nida, Eugene A., and William A. Smalley. *Introducing Animism.* New York: Friendship Press, 1959.

Nida, Eugene A., and Charles R. Taber. *The Theory and Practice of Translation.* Leiden: E. J. Brill, for the United Bible Societies, 1969.

Nida, Eugene A., J. P. Louw, A. H. Snyman, and J. v. W. Cronje. *Style and Discourse: With Special Reference to the Text of the Greek New Testament.* Cape Town: Bible Society of South Africa, 1983.

North, Eric M. ''Eugene A. Nida: An Appreciation.'' In *Language, Culture, and Religion,* ed. Black and Smalley, vii-xx.

_____, ed. *Book of a Thousand Tongues.* New York: Harper & Brothers, for the American Bible Society, 1938.

O'Connor, Gulbun Coker. *The Moro Movement of Guadalcanal.* Ann Arbor: University of Michigan Press, 1974.

Ogbu, John. "Opportunity Structure, Cultural Boundaries and Literacy." In *Language, Literacy, and Culture*, ed. Judith A. Langer, 149-77.

Omanson, Roger L. "Problems in Bible Translation." *The Christian Century* (22-29 June 1988): 605-607.

Ong, Walter J. *Orality and Literacy: The Technologizing of the Word*. London: Methuen, 1982.

Oosthuizen, G. C. *Post-Christianity in Africa: A Theological and Anthropological Study*. Grand Rapids MI: Eerdmans, 1968.

Oussoren, A. H. *William Carey, Especially His Missionary Principles*. Leiden: A. W. Sijthoff's Uitgeversmaatschappij N.V., 1945.

Owen, John. *The History of the Origin and First Ten Years of the British and Foreign Bible Society*. Vol. 1. London: Tilling and Hughes, 1816.

Page, Jesse. *The Black Bishop: Samuel Adjai Crowther*. Repr. Westport CT: Greenwood Press, 1979; orig. 1908.

Peacock, Heber F. "Current Trends in Scripture Translation." In *Current Trends in Scripture Translation*, ed. Peacock, 5-9.

_____., ed. *Current Trends in Scripture Translation*. Special issue of *United Bible Societies Bulletin* 124-125 (1981).

Phillips, Godfrey E. *The Old Testament in the World Church, with Special Reference to the Younger Churches*. London: Lutterworth Press, 1942.

Phillips, J. B. *Four Prophets: Amos, Hosea, First Isaiah, Micah. A Modern Translation from the Hebrew*. New York: The Macmillan Co., 1963.

_____. *Letters to Young Churches*. New York: The Macmillan Co., 1947.

_____. *The New Testament in Modern English*. Rev. ed. New York: MacMillan Publishing Co., 1972; ¹1958.

Pickett, J. Wascom. *Christian Mass Movements in India*. New York: Abingdon Press, 1933.

Pike, Eunice V. *Ken Pike: Scholar and Christian*. Dallas: Summer Institute of Linguistics, 1981.

_____. "William Cameron Townsend." In *A William Cameron Townsend en el vigésimoquinto aniversario del Instituto Lingüístico de Verano*. Mexico DF, 1961.

Pike, Kenneth L. *Language in Relation to a Unified Theory of the Structure of Human Behavior*. 2nd ed. The Hague: Mouton, 1967.

_____. *Linguistic Concepts: An Introduction to Tagmemics*. Lincoln NE: University of Nebraska Press. 1982.

_____. *Phonemics: A Technique for Reducing Languages to Writing.* Ann Arbor: University of Michigan Press, 1947.

_____. *Phonetics: A Critical Analysis of Phonetic Theory and a Technic for the Practical Description of Sounds.* Ann Arbor: University of Michigan Press, 1943.

_____. *Tone Languages: A Technique for Determining the Number and Type of Pitch Contrasts in a Language, with Studies of Tonemic Substitution and Fusion.* Ann Arbor: University of Michigan Press, 1948.

Pike, Kenneth L., and Evelyn G. Pike. *Grammatical Analysis.* Rev. ed. Dallas: Summer Institute of Linguistics, 1982.

Poggie, J., and R. Lynch, eds. *Rethinking Modernization: Anthropological Perspectives.* Westport CT: Greenwood Press, 1974.

Potts, E. D. *British Baptist Missionaries in India 1793-1837.* Cambridge, 1967.

Prasithrathsint, Amara. "Change in the Passive Constructions in Standard Thai from 1802–1982." *Language Sciences* 10/2 (1988): 363-93.

Prickett, Stephen. *Words and* The Word: *Language, Poetics and Biblical Interpretation.* Cambridge: Cambridge University Press, 1986.

Reed, William R. "Church Growth as Modernization." In *God, Man, and Church Growth,* ed. Alan R. Tippett.

Rensch, Calvin R. "The Contributions of SIL in Linguistics." In *Summer Institute of Linguistics,* ed. R. Brend and K. Pike, 85-128.

Reports of the British and Foreign Bible Society with Extracts of Correspondence, &c. Vol. 1. *1805–1810.* London: British and Foreign Bible Society, 1811.

Revised Standard Version. *The Oxford Annotated Bible with the Apocrypha.* New York: Oxford University Press, 1965.

Revised Standard Version, Catholic Edition. *The Holy Bible Containing the Old and New Testaments.* Toronto: Thomas Nelson & Sons, 1966.

Rey Lescure, Philippe. *Vos racines. . . . Essai d'histoire des débuts de l'évangélisation de la Nouvelle-calédonie.* Alençon, France: Imprimerie Corbière et Jugain, 1967.

Reyburn, William D. "Motivations for Christianity." In *Readings in Missionary Anthropology,* ed. William A. Smalley, 73-76.

_____. "The Transformation of God and the Conversion of Man." In *Readings in Missionary Anthropology,* 2ed. William A. Smalley, 481-85.

Richie, John, "The Gospels in Aymara." *Bible Society Record* 85/1 (January 1940): 8-9.

Rijks, Piet. *A Guide to Catholic Bible Translations*. Vol. 1. *The Pacific*. Stuttgart: World Catholic Federation for the Biblical Apostolate, n.d.

Ritson, John H. *The World Is Our Parish*. London: Hodder & Stoughton, 1939.

Robbins, Frank E. "Training in Linguistics." In *Summer Institute of Linguistics*, R. Brend and K. Pike, 57-68.

Ross, Harold M. "Competition for Baegu Souls: Mission Rivalry on Malaita, Solomon Islands." In *Mission, Church, and Sect in Oceania*, ed. James A. Boutilier et al., 163-200.

Rossi, Sanna Barlow. *God's City in the Jungle*. Huntington Beach CA: Wycliffe Bible Translators, 1975.

Roxburgh, William. *Flora Indica*. 3 vols. Serampore, India: Mission Press, 1832.

_____. *Hortus Bengalensis, or a Catalogue of the Plants of the Honourable East India Company's Botanic Garden in Calcutta*. Serampore, India: Mission Press, 1814.

Rubadiri, David. "The Development of Writing in East Africa." In *Perspectives in African Literature*, ed. Christopher Heywood, 148-56.

S.I.L. Bibliography. Dallas: Summer Institute of Linguistics, 1986.

Salamone, Frank A., ed. *Missionaries and Anthropologists*. Studies in Third World Societies 26. Williamsburg VA: Department of Anthropology, College of William and Mary, 1985.

Samarin, William J. *Tongues of Men and Angels: The Religious Language of Pentecostalism*. New York: Macmillan, 1972.

Sanneh, Lamin. *Translating the Message: The Missionary Impact on Culture*. Maryknoll NY: Orbis Books, 1989.

Sapir, Edward. *Culture, Language, and Personality*. Berkeley: University of California Press, 1956.

_____. *Language: An Introduction to the Study of Speech*. New York: Harcourt, Brace, 1939.

Sayers, Dorothy L. *The Man Born to Be King: A Play-Cycle on the Life of our Lord and Saviour Jesus Christ*. London: Victor Gollancz, 1943.

Schmidt, Wilhelm. *The Origin and Growth of Religion*. London: Methuen, 1931.

Schwarz, W. *Principles and Problems in Biblical Translation: Some Reformation Controversies and their Background*. Cambridge: Cambridge University Press, 1955.

Scribner, Sylvia, and Michael Cole. *The Psychology of Literacy*. Cambridge MA: Harvard University Press, 1981.

Sen Gupta, Kanti Prasanna. *The Christian Missionaries in Bengal 1793-1833*. Calcutta: Firma K. L. Mukhopadhyay, 1971.

Shannon, Claude L., and Warren Weaver. *The Mathematical Theory of Communication*. Urbana: University of Illinois Press, 1949.

Shaw, R. Daniel. *Transculturation: The Cultural Factor in Translation and Other Communication Tasks*. Pasadena CA: William Carey Library, 1988.

Singh, Shri Ram Briksh. "Notice." *Bangkok World* (3 December 1975).

Slocum, Marianna C. "Goal: Vernacular Scriptures in Use." *Notes on Scripture in Use* 15 (October 1987): 7-11.

Slocum, Marianna C., and Grace Watkins. *The Good Seed*. Orange CA: Promise Publishing Co., 1988.

Smalley, William A. "Adaptive Language Strategies of the Hmong: From Asian Mountains to American Ghettos." *Language Sciences* 7/2 (1985): 241-69.

_____. *Linguistic Diversity and National Unity in Thailand*. Forthcoming.

_____. "Multilingualism in the Northern Khmer Population of Thailand." *Language Sciences* 10/2 (1988): 393-408.

_____. "Phillips and the NEB: Some Comments on Style." *The Bible Translator* 16/4 (July 1965): 165-70.

_____. "Thailand's Hierarchy of Multilingualism." *Language Sciences* 10/ 2 (1988).

_____. "Translating the Psalms as Poetry." In *On Language, Culture, and Religion*, ed. Black and Smalley, 337-71.

_____. "The Use of Non-Roman Script for New Languages." In *Orthography Studies*, ed. Smalley, 71-107.

_____, ed. *Orthography Studies: Articles on New Writing Systems*. London: United Bible Societies, 1963.

_____, ed. *Phonemes and Orthography: Language Planning in Ten Minority Languages of Thailand*. Canberra: Department of Linguistics, Australian National University, 1976.

_____, ed. *Readings in Missionary Anthropology II*. Pasadena CA: William Carey Library, 1978.

Smalley, William A., Chia Koua Vang, and Gnia Yee Yang. *Mother of Writing: The Origin and Development of a Hmong Messianic Script*. Chicago: University of Chicago Press, 1990.

Smith, Edwin W. *African Beliefs and Christian Faith*. London: United Society for Christian Literature, 1936.

_____. *The Golden Stool: Some Aspects of the Conflict of Culture in Modern Africa.* New York: Doubleday Doran, 1926.

_____. *The Secret of the African.* London: Student Christian Movement, 1929; orig. 1907.

_____. *The Shrine of a People's Soul.* New York: Friendship Press, 1947; orig. 1929.

Smith, George. *The Life of William Carey.* London: J. M. Dent & Sons, 1909.

Smith, J. M. Powis, and Edgar J. Goodspeed. *The Bible: An American Translation.* Chicago: University of Chicago Press, 1927.

Snell-Hornby. *Translation Studies: An Integrated Approach.* Amsterdam: Johns Benjamins Publishing Co., 1988.

Somerville, W. C. "The UBS Story." *United Bible Societies Bulletin* 91 (3rd quarter 1972): 148-63.

Song, C. S. *Theology from the Womb of Asia.* Maryknoll NY: Orbis Books, 1986.

Stamoolis, James J. *Eastern Orthodox Mission Theology Today.* Maryknoll NY: Orbis, 1986.

Steven, Hugh. *They Dared to Be Different.* Irvine CA: Harvest House Publishers, 1976.

Stine, Philip C. "To Read or Not to Read. A Consideration of Literacy in Secondary and Tertiary Languages." Paper presented to the 19th African Linguistic Conference, Boston University, 1988.

_____. "The UBS Translation Program in 1987." *United Bible Societies Bulletin* 150-151 (1st-2nd quarters 1988): 191-95.

_____, ed. *Current Trends in Scripture Translation.* Special issue of *United Bible Societies Bulletin* 148-149 (3rd-4th quarters 1987).

_____, ed. *Issues in Bible Translation.* UBS Monograph Series 3. London: United Bible Societies, 1988.

Stipe, Claude E. "The Anthropological Perspective in *Is God an American?*" In *Missionaries and Anthropologists,* ed. Frank A. Salamone, 117-83.

Stoeffler, F. Ernest. *German Pietism during the Eighteenth Century.* Leiden: E. J. Brill, 1973.

Stoll, David. *Fishers of Men or Founders of Empire?* London: Zed Press, 1982.

_____. "The Wycliffe Bible Translators: Not telling the Whole Story." *The Other Side* (February 1983): 5-7.

Swartley, Willard M. *Slavery, Sabbath, War, and Women: Case Issues in Biblical Interpretation.* Scottdale PA: Herald Press, 1983.

Taylor, Robert. "The Summer Institute of Linguistics/Wycliffe Bible Translators in Anthropological Perspective." In *Missionaries and Anthropologists,* ed. Frank A. Salamone, 93-116.

Tippett, Alan R. *Solomon Islands Christianity: A Study in Growth and Obstruction.* Pasadena CA: William Carey Library, 1967.

_____., ed. *God, Man, and Church Growth: A Festschrift in Honor of Donald Anderson McGavran.* Grand Rapids: Eerdmans, 1973.

Torre, Elisa. "My First Attempts at Translating." *The Jerome Quarterly* 4/2 (February-March 1989): 8.

Turner, Harold W. *African Independent Church.* Vol. 1. *History of an African Independent Church: The Church of the Lord (Aladura).* Vol. 2. *African Independent Church: The Life and Faith of the Church of the Lord (Aladura).* Oxford: Clarendon Press, 1967.

_____. *Profile through Preaching.* London: Edinburgh House, 1965.

_____. *Religious Innovation in Africa: Collected Essays on New Religious Movements.* Boston: G. K. Hall & Co., 1979.

_____. "A Typology for African Religious Movements." In his *Religious Innovation in Africa,* 79-108.

Tutu, Desmond M. "Whither African Theology?" In *Christianity in Independent Africa,* ed. Fasholé-Luke, Gray, Hastings, and Tasie, 364-69.

Twentieth-Century New Testament, The: A Translation into Modern English. Rev. ed. New York: Fleming H. Revell, 1904; orig. 1899-1901.

Ugang, Hermogenes. "Translating 'God' into the Ngaju Language: Problems and Possibilities." In *Current Trends in Scripture Translation,* ed. Philip C. Stine, 61-68.

United Bible Societies. "1987 Scripture Language Report." New York: United Bible Societies Service Center, 1988.

_____. "World Translations Progress Report, 1989." New York: United Bible Societies, 1989.

_____. *Scriptures of the World.* New York: United Bible Societies, 1989.

_____. *1988 Annual Report.* Reading, England: United Bible Societies, 1988.

Van Bruggen, Jakob. *The Future of the Bible.* New York: Nelson, 1978.

Versión Popular. *El Nuevo Testamento.* Mexico City: Bible Societies in Latin America, 1966.

Walker, F. Deaville. *William Carey: Missionary Pioneer and Statesman.* London: Student Christian Movement, 1926.

Walker, Sheila S. "The Message as Medium: The Harris Churches of the Ivory Coast and Ghana." In *African Christianity*, ed. George Bond et al., 9-64.

Walker, Williston, Richard A. Norris, David W. Lotz, and Robert T. Handy. *A History of the Christian Church*. 4th ed. New York, Charles Scribner's Sons, 1985.

Wallace, Anthony F. C. "Revitalization Movements." *American Anthropologist* 58/2 (April 1956): 264-81.

Walls, Andrew F. "Culture and Coherence in Christian History." *Evangelical Review of Theology* 9/3 (July 1985): 214-23.

_____. "The Gospel as the Prisoner and Liberator of Culture." *Faith and Thought* 108/1-2 (October 1981): 39-52.

_____. "The Nineteenth Century Missionary as Scholar." In *Misjonskall og Forskerglede*, ed. Bloch-Hoell, 209-21.

Walsh, J. P. M. "Contemporary English Translations of Scripture." *Theological Studies* 50/2 (1989): 336-58.

Ward, William. *A View of the History, Literature, and Mythology of the Hindoos, Including a Minute Description of their Manners and Customs, and Translations from their Principal Works*. 2nd ed. 2 vols. Serampore, India: Mission Press, 1818.

Watkins, Morris. *Literacy, Bible Reading, and Church Growth through the Ages*. South Pasadena CA: William Carey Library, 1978.

Wendland, Ernst R. *The Cultural Factor in Bible Translation*. UBS Monograph Series 2. London: United Bible Societies, 1987.

_____. *Language, Society, and Bible Translation, with Special Reference to the Style and Structure of Direct Speech in the Scriptures*. Cape Town: Bible Society of South Africa, 1985.

Westermann, Diedrich. *Africa and Christianity*. London: Oxford University Press, 1937.

Weymouth, Richard F. *The New Testament in Modern Speech: An Idiomatic Translation into Everyday English from the "Resultant Greek Testament."* Boston: The Pilgrim Press, 1936; orig. 1903.

Whiteman, Darrell. *Melanesians and Missionaries: An Ethnohistorical Study of Social and Religious Change in the Southwest Pacific*. Pasadena: William Carey Library, 1983.

_____, ed. *Missionaries, Anthropologists, and Culture Change*. Studies in Third World Societies 25. Williamsburg VA: Department of Anthropology, College of William and Mary, 1985.

Wilson, H. H. "Remarks of the Character and Labors of Dr. Carey as an Oriental Scholar and Translator." In *Memoir of William Carey,* ed. Eustace Carey, 393-422.

Wolfensberger, G. H. *Multiplying the Loaves: The Bible in Mission and Evangelism.* London: Fontana Books, 1968.

Wolfson, Nessa, and Joan Manes, eds. *Language of Inequality.* Berlin: Mouton 1985.

Wonderly, William L. *Bible Translations for Popular Use.* New York: United Bible Societies, 1968.

Wonderly, William L., and Eugene A. Nida. "Linguistics and Christian Missions." *Anthropological Linguistics* 5/1 (January 1963). Repr. in *The Bible Translator* 15/2 (April 1964): 51-69; 15/3 (July 1964): 107-16; 15/4 (October 1964): 154-66.

Yamamori, Tetsunao, and Charles R. Taber, eds. *Christopaganism or Indigenous Christianity?* South Pasadena CA: William Carey Library, 1975.

Yonge, C. D., ed. and trans. *The Works of Philo Judaeus, the Contemporary of Josephus.* Vol. 3. London: Henry G. Bohn, 1855.

Young, Richard Fox. "Church Sanskrit: An Approach of Christian Scholars to Hinduism in the Nineteenth Century." *Wiener Zeitschrift für die Kunde Sudasiens* 23 (1979): 205-31.

_____. *Resistant Hinduism: Sanskrit Sources on Anti-Christian Apologetics in Early 19th-Century India.* Nobili Research Library 8. Vienna: Institut für Indologie der Universität Wien, 1981.

Yost, J. "We Have a Mandate." *The Other Side* (February 1983): 7-9.

INDEX

accessibility
  as purpose of translation, 2-6, 18, 49-50, 96, 152
  by translation, 253-55
  in modern translations, 98, 109
  of interactional meaning, 120
  of original meaning, 84, 122, 175, 181, 233
  priority in, 10-15, 124, 125
African independent churches, 170-71, 205, 226, 229-30, 238. *See also* Church of the Lord (Aladura); Kimbanguism
Aguaruna, 167-68, 216-17, 251
Aladura. *See* Church of the Lord (Aladura)
American Bible Society, 28-29, 67, 99-100, 174
American Standard Version, 11-12, 96, 107, 108, 109
analysis. *See* interpretation; translation process
anthropology
  in dynamic equivalence theory, 68
  in missiology, 241-42
  Nida, 28, 69
  Practical Anthropology, 146, 242
  Summer Institute of Linguistics, 75-76
  translator scholarship in, 40, 53-58, 67
apocrypha, 99-100
Arabic, 2, 24, 61, 88
Armenian, 24, 25
attitude
  toward dialect, 134, 135
  toward language, 136-37, 142-43, 143-44, 144-47
  toward language level, 134, 150-51
  toward literacy, 198
  toward translation, 136-37, 216-33

See also bounded categories; centered categories; hierarchy of languages
Augustine, 94
Authorized Version. *See* King James Version
Aymara, 30, 32

backgrounds of translators, 15, 16, 41-42, 54, 105, 246-47
Bailey, Benjamin, 22
baptism controversy, 51, 64, 169
base community movement, 186-90, 208, 219
Bengali, 40, 42, 44, 48, 49
Bible
  behavioral manual, 228-30
  cultural artifact, 224, 248
  devotional book, 230-31
  distribution of, 221-24
  fetish, 224-25
  fruits of its translation, 215-33
  law book, 225-27
  male focus in, 4-5
  oracle, 231-33
  reference book, 228
  textbook, 227-28
  theology concerning, 91, 97-101
  translation of, 1-19
  uniformity or diversity of, 100, 177-78
Bible societies, 62-73, 81, 148, 244, 245, 246
  effect on missionary attitudes, 146
  era of, 27-28, 62
  origin of, 27-28, 62-64
  See also individual Bible societies; help for translators
Bible Translator, The, 70, 77